BREEDING
BIOLOGY
OF THE
ADÉLIE
PENGUIN

BREEDING BIOLOGY OF THE ADÉLIE PENGUIN

David G. Ainley,
Robert E. LeResche,
and
William J. L. Sladen

University of California Press
Berkeley Los Angeles London

University of California Press
Berkeley and Los Angeles, California

University of California Press, Ltd.
London, England

Copyright © 1983 by The Regents of the University of California

Library of Congress Cataloging in Publication Data

Ainley, David G.
  Breeding biology of the Adélie penguin.

  Bibliography: p. 227
  Includes index.
  1. Adélie penguin—Reproduction.   2. Birds—Reproduction.
I. LeResche, Robert E.   II. Sladen, William J. L.   III. Title.
QL696.S473A36 1983   598.4'41   82-17573
ISBN 0-520-04838-5

Printed in the United States of America

1   2   3   4   5   6   7   8   9

CONTENTS

8
Factors Other Than Age and Experience That Affect Productivity   151

9
Demography of the Crozier Population   183

10
Age at First Breeding and the Balance among Demographic Variables   198

PREFACE

The few long-term studies of birds that exist have all been done by individual or small groups of researchers. In many, especially those that have yet to be published, the project has by and large been a hobby. Prime examples, which fortunately have been published, are M. M. Nice's study of Song Sparrows and L. E. Richdale's study of Yellow-eyed Penguins. The avocational character of long-term population research is not surprising given the reluctance of funding institutions to support such work. While this is to some degree understandable, it is unfortunate because some ideas about bird ecology based on short-term studies have had a tendency to crumble when tested against long-term data. As this monograph will reveal, even we, with several years of data, experienced this with some of the ideas in our earlier "preliminary" publications.

Since this project was supported financially and logistically by large organizations, it is not typical of the hobbies that have evolved into long-term studies. This can be accounted for only through the efforts of two persons (in addition to ourselves), and to them we wish to dedicate this volume:

Robert C. Wood spent ten consecutive austral summers* at Cape Crozier, 1961 1962 to 1970–1971. He took time from the busiest part of his own studies each summer to organize and orchestrate the several people needed in the banding of 2,000 to 5,000 penguin chicks. In the mud, snow, and wind the appropriate birds received the correct marks that would identify them in years to come. Later, in the comforts of his Baltimore office, he accurately translated field notes into banding records. Equally important, Bob served as unofficial station leader at Cape Crozier and provided the continuity needed to integrate the comings and goings of all the graduate students, field assistants, and researchers who visited there.

*See *season* in Definitions, p. 19.

George A. Llano was Program Manager for Biology at the Division of Polar Programs, National Science Foundation, from the inception of this study in 1960 until the completion of most of its fieldwork in the 1975–1976 summer season. We did not always see eye to eye with him, but to a great extent, it was through George's interest and effort that the funding for this project materialized year after year.

ACKNOWLEDGMENTS

This project was carried out through the Johns Hopkins University, 1961 to 1970, and the Point Reyes Bird Observatory, 1970 to 1982. In addition to Bob Wood and George Llano, many persons made important contributions to its success. The various grants were administered by M. Gambrill, H. Strong, J. Church, J. Smail, H. Crandall, and B. Heneman. Field assistance and comradeship in the field were supplied by M. C. Smith, S. H. Morrell, R. J. Boekelheide, R. P. Schlatter, W. B. Emison, D. A. Saunders, F. J. Pitzman, and R. L. Penney. Many additional persons helped in the banding of chicks, an operation brought from an impossible task to one of efficiency when A. G. Parker applied his sheep-herding techniques to penguins.

D. P. DeMaster helped a great deal with the data analysis that resulted in chapter 9. He, J. P. Church, and R. W. Schreiber each read the entire manuscript and, with J. P. Croxall and W. Z. Trivelpiece who read the last two chapters, offered many useful criticisms that were quite sobering at a time when we thought our writing efforts were near completion. W. C. Riggs helped in the drawing of figures. Last, O'B. Young, with assistance from M. Sanders and B. Willow, undauntedly overcame the tedium of producing the several drafts of this monograph.

Logistic support was supplied by the U. S. Antarctic Research Program, U. S. Navy Operation Deepfreeze, and U. S. Navy Squadron VXE-6. For coordination of the efforts of these organizations, we thank D. Bresnahan, G. Huffman, P. Lewis, Jr., and K. Moulton.

Fieldwork was supported by grants from the National Science Foundation, Division of Polar Programs (DPP), to the Johns Hopkins University and Point Reyes Bird Observatory (PRBO). Data analysis was supported by DPP and PRBO. Costs for publication were in part funded by NSF grants DPP 7906906 and 7920796-01. This is contribution no. 233 of the Point Reyes Bird Observatory.

1
INTRODUCTION

 Seabirds are slow to mature, are rather long-lived compared to most terrestrial birds, and are sensitive to continually fluctuating factors in their marine environment. Because of this, correct knowledge about many aspects of their lives can be gained only through studies that persist for at least several years. The added fact that subadult seabirds of most species wear the same plumage worn by adults means that these studies require marked individuals so that the influence of age and inexperience can be detected.

These points were clearly illustrated in Richdale's (1949*a, b*, 1954, 1955, and 1957) pioneering, twenty-year study of Yellow-eyed Penguins *Megadyptes antipodes* breeding on the Otago Peninsula, New Zealand. Led by this classic work, much interest in long-term research on seabirds was generated during the 1950s and early 1960s. Studies were initiated and their results published on the Short-tailed Shearwater *Puffinus tenuirostris* (Serventy 1956, 1957, 1961, 1963), Black-legged Kittiwake *Rissa tridactyla* (Coulson and White 1958*a, b*, 1959, 1960, 1961; Coulson 1963, 1966; Wooller and Coulson 1977), Manx Shearwater *P. puffinus* (Harris 1966*a, b*; Perrins 1966), and Atlantic Gannet *Sula bassana* (Nelson 1966*a, b*; 1978*a, b*). Similar studies were begun during this period on Leach's Storm-Petrel *Oceanodroma leucorhoa* (Huntington 1963), Royal Penguin *Eudyptes chrysolophus* (Carrick and Ingham 1967, Carrick 1972), Red-billed Gull *Larus novaehollandiae* (Mills 1973, 1979), South Polar Skua *Catharacta maccormicki* (Wood 1971), and Sooty Tern *Sterna fuscata* (Robertson 1964). The major results of these works, however, have yet to be reported. If the investment of time and the financial resources required to bring them to fruition do not become insurmountable barriers, the effort to publish results will be well worthwhile because of the paucity of long-term data on avian life history.

Also growing out of the 1950s interest in long-term seabird research was the study we report on here. Beginning in the austral summer of 1961–1962, we examined the breeding biology of Adélie Penguins *Pygoscelis adeliae* at Cape Crozier, Ross Island, Antarctica. Of particular interest was the way in which age and experience influenced breeding behavior. We were also well aware that a comparison with Richdale's information on Yellow-eyed Penguins would be rewarding—long-term data on one species are important enough by themselves, but to have similar information on two closely related species was an exciting prospect. From that first season to the austral summer of 1975–1976, fourteen years later, we spent eleven summers at Cape Crozier; during four consecutive summers, 1970–1971 to 1973–1974, we were not present there. Supplemental observations were added during December of 1980–1982. Individually marked, known-age penguins were studied throughout; in all, 4,485 individuals were observed in years after being banded as chicks, many during several seasons, for a total of 7,860 bird seasons.

Other factors also led to this study. An indirect one was the signing of the Antarctic Treaty in 1959, which set aside Antarctica as a place only for research and which led to the establishment of national research programs by several countries including the United States.

The Adélie Penguin became a convenient subject of study in these programs by virtue of its need for ice-free areas in which to nest, a need also shared by humans for the construction of logistic facilities. Thus a great deal of research has been conducted on this species, as reviewed below. Other avian species also nest near Antarctic research facilities, but the Adélie's large size, flightlessness, dense coloniality, and habit of nesting in the open made it easy to observe, to mark for individual recognition, to recapture, and to locate in large numbers. Few other birds, or even penguin species, share these characteristics. Soon to be apparent is that in this study large sample sizes were often attained for analysis. The traditionality of the birds in returning to the same colonies and even nest sites allowed us to follow individuals for several consecutive years.

PREVIOUS STUDIES ON ADÉLIE PENGUINS

The Adélie, perhaps the most numerous of any penguin, breeds at rookeries scattered along the Antarctic coast and on islands south of lat. 60° S (fig. 1; Watson et al. 1971). It is migratory, spending from mid-February through September and early October at sea in the pack ice and returning to land from distances of up to several hundred kilometers (Emlen and Penney 1964, 1966). Their postbreeding migration during fall is largely accomplished by swimming through open water from rookeries to the areas of residual pack ice. Their return to rookeries as prebreeding migrants is accomplished in the spring by walking long distances over seas covered by pack ice that extends outward from Antarctica. The persistence of the pack during spring, largely a factor of weather, can have a great influence on breeding success because extensive ice cover, which forces the birds to walk, slows movement between rookeries and feeding areas (Ainley and LeResche 1973; Yeates 1968, 1975; Spurr 1975b).

The basic breeding biology of the Adélie Penguin has been described several times, in most detail by Taylor (1962) but also by Sladen (1958), Sapin-Jaloustre (1960), Penney (1968), Reid (1968), Tenaza (1971), and Spurr (1975b). Longevity and mortality rates for the species have been reported by Ainley and DeMaster (1980). Adélies usually lay two eggs (sometimes one); they lay a third if the first is lost before the second is laid. Egg laying begins in the last days of October and extends through November, the peak occurring in about the second week (Emison 1968). Males,

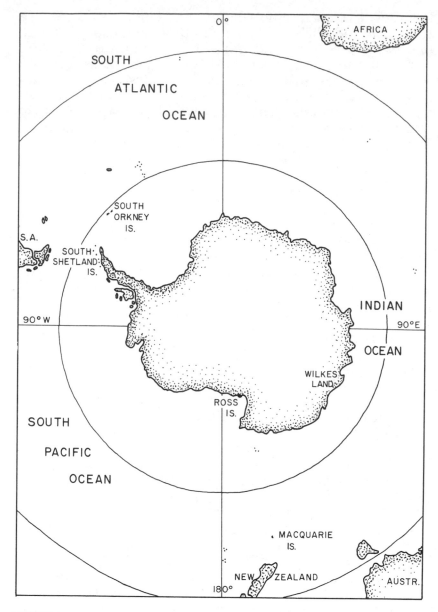

FIGURE 1   **Antarctica and the location of Ross Island; other localities mentioned in the text are shown.**

which usually arrive at the rookery earlier than females (Levick 1914), normally incubate the eggs for the first two to three weeks. They are then relieved by the females and go to sea to feed, returning to resume incubation duties after one to two weeks. Incubation watches shorten toward the end of the thirty-three to thirty-six-day incubation period, becoming only two to three days in length by the time of hatching. Newly hatched chicks are closely brooded by parents, which alternate trips to sea for a period of about ten days; then they are merely guarded by parents for an additional eight to ten days (Taylor 1962, LeResche and Boyd 1969). At the end of that time chicks reach a period of development during which they grow most rapidly and, because of their size, no longer need to be guarded. Both parents then forage simultaneously. Chicks left alone form groups, called crêches, and parents continually journey from rookery to sea to secure food, which they feed only to their own chicks (Sladen 1958, Thompson 1974). Feedings occur approximately twice every three days. Crêche stage starts in early January, when chicks are approximately twenty days of age, and lasts until early February, when chicks molt into juvenile plumage and depart to sea at about fifty days. The growth of Adélie chicks has been studied by Taylor and Roberts (1962), Ainley and Schlatter (1972), and Volkman and Trivelpiece (1980). Though each of these studies was conducted in a different place and year, little difference occurred in calculated growth curves.

Following the breeding season most adults molt at sea on ice floes (Murphy 1936, Ainley unpub. data), but a few return to the rookery or molt ashore at other rookeries (Penney 1967). Near the outer periphery of the pack ice (e.g., the northern Antarctic Peninsula and Scotia Sea), Adélies may visit rookery sites during mild periods of the winter (Parmelee et al. 1977).

The social behavior of Adélie Penguins has also been studied rather intensively beginning with Levick (1914). Sladen (1958), Sapin-Jaloustre (1960), Penney (1962, 1968), Spurr (1975a, b), and Müller-Schwarze and Müller-Schwarze (1980) described social displays on the basis of the motivational approach of Tinbergen (1960). Ainley (1975b) took a different approach, that of Smith (1977), in which he investigated the message content of displays and the importance of context in modifying the meaning of messages. The species possesses a repertoire of rather concise visual and vocal displays; the usage of these is affected by the dense spacing of nests, the very short breeding season, the fact that members of a pair see each other so little throughout the nesting period, the strong tendency to flock when away from breeding areas, and the vigorous maintenance of individual distances. Ainley (1974, 1975*a, b,* 1978) investigated the maturation process of social behavior, using known-age birds, and the comfort or maintenance behavior of Adélie Penguins. Some individuals matured more quickly than others, and immature behavior prevented some young but reproductively mature birds from pairing. Bekoff et al. (1979) studied the ontogeny of their comfort behavior, finding that the most complete sequences of behaviors matured most slowly. Derksen (1977) and Weinrich and Baker (1978) investigated their incubation behavior.

PREVIOUS STUDIES ON SEABIRDS

Unlike Richdale, who as a pioneer had few other long-term studies with which to compare his data on Yellow-eyed Penguins, we have for reference the several studies on other species mentioned earlier as well as a few on additional species. Trying to deduce the significance of many life history patterns in a species without reviewing the way that others accomplish the same functions is difficult and can lead to an inaccurate conclusion. Therefore, in the following pages we draw heavily on the pertinent seabird literature, and in the final chapter we will try to draw together the several long-term studies thus far published.

We will also in the following chapters attempt to draw together the many studies thus far published on the breeding biology and ecology of the Adélie Penguin. The above review of literature on this species was by no means exhaustive, but the reader should have been impressed by the amount of research that has so far been conducted on the Adélie (see also, Young 1981). Thus, the life history of this species is fairly well known, and in fact, the extent of our knowledge of it can hardly be rivaled by that of any other seabird species, except perhaps the Herring Gull *Larus argentatus*. The Adélie Penguin derives this status from its close proximity to research stations in the Antarctic; and the Herring Gull, from its accessibility and close proximity to human population centers in eastern North America and Europe. Unlike the studies on other species reviewed earlier, those on the Adélie and Herring Gull have been the work of many researchers rather than just one or two. Surprisingly, however, the Herring Gull has escaped being the subject of a project in which known individuals have been studied over a long period. For this reason, and because this gull is among the least marine of "seabirds," our comparisons to it will be minimal.

2
METHODS AND
DEFINITIONS

THE CAPE CROZIER ROOKERIES AND POPULATION

The Cape Crozier rookeries are situated at the base of the northern and seaward slopes of Mt. Terror, on the eastern tip of Ross Island (lat. 77°20′ S, long. 169°15′ E; fig. 2). To the east lies the Ross Ice Shelf, an immense portion of the polar ice cap that floats upon the southernmost reaches of the Ross Sea; toward the southeast and around to the southwest lies Ross Island, which is composed of three large volcanoes; and toward the northeast around to the northwest extends the Ross Sea. The terrain is steep and starkly beautiful with its glaciers and its red or black volcanic cones. Without these small, protruding peaks to divert glaciers to one side or another and the incessant gale-force winds that sweep snow from the slopes and blow the pack ice out to sea, the terrain would also be quite bleak, for then Adélie Penguins would not breed there.

At the Cape there are actually two Adélie Penguin rookeries (see definition, p. 19), the East and West, separated by a 45 m high ridge and a steep ice field across which Adélies do not travel. The two rookeries are about a kilometer apart (fig. 2). Fewer than 200 pairs of Emperor Penguins *Aptenodytes forsteri* and about 1,000 pairs of South Polar Skuas

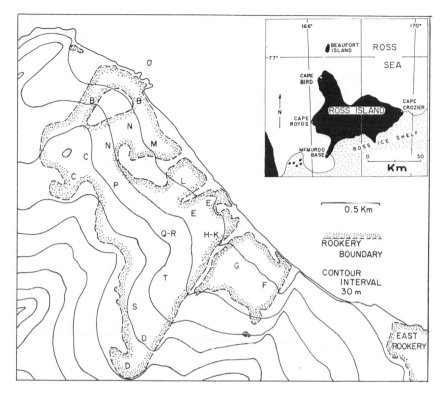

FIGURE 2 **The Cape Crozier rookery showing approximate locations of study areas; and (insert) the location of Adélie Penguin rookeries in the southwestern Ross Sea (from Ainley and DeMaster 1980, copyright © 1980, the Ecological Society of America).**

comprise the only other birds that nest in the vicinity (Ainley et al. 1978).

West Rookery has a coastline of 1.6 km, comprised of three beaches separated by rock outcrops. These interruptions were no more than 30 m each, so most of the seaward edge of the rookery provided suitable landing areas for Adélies. Rough dimensions of the West Rookery were 1.6 km × 1.1 km, or 1.81 km² in area, but breeding Adélies occupied only about 1 km². About 89,000 pairs of Adélie Penguins, or about 178,000 birds, bred within this area. Birds were counted in aerial photos taken 16 November 1966, and corrections for seasonal population fluctuations were made on the basis of ground counts (Butler and Müller-Schwarze 1977). Using similar means, Oelke (1975) estimated about 85,000 pairs in 1970.

East Rookery, by contrast, has only one small (ca. 50 m wide) rocky landing beach and 550 m of sea cliffs that were insurmountable from the sea except when early-season snowdrifts made climbing to the rookery temporarily possible. This rookery was 0.6 km x 0.25 km or 0.15 km²; about 0.1 km² was occupied by breeding Adélies. Butler and Müller-Schwarze (1977) estimated the breeding population in East Rookery to be about 13,600 pairs, or 27,200 birds.

Each rookery contained many breeding colonies that varied in size to over 4,000 contiguous nests. West Rookery contained about 880 colonies; and East Rookery, about 220. Although most colonies contained fewer than 200 nests and half contained fewer than 50, some were large, spreading clusters and lines of 4,000 to 5,000 nests. For convenience in recording activities of birds, the West Rookery was divided into 21 study areas that included breeding areas, snow slopes, and landing beaches (fig. 2). Each study area was designated by a letter, and colonies within the most intensively studied areas were numbered consecutively beginning with number one. Portions of some colonies, recognizable by physical features, were given decimal designations; for example, colony B12 was divided into B12.0, 12.1, and 12.2.

Chicks were banded in four study areas (B, C, D, and E), and subsequent study of known-age Adélies was most intensive in these and adjacent areas.

Study area B was composed of 29 colonies that ranged in size from fewer than 30 (B1) to more than 1,100 nests (B5); it stretched along the shore to the base of North Hill and was characterized by discrete colonies, mostly surrounded by snow. It was located along the western periphery of the rookery. The largest colonies (B3, 4, 5, and 12) were poorly drained or in snowdrift areas and became quite wet during December and January. Over the course of this study about half the colonies in area B were reduced significantly in size by the encroachment of persistent snowbanks (see chap. 7). At some time between 1970 and 1974 one new colony was formed in a snow-free area near B11, but colonies B1 through B9 continued to decline in size even through 1980.

Study area C bordered the southern periphery of the rookery but extended north and east well into the rookery center. It contained 46 colonies of all sizes, but most were larger than those in area B. Almost all these colonies were well drained and drift free. Colony C2, 40 m from the hut we used from 1962–1963 to 1969–1970, was used as a source for experimental birds by various researchers (e.g., Emlen and Penney 1964) and was also adjacent to a helicopter landing site used between 1962 and 1970. Owing largely to this disturbance during this period, it all but disappeared. One new colony formed in Area C between 1970 and 1974, but others along the rookery edge continued to decline through 1980.

Study area D, in the far southeastern corner of West Rookery, contained about 49 colonies and was protected from storms by Post Office Hill to the south and a high snow ridge to the east. The area, also along the rookery edge, adjoined a skua breeding area of about 200 pairs. Area D was essentially used as a control area by restricting visits to only four or five each season.

Study area E contained 37 colonies, most rounded rather than elongate, containing 200 to 400 pairs. It extended from the beach well into the rookery. Adélies commonly reached area E from either of the two easternmost major beaches; colonies were well exposed to prevailing winds and almost without exception were drift free and well drained.

Study areas H-K, L, M, N, and P (fig. 2) were also used for studies of known-age birds, although no Adélie chicks were banded there. These areas were searched daily for marked birds, and nests were marked when known-age breeders were found. At least one and possibly two colonies appeared in area N sometime between 1970 and 1974. Areas Q-R, S, F, and G were visited four or five days each season during intensive searches for known-age birds. Area Q-R was also visited once a week to observe nests being used by us to assess the effects of disturbance (see below).

Adélie chicks were banded in late January and early February for nine consecutive seasons, beginning in 1961–1962 (Wood et al. 1970). This report is based on the survivors of about 40,000 chicks banded through the 1969–1970 season. We and our field assistants observed 4,485 individually marked Adélies aged two to eighteen years. Some were seen more than one season for a total of 7,860 bird seasons. In addition, many chicks-of-the-year and more than 600 mates of known-age birds were also studied. Many unbanded adults were temporarily marked for specific objectives as described below.

MARKING METHODS

It was important to have identifiable individuals for study, and several permanent and temporary marking methods were used. Throughout this report, when a bird is referred to as an individual, its identification was positive.

The primary marking method was the flipper band described by Sladen and Penney (1960), Sladen, Wood, and Monaghan (1968), and Sladen and LeResche (1970). These bands, with 6.5 mm tall numerals, were easily legible with 8x binoculars without disturbing the bird. Each year just before the first chicks fledged, crêched chicks were encircled in sheep pens, banded, and released. At the time of banding, chicks were also permanently web-punched to distinguish their hatching year. A leather punch was used to cut these small holes, and this did not seem to bother the chicks. In later years we looked for web-punched birds without bands to determine the extent of band loss (see Ainley and DeMaster 1980). Two partial days during 1969–1970 and 1974–1975 were spent walking the peripheries of all colonies in areas B, C, and E. The feet of as many birds as possible were observed, and if punched ones were seen, we looked for a band on the bird's wing. The punch combinations used are shown in table 2.1.

Adults were sometimes marked temporarily by numbers placed in indelible ink on the underside of flippers or on the breast or by dyes squirted or sprayed on various parts of their bodies. Chicks were marked temporarily with dyes,

TABLE 2.1   The web-punch combinations used to identify a bird's hatching year.

YEAR	WEB-PUNCH
1961–1962	Outer web left foot
1962–1963	Inner web left foot
1963–1964	Inner web right foot
1964–1965	Outer web right foot
1965–1966	Both webs left foot
1966–1967	Outer web left foot, inner web right foot
1967–1968	Outer web both feet
1968–1969	Inner web both feet
1969–1970	Inner web left foot, outer web right foot

also, or with rubber bands holding numbers embossed on plastic tape. These were placed on flippers and changed as the chicks grew.

Colonies and some subcolonies in areas B, C, and D were permanently marked by electrical conduit 1 m high. These poles were placed firmly in the ground and supported stainless steel plates with engraved colony designations (e.g., C2.1).

Nests of known-age breeders and other nests of interest were marked by driving 40 cm x 1 cm rods into the ground until only 20 cm emerged. When nests were active, 1 m high bamboo poles were placed over the rods to facilitate finding them. Rods marking inactive nests were tipped with plastic tubing to prevent injury to penguins and were marked with metal tags embossed with the band number and year of breeding of the bird that had occupied the nest. Rods were left in place as permanent records of breeding sites.

SEXING TECHNIQUES

Definitions of criteria for sexing are recorded at length in the definitions section, which follows (pp. 17–20). Techniques included cloacascopic examination (Sladen and LeResche 1970, Ainley 1975a), observation of copulation, and several behavioral techniques. The cloacascope was the most reliable means of sexing birds never observed copulating or never observed in other telltale situations described later. In order to minimize disturbance, breeders were cloacascoped only when chicks had been lost or had joined the crêche. Properly executed, cloacascopy could be accomplished in less than a minute and was seemingly painless for the birds.

OBSERVATION TECHNIQUES

Most of our data were gathered while searching for banded birds on systematic walks through the rookery. When a bird was located, its behavior was recorded, as explained in a following section, and in a few cases it was then handled for rebanding, marking, sexing, nest marking, or other reasons. Throughout the study, disturbance was kept at the absolute minimum consistent with accomplishing study objectives. This precluded systematic weighing of birds and regular handling but allowed us to study relatively undisturbed birds.

Specific procedures for general observation and specific experiments were as follows:

Disturbed Controls

A sample of nests was selected to obtain both (a) an index of how productive the *established* breeders were (see definitions), their dates of laying, and related information for comparison with known-age birds and (b) an idea of how much disturbance we caused by a careful visit to a nest each day or every other day (since this is how we had been studying the known-age birds). A field assistant who had never been at Crozier before chose fifty nests in study colonies early in the occupation period (4 November in 1968, 1969, and 1974) and marked them with nest poles. When the nests of known-age birds were checked, these nests, too, were visited and their status determined (number of adults, number of eggs, number of chicks, any special behavior, etc.). We tried to disturb these birds, as well as the known-age birds, as little as possible. When one bird was left alone on eggs, dye was squirted on its breast in order to know at a glance which bird of the pair was at the nest on any given date (i.e., when changeovers occurred).

The controls were distributed throughout the study areas (except in colony B5) in approximately the same ratio as were studied nests of known-age birds. For example, the distribution of control nests in 1968 was as shown in table 2.2.

"Undisturbed" Controls

To obtain further information on productivity and chronology of established breeders and an evaluation of the effect of less frequent disturbance to compare with "disturbed" controls, 100 nests were selected in as straight a line as possible in area Q-R during early November 1968, 1969, and 1974. The line ran directly through colonies in different situations, and every nest intersected by it was studied unless it was inaccessible. A large nail was driven through a 9 cm length of rubber tubing and was then driven into the ground between every two nests. Every tenth nest was marked with a numbered bamboo pole to further guide the observer.

Visits were made once per week, and nest status (number of eggs, number of chicks, number of adults, any special

TABLE 2.2   The distribution of control nests in various colonies during 1968.

COLONY	NUMBER OF NESTS	COLONY	NUMBER OF NESTS
C2.0	2	B2.0	2
C6.0	2	B2.1	1
C15.0	3	B3.0	2
C7.0	1	B4.0	2
C8.0	1	B6.0	2
C10.0	2	B7.0	2
C11.0	2	M	3
C12.0	2	L	2
N	9	E	5
B11.0	2	P	3

behavior, etc.) was recorded. The birds were not handled and were disturbed as little as possible (see chap. 7).

Area D and East Rookery provided a relatively undisturbed area for banding, logging the returns of banded birds, and assessing the effect of our work on the more intensively studied areas B, C, and E. Visits to the East Rookery also provided data on rates of emigration to the nearest rookery (see Ainley and DeMaster 1980). Three visits were made to each during the course of the season, particularly during seasonal peaks in the rookery population size. We made an exhaustive search for bands each time and noted the status of each banded bird. Dates of the visits were approximately the following, depending upon competing activities: 20–25 November, 20–25 December, and 10–15 January.

January Chick Counts

To assess yearly productivity in various areas of the rookery, including those maximally disturbed (B and especially C), moderately disturbed (E), and virtually undisturbed (D and F), as soon as possible after 7 January all chicks in the following colonies were counted: C1 through C6.10; C7, C7.1, C7.2, C8.0, C13, and C15; all colonies in area B, including B10; subcolonies D1, D2, D3, D4, and D8; and F1 and F2.

GENERAL PROCEDURE FOR RECORDING THE STATUS OF BANDED BIRDS

1. Band number was read with binoculars with the least possible disturbance
2. Area, colony, and subcolony (if any), and whether nest had been marked was recorded
3. Status was recorded as follows:
   AoN: alone on nest
   PoN: paired on nest (either of the following was recorded: "with UB," if partner was unbanded; "with [partner's band number]")
   Wand: not attached to territory, wandering

OC, 1C, or 2C: if no chicks, one chick, or two chicks
OE, 1E, or 2E: if no eggs, one egg, or two eggs

4. Kind of nest was recorded as follows (see Ainley 1978):
   Sc: scoop; a depression scratched into the substrate
   PBN: poorly built nest; a few stones dumped haphazardly into the scoop
   FBN: fair-built nest; moderate number of stones arranged into a nest shape
   WBN: well-built nest; many stones in a well-formed bowl; the nest was equal to the best in its respective colony

5. Indication of sex was recorded as follows (see definition of *sex* in following section):
   DC: dilated cloaca just after egg laying
   TMKS: definite, muddy tread marks on back
   s1 TMKS: only slight traces of tread marks on back

The above abbreviations were only guidelines. Any abnormal or interesting behavior not describable by the use of the abbreviations was recorded at length.

DEFINITIONS

We have defined all terms used in this study that could be peculiar to it or to penguins. Some were previously defined by other researchers (as noted), and we include them for the sake of completeness.

ADULT: A bird mature both physically and behaviorally; adults showed modal behavior. Unbanded birds (of unknown age) that arrived early at the rookery were considered adults for the purposes of "control" comparisons.

AGE: Given in years for birds banded as chicks and later identified by band number or web-punch code. Age was calculated from the bird's nearest birthday; for example, a bird hatched in December 1964 was called a four-year-old during the 1968–1969 breeding season, from October 1968 through February 1969. When a chick's age was referred to, it was expressed in days since hatching.

AREA: (e.g., *natal area, breeding area*). Natal area: in large rookeries the area within 200 m in all directions from the site of hatching.

The size of the area designated, necessarily arbitrary in large rookeries, was taken as approximately the maximum dimension of the Cape Royds rookery (from colony 1 to colony 10 of Taylor 1962). Thus all chicks from Cape Royds have the same natal area. *Area* used with other prefixes has the same meaning: within a 200 m radius.

BREEDING: A bird was spoken of as breeding, or attempting breeding, only with evidence that at least one egg had been laid. When chicks were mobile (and sometimes brooded by adults other than their parents), observation of a complete act of feeding chicks (swallowing of food by the chick) established parenthood. (See *successful breeding, prebreeder, nonbreeder,* below).

CHICK: A bird from the time of its complete emergence from the egg until it swam off to sea the first time.

CLUTCH SIZE: Number of eggs laid in one season by an individual female or male's mate. Clutch size was recorded only when observation began before the first egg and when egg loss had not occurred.

COHORT: A group of birds hatched the same season.

COLONY: A discrete and contiguous group of breeding penguins (Penney 1968). The number of nests in a colony varied from a few to many thousand. Since nest-to-nest distances varied and therefore "contiguousness" was sometimes open to question, the delineation of colonies was at times arbitrary.

COLONY GROUP: A naturally discrete group of colonies, each closer to its neighbor within the group than to any colony in another group. These were arbitrarily defined by topography and shape of colonies and were in size somewhere between colonies and areas. The typical area contained ten to fifteen colonies and three to four colony groups.

CRÊCHE: More than a normal brood of two chicks gathered together in a group; they were normally unguarded by adults (Sladen 1958).

DISUNITED: Mates were disunited when, after breeding together, they did not breed together when both returned to the rookery the following season (Penney 1968). This term is analogous to Richdale's (1957) *divorced.*

ESTABLISHED: Established breeders exhibited modal adult behavior in all breeding characteristics (e.g., early arrival, two-egg clutch, chick or chicks hatched or fledged). This term is analogous to Sladen's (1953, 1958) *experienced.*

EXPERIENCED: A bird was experienced in a behavior (e.g., breeding) if it had been observed *performing that behavior* in a previous season (Sladen 1953, 1958). Its experience at the rookery was measured by the number of seasons it had been sighted there (see *inexperienced*).

FIRST SIGHTED: A bird during its first season at the rookery. It may have been observed twenty times that season, but it was still *first sighted* or *inexperienced.*

FLEDGLING: A chick that left the rookery and swam off to sea.

FORMER MATE: Used only in reference to mates of known-age birds; a bird that had bred with a known-age bird during at least one previous season.

INCIDENCE: The proportion of birds in a (usually age- or sex-) group observed performing a behavior *at least once* in a given season (e.g., if two of ten five-year-olds were seen wandering one or more times, incidence of wandering was 20 percent).

INCUBATION PERIOD: The length of time (in days ± 1 because we often checked nests every other day) from laying of an egg to complete emergence of a chick.

INEXPERIENCED: A bird was inexperienced in a behavior (e.g., breeding) if it had never been observed performing that behavior in a previous season. Inexperienced birds in relation to presence in the rookery were those that were observed for the first season.

KEEPING COMPANY: The partnership, which may or may not have led to the establishment of a mated pair, of two birds of opposite sex at a nest site (Sladen 1953, 1958). Duration of *keeping company* varied from a few hours to several weeks, but the term does not include brief (less than 30 min) associations between wandering birds at a site. Keeping company was often accompanied by displays such as Loud Calls (Ainley 1975*b*), but occurrence of such displays did not confirm this status, nor did their absence preclude it.

KNOWN-AGE BIRD: A bird banded and/or web-punched as a chick and recognizable as a member of a specific cohort by these markings.

MATE: A bird breeding with another was its mate; the association led to the laying of eggs.

NATAL: This refers to the site, whether rookery, area, or colony, where a bird was banded as a chick.

NESTLING: A chick during guard stage, from hatching until it had entered the crèche.

NONBREEDER: A bird that had not bred during the current breeding season. This designation was not assigned until egg laying was finished and referred only to birds observed since their arrival at the rookery. It did not include *failed breeders.*

PAIRED: Two birds keeping company at a nest site were paired, as opposed to *mated* (which includes breeding).

PARTNER: A bird keeping company (not breeding) with another was its partner.

PREBREEDER: A bird unknown ever to have bred.

ROOKERY: An aggregation of colonies to which breeding birds have access from the same landing beach or beaches (Penney 1968).

SEASON: The breeding season, from mid-October through mid-February, from the arrival of the first birds until final departure of all adults and chicks.

SEX: Sex was stated unequivocally only when one or more pieces of evidence were available. This replaced and added to Sladen's (1958) methods of sexing Adélies. Sex was known unequivocally based on the following: (1) cloacascopic examination (see *sexing techniques*, p. 13); (2) dissection (a method used only when a bird was found dead); (3) copulation position; (4) mate or partner was positively sexed; (5) clearly discernible tread marks on the back of the smaller member of a pair (the male on top often leaves muddy tread marks on a female's back) *in conjunction with* a normal incubation routine (male incubates first: Ainley and LeResche 1973). Probable sex was inferred from the following criteria (in order of reliability): (1) within 24 h after an egg had been laid in the nest, a clean contracted cloaca (♂) compared to the mate's flaccid or bloody cloaca (♀); (2) complete and repeated Ecstatic Vocalizations (see Ainley 1975*b*) while on a nest site during the egg-laying period (♂); (3) long (10+ days) occupation of an empty, well-built nest, usually alone, and accompanied by complete or incomplete vocalizations (♂); and (4) larger size and greater aggressiveness (♂) when compared with partner or mate (♀).

SUCCESSFUL BREEDING: In a given season, successful breeding was defined in specific reference to one of three stages of the annual cycle, the criterion being explicitly stated each time (Sladen 1953, 1958). (1) Hatching: the successful hatching of at least one egg to a viable chick (see *chick*); (2) crèche chicks: the hatching and rearing of at least one chick until it entered the crèche, or for four weeks, whichever came first (see *crèche*); and (3) fledged chicks: the hatching and rearing of at least one chick to a stage at which it had molted half or more of its down and was robust enough to swim to sea. The latter was a necessarily arbitrary criterion but was used to exclude obviously emaciated chicks, since positive evidence of fledging (sighted on beach or actually swimming away) was seldom possible (see *fledgling*).

TERRITORY: A defended space with geographic reference.

WANDERER: A bird that exhibited little, if any, affinity to a single nest site (Sladen 1958).

YEARLING: A bird in white-chinned plumage, worn from fledging at about ten weeks to about age fifteen months.

3
OCCUPATION
OF THE ROOKERY

 In sedentary penguins such as the Yellow-eyed (Richdale 1949*a*, 1957), both pre-breeders in juvenile or adult plumage and adults visit the rookery continually throughout the year; for several months, however, fewer juveniles than adults occur. In migratory species such as Adélie and Royal penguins, first arrival at the rookery and eventual final departure are precise annual events. The timing of arrival has profound effects upon the activities of a bird at the rookery— where it will procure a nest site, with whom it will mate, if at all, and whether it will breed successfully. We know much less about what Adélies do after their departure, but the timing of that event is likely to be critical, too, because they need time to recover from the demands of breeding and to molt before the long winter begins.

Sladen (1958) was the first to describe the periodic fluctuation in the numbers of Adélies at a rookery. The *occupation period* starts when breeders return in the spring to establish nests, pair, and mate. The population increases rapidly as females begin to lay eggs. The penguins begin to depart shortly thereafter, soon more birds depart than arrive, and numbers decline. Later, about the time that chicks hatch, the *reoccupation period* starts, when the population of birds in adult plumage begins to swell again, moving toward its highest peak of the summer. Some birds arrive for their first visit of the season, breeders who had lost their eggs return to reoccupy their nests, and both members of successful pairs are more often present together than earlier in the season because attendance periods at the nest for individuals last only a few days. After remaining in peak numbers for several days, birds then leave the rookery in increasing numbers, parents begin to make only brief visits to feed their chicks, and thus the population declines. Just large, fully feathered chicks, the occasional parent, and a few molting adults are left. Finally even the chicks leave, and the rookery is quiet, except for the calls of scavenging skuas, until the following spring.

Ainley et al. (1978) described the annual fluctuation in the Adélie population at Cape Crozier, and Taylor (1962) described the phenomenon at Cape Royds on the opposite side of Ross Island. When compared to Sladen's (1958) description for Signy Island in the South Orkneys, 16° north of Ross Island, some differences become apparent. At Ross Island the interval between the arrival of the first birds and the population peak is about two weeks shorter, and the dip in numbers between the occupation and reoccupation peaks is much smaller. Interestingly, because the population peak during the reoccupation period and final departure occurs at similar times for both islands, the breeding season is two to three weeks shorter at Ross Island (Cape Crozier) at lat. 77° S, mainly because the occupation period is later. Its lateness would also account for the smaller dip in numbers between the occupation and reoccupation periods. It is unknown if the breeding season of individual pairs is also shorter farther south at Ross Island; if it is, this might increase the stress of breeding, which in turn might affect predation pressure and mortality (see ch. 9).

Incubation periods are similar at Signy and Ross islands for single-egg clutches and second eggs of two-egg clutches: 34 days (range 33–37; n = 7) at Signy (Sladen 1958) and 33.3 $\pm$ 1 days (range 30–37; n = 78) at Cape Royds (Taylor 1962); in two-egg clutches full incubation does not begin until the second egg is laid (Derkson 1977, Weinrich and Baker 1978). Because of this, any curtailment of the breeding season must occur during the nest-building and pair formation/reformation period or, more critically, during the growth period of chicks. What little comparative data are available indicate equal growth periods: three chicks at Signy Island fledged at 48 to 53 days; 91 chicks at King George Island in the South Shetlands fledged at 50 to 55 days (Volkman and Trivelpiece 1980); and 113 chicks at Cape Royds fledged at 41 to 56 days (mean = 50.6). There is thus no evidence that the time required to incubate eggs and raise chicks is affected by the latitude of a breeding site. The apparent differences in the shorter annual rookery period of a population at higher latitudes are an increased synchrony of activity among breeders and a greater overlap between their activities and those of younger breeding birds that, as shown below, arrive later.

AGE OF FIRST RETURN

Each year a few yearlings, distinguishable by their white chins and throats (Sladen 1958), returned to the Cape Crozier rookeries, usually in January and February and usually to molt. Never did we sight a yearling that was banded, and the proportion of one-year-olds returning accounted for much less than 1 percent of all birds visiting each year. During December and January 1976 through 1980, however, yearlings accounted for the great majority of Adélie Penguins seen in pelagic waters of the Ross Sea distant from any rookeries (Ainley and O'Connor in press). Interestingly, though they did not visit rookeries, these youngest birds still moved toward breeding areas and left vacant large portions of seemingly suitable habitat during December. By January, they spread out to occupy all of the available pack ice and concentrated where food was abundant. Ainley and O'Connor hypothesized that these youngsters were drawn along by the mass movement of older birds toward rookeries during the reoccupation period and/or, building on the earlier hypothesis of Ainley (1975a), they underwent an "incipient" migratory movement stimulated by a slight increase in hormone levels.

Based on records for 1,064 birds of known sex gathered from the 1963–1964 to the 1969–1970 seasons, about 29 per-

TABLE 3.1   Age at first observed visit to the Cape Crozier rookery for the 1963–1964 through 1969–1970 seasons.

Age	Male		Female	
(yrs)	*Percent*	*n*	*Percent*	*n*
1	0.0	0	0.0	0
2	28.6	157	30.7	158
3	43.4	238	49.7	256
4	18.9	104	14.6	75
5	7.5	41	3.3	17
6	1.6	9	1.0	5
7	0.0	0	0.6	3
8	0.0	0	0.2	1
Totals	100.0	549	100.1	515
Mean ± SE	3.1 ± 0.008		2.9 ± 0.08	

cent of males and 31 percent of females ($P<.05$) that eventually returned to Crozier arrived first when two years old (table 3.1). Among the next oldest birds a slight difference was apparent between males and females in their return rates: 72 percent of males and 81 percent of females ($P<.05$; t-test, Sokal and Rohlf 1969:608) had visited at least once by the time they were four years old. The slightly earlier return of females was probably related to their earlier development in reproductive physiology (Ainley 1975*a*). For a number of reasons, we probably overlooked most of the several females recorded as making first visits when six to eight years old. Older males usually remained for several days, but older females that arrived later than average in the spring visited for only a few days and hence the chances of their being detected were lessened. We discuss this more fully below (see also Ainley 1978). In addition, all females were known to have bred at least once by the age of seven (see ch. 6). The five- to eight-year-old females in table 3.1 would have to have bred without any previous experience in the rookery; this, though possible, was unlikely. We believe that almost all Adélies that were going to visit Crozier did so at least once by the time they were seven years old.

ARRIVAL DATE IN THE BREEDING SEASON

Older Adélies arrived at Cape Crozier earlier in the spring than younger birds, and individual birds usually arrived earlier the following spring than they had the previous year. These patterns continued only up to a certain age depending on sex and were related to whether a bird arrived for the first time or whether it had visited during a previous year, as well as its breeding status.

Both the date the first member of each age group was seen at the rookery (table 3.2) and the average date of arrival for each age group (table 3.3) were later for younger birds. The date the first bird of any given age was seen at Crozier varied from year to year and did not follow a precise age sequence in birds five years old and older because of individual variation within age groups. The average date of arrival, however, demonstrated clearly that older birds arrived earlier. The trend was most dramatic through ages seven and six for males and females, respectively; and then the differences between progressively older birds decreased. Among males seven to eleven years old, arrival dates differed little for birds that had visited in a previous year, but the three oldest age classes arrived even earlier; for females older than six, there was little actual difference in arrival dates. Ainley (1978) reported that breeders in a given season arrived earlier on the average than nonbreeders; this is also true for birds within the same age classes (table 3.4). The greater proportion of females breeding in the youngest age-groups (Ainley 1978, Ainley and DeMaster 1980; see ch. 6) would account for their average arrival being earlier than that of males in those groups.

The trend toward earlier arrival of older birds also applied to individuals, subject to variation, with some birds returning consistently early, some consistently late, and a few at widely varying dates. The overall pattern, however, was also one of earlier return with added age and experience but of less change with each added year of age. This is illustrated in figure 3: for birds between the second and third years of age, the median date (i.e., for 50 percent of the birds) advanced at least 21 to 25 days; between the third and

TABLE 3.2 Dates of first arrival and first egg at Cape Crozier, 1962–1975.

Age (yrs)	1962–63	1963–64	1964–65	1965–66	1966–67	1967–68	1968–69	1969–70	1974–75	1975–76
unknown	22 Oct.		20 Oct.		25 Oct.	18 Oct.	20 Oct.	19 Oct.	22 Oct.	21 Oct.
1		19 Dec.	15 Dec.	14 Dec.	25 Dec.	26 Dec.	19 Dec.	18 Dec.	27 Dec.	
2		19 Dec.	19 Nov.		6 Dec.	6 Dec.	11 Dec.	22 Nov.		
3			4 Nov.		7 Nov.	7 Nov.	8 Nov.	1 Nov.		
4					4 Nov.	30 Oct.	2 Nov.	29 Oct.		
5					7 Nov.	28 Oct.	28 Oct.	24 Oct.	25 Oct.	
6						30 Oct.	31 Oct.	25 Oct.	24 Oct.	23 Oct.
7							5 Nov.	24 Oct.	22 Oct.	23 Oct.
8								25 Oct.	27 Oct.	22 Oct.
9									24 Oct.	24 Oct.
10									24 Oct.	25 Oct.
11									28 Oct.	23 Oct.
12									25 Oct.	23 Oct.
13									25 Oct.	24 Oct.
14										24 Oct.
First egg			2 Nov.	30 Oct.	5 Nov.	3 Nov.	3 Nov.	5 Nov.	3 Nov.	3 Nov.

TABLE 3.3 Average date of arrival (± SD in days) at Cape Crozier, 1967 to 1975.

Age	MALE						FEMALE					
	First time			Returnees			First time			Returnees		
(yrs)	Date ± SD		n	Date ± SD		n	Date ± SD		n	Date ± SD		n
2	1 Dec. ± 10.6		104				30 Dec. ± 11.2		115			
3	18 Dec. ± 16.2		183	4 Dec. ± 19.5		61	14 Dec. ± 18.0		173	1 Dec. ± 17.6		55
4	9 Dec. ± 20.8		95	22 Nov. ± 18.0		194	4 Dec. ± 21.2		65	24 Nov. ± 19.3		161
5	6 Dec. ± 21.8		40	16 Nov. ± 16.7		409	15 Dec. ± 26.9		16	18 Nov. ± 14.6		317
6	26 Nov. ± 24.1		9	11 Nov. ± 12.8		518	22 Nov. ± 20.6		5	15 Nov. ± 12.6		408
7				9 Nov. ± 12.7		391				14 Nov. ± 10.7		331
8				6 Nov. ± 10.6		198				12 Nov. ± 7.1		164
9				7 Nov. ± 9.5		78				13 Nov. ± 5.7		46
10				8 Nov. ± 12.6		64				14 Nov. ± 12.1		36
11				6 Nov. ± 12.3		59				14 Nov. ± 15.4		33
12				3 Nov. ± 7.7		38				11 Nov. ± 6.4		24
13				2 Nov. ± 8.2		15				14 Nov. ± 2.0		8
14				4 Nov. ± 10.4		3						
8–14 ($\bar{x}$)				6 Nov. ± 10.1		455				13 Nov. ± 8.1		311
All ($\bar{x}$)	18 Dec. ± 19.5		431	12 Nov. ± 15.4		2,028	17 Dec. ± 19.9		374	17 Nov. ± 13.8		1,583
r*	−.9786			−.9523			−.8406			−.9357		

*Regressions of age vs. arrival date, using a weighted average date of arrival for 8- to 14-year-olds; all are significant (P<.05).

TABLE 3.4   Dates by which 50 percent of the mates* of known-age birds, known-age breeders, and known-age nonbreeders arrived at Cape Crozier, 1967.

Age	Date of 50% arrival†		
(yrs)	Breeders	Nonbreeders	Mates*
?			7 Nov.
1		29 Jan.	
2		30 Dec.	
3	22 Nov.	14 Dec.	
4	19 Nov.	28 Nov.	
5	17 Nov.	23 Nov.	
6	16 Nov.	2 Dec.	

*Unknown age

†Regression of age vs. arrival date, for breeders r $=$ $-.9759$ and for nonbreeders r $=$ $-.8847$ (P$<$.05). A comparison of dates for breeders and nonbreeders three to six years of age indicates that the former arrive earlier (X^2 $=$ 42.48, P$<$.05).

fourth years, 16 to 20 days; between the fourth and fifth years, 11 to 15 days; between the fifth and sixth years, 6 to 10 days; and between the sixth and seventh years, 0 days. Among Adélies three years of age, more than four-fifths arrived earlier than they had the previous year; but among those seven years old, half arrived earlier and half arrived later.

Ice conditions in spring also affected arrival dates. Although to a large extent its ability to fast for long periods allows the Adélie Penguin to cope with extensive areas of frozen sea, especially heavy ice cover has its effects. At Crozier, Ainley and LeResche (1973) compared a year of extensive pack ice cover, 1968–1969, with one of minimal cover, 1969–1970. The average arrival date for the population was delayed a week the first year, and individual Adélies were affected differently depending on their age and experience but not their sex. Arrival dates of those two, three, and four years old showed little year-to-year variation, probably because the ice was gone or greatly dissipated by the time they migrated to the rookery in late December. This is indi-

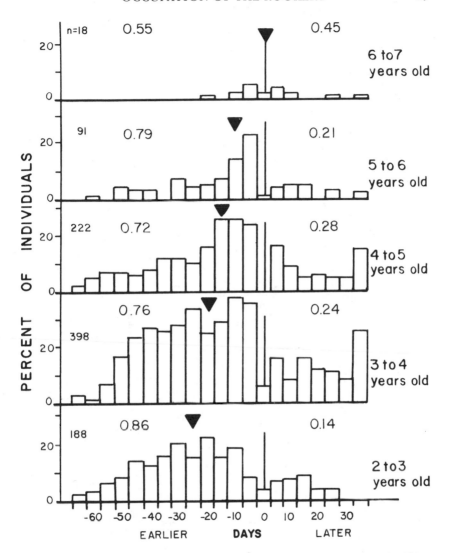

FIGURE 3   The advancement in arrival dates of individual Adélies in successive years, 1963 to 1969. Each histogram shows the percent of individuals whose date of return was advanced or retarded compared to the previous season. The percentage of total individuals that advanced or retarded their dates is also shown; arrows indicate the median number of days advanced.

TABLE 3.5 Anomalies (in days) between the mean arrival dates at Cape Crozier for all years and the mean arrival dates for individual years. Analysis is broken down by age, sex, and experience (First time visitors = F; Returnees = R; the negative sign (−) = date earlier than long-term average; and the positive sign (+) = date later than long-term average).

Age (yrs)	S*	1967–68				1968–69				1969–70				1974–75				1975–76			
		♂		♀		♂		♀		♂		♀		♂		♀		♂		♀	
		F	R	F	R	F	R	F	R	F	R	F	R	F	R	F	R	F	R	F	R
2	1.94	−2		−2		−1		+3		+1		0									
3	2.84	−4	−2	−2	+6	+3		+1	0	+4	+1	+1	−2								
4	2.86	+2	+3	+1	+3	−5		0	−5	0	0	+4	0								
5	12.62	+12	+3	+22	+2	+24	+2	+37	+1	+20	−2	+7	−3		−4		−7				
6	10.16	+6	+17	+10	+11	+29	+4	+4		−4	−2	−3			0		0				
7							+12		+10		+4		−3		0		0		−1		0
8											−1		−10		+4		+3		−1		0
9															+2		+1		−1		+1
10															+1		+3		−1		−1
11															+4		+3		−5		−5
12															−2		+1		+1		−2
13															+6				+2		−5

* Standard deviation of the mean anomaly for the three seasons, 1967–1968 to 1969–1970; S^2 for two- to four-year-olds is 6.87 (n = 30), which is not similar statistically to S^2 for four- and five-year-olds at 130.33 (n = 22; F = 18.97; P < .05).

cated by averaging the arrival date anomalies for each age class during the years 1967–1968 to 1969–1970. The standard deviation of the mean anomaly for those two, three, and four years old was much smaller than that for older birds in those years (table 3.5). Earlier in the year, ice conditions were much more of a delaying factor. Among the older birds migrating then, anomalies in arrival dates varied much more for first time visitors than for those who had visited in at least one previous year.

Pack ice cover was very extensive and long lasting in the springs of 1967–1968 and 1968–1969, and fairly extensive in 1974–1975 compared to the other two years. In the years of heavy ice, migration was delayed in all older age groups, especially among inexperienced birds; in the years of light ice, migration was advanced. The late arrival dates for four- and five-year-olds and the late egg date shown in table 3.2 indicate that ice cover was also extensive during spring 1966–1967.

TIME SPENT IN THE ROOKERY

An Adélie's age, sex, and breeding status also had bearing on when it departed the rookery but not as dramatically as they did on when it arrived. The date of last observation of nonbreeders went from 5 January for two-year-olds to 10 January for males nine and older and to 8 January for females six and older (table 3.6; $P<.05$). Among breeders, the date of last observation was similar to that for the oldest nonbreeders; for breeding males but not females, the date increased slightly with age ($P<.05$). Many of the oldest nonbreeding birds were departing just prior to or just as the youngest birds were arriving. Most of these older birds had been in the rookery for two extended periods during which they fasted (Ainley 1978). Among nonbreeders, females departed slightly earlier on the average than did males (t = 4.015, df = ∞; $P<.05$); no such difference was apparent among breeders.

The average date when breeding birds were last seen was more a measure of when they discontinued guarding and brooding their chicks (who then formed crèches);

TABLE 3.6 Average date in January when Adélie Penguins were last seen at Cape Crozier, 1967 to 1974.

Age (yrs)	NONBREEDING BIRDS				BREEDING BIRDS			
	Male		Female		Male		Female	
	Date ± SD	n	Date ± SD	n	Date ± SD	n	Date ± SD	n
2	5 ± 8.3	102	5 ± 7.8	112			11 ± 8.3	34
3	6 ± 9.4	220	3 ± 9.3	177			11 ± 12.4	102
4	8 ± 9.5	217	5 ± 10.1	89	8 ± 13.0	28	8 ± 8.1	205
5	8 ± 9.2	217	6 ± 9.1	71	9 ± 9.0	147	9 ± 8.1	213
6	9 ± 7.4	104	8 ± 7.0	45	9 ± 6.7	214	8 ± 7.4	175
7	8 ± 8.4	35	9 ± 7.7	13	10 ± 6.4	176	9 ± 5.0	90
8–13	11 ± 5.3	20	7 ± 3.6	11	10 ± 4.6	131		
All	7 ± 9.1	915	5 ± 9.0	518	9 ± 7.3	696	9 ± 8.5	819
r_{2-8}	.9092*		.7960*		.9449*		.7042*	

*P<.05.

thereafter, into early February, although parents continued to feed chicks, their visits to nest sites were as short as our daily observations, and thus we usually failed to detect them. A more valid comparison of departure dates is given by combining all birds regardless of breeding status (fig. 4). We could do this only with data from the 1967–1968 season, when special attention was given to departure dates. The figure shows the rapid but early departure of two-year-olds and the later departure of older birds.

As indicated by earlier arrival and later or similar departure dates, older penguins stayed longer than younger ones at Crozier. This was also evident in the interval between first and last sightings of individuals in a given season. Among nonbreeding birds, two-year-olds were present over a span of four to six days (64 percent spent only one day; table 3.7). By age five, males were seen over a period averaging 35 days; and by age six, females were seen 29 days. Many of these birds, however, visited over periods exceeding 65 days. In their respective age classes, nonbreeding females

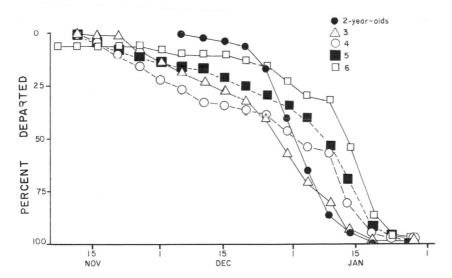

FIGURE 4   The progression in departures from Cape Crozier by Adélie Penguins two to six years of age. The ordinate represents the cumulative proportion of birds last seen by a given date, 1967–1968.

TABLE 3.7 **Relationship between age and the average number of days between dates first and last seen at Cape Crozier for nonbreeding Adélie Penguins, 1967 to 1974.**

Age	Male		Female	
(yrs)	Days ± SD	n	Days ± SD	n
2	4.3 ± 6.7	104	6.0 ± 8.8	115
3	19.1 ± 19.1	244	17.9 ± 17.8	189
4	33.4 ± 25.4	256	21.9 ± 23.0	117
5	38.6 ± 25.6	270	23.9 ± 22.4	105
6	44.9 ± 25.2	128	29.2 ± 23.9	61
7	36.1 ± 25.1	46	22.4 ± 21.0	18
8	34.9 ± 32.5	10	30.0 ± 24.3	5
9	50.0 ± 27.8	9	49.0 ± 13.9	4
All	30.0 ± 26.0	1,067	18.9 ± 20.7	614
r	.8257*		.8779*	

*$P < .05$.

spent less time at Crozier than nonbreeding males (see also Ainley 1978). In contrast, age had little effect on the amount of time breeding birds were seen (table 3.8): males were seen over a period of 52 to 63 days; females, 47 to 58 days. When we add the additional month they were visiting chicks but were rarely seen by us, the time they spent in breeding activities exceeds three months. Thus older birds visited over a longer period each year than younger ones, breeders longer than nonbreeders, and males longer than females.

The number of visits a bird made was also related to its age and breeding status. Ainley (1978) reported that most nonbreeders younger than five made only one visit, in December, but that older nonbreeders visited twice, arriving in November for about three weeks, leaving for three weeks, and then returning in late December for another three-week stay. Thus the younger birds were only present during the reoccupation period, but the older birds were present then as well as during the occupation period. The pattern was completely different for breeding birds who made thirty-five to forty different visits over the course of a season (Taylor 1962; Ainley and DeMaster 1980). For breeders and non-

TABLE 3.8 **Relationship between age and the average number of days between dates first and last seen at Cape Crozier for breeding Adélie Penguins, 1967 to 1974.**

Age	Male			Female		
(yrs)	Days ± SD		n	Days ± SD		n
3				46.7 ± 19.3		38
4	48.9 ± 23.3		33	50.8 ± 20.2		109
5	52.3 ± 22.5		179	50.2 ± 18.6		227
6	60.2 ± 16.4		227	55.2 ± 15.6		221
7	63.0 ± 15.1		183	56.2 ± 13.8		179
8	62.6 ± 15.6		50	56.3 ± 14.0		40
9	60.2 ± 25.9		28	60.6 ± 6.1		18
10	59.5 ± 20.7		34	55.1 ± 8.1		17
11	57.5 ± 20.6		24	45.9 ± 22.5		9
12	72.4 ± 6.0		10	57.8 ± 6.6		10
13	55.8 ± 17.8		4			
All	58.4 ± 19.3		772	53.3 ± 16.9		868
r	.5045*			.4026*		

*P>.05

breeders of both sexes, the amount of time spent in the rookery during the first or only visit was inversely correlated to arrival date (Ainley 1978) and to weight (Ainley 1975a). Simply stated, if a bird had more energy stored in the form of fat, it could remain longer and usually did. On the average, breeders remained much longer on their first visit than nonbreeders and much longer than young nonbreeders; in all groups, the amount of time present increased with age (P<.05; table 3.9).

CHAPTER SUMMARY/SYNTHESIS: SIGNIFICANCE OF DELAYED ARRIVAL

Several significant facts emerge from the above: (1) Adélies return to their natal area only after two or more years at sea; (2) females return at younger ages than males; (3) older birds return earlier in the season than younger birds; (4)

TABLE 3.9 Average number of days between arrival and first departure; Cape Crozier, 1967 to 1974.

Age (yrs)	MALE Breeders		MALE Nonbreeders		FEMALE Breeders		FEMALE Nonbreeders	
	Days ± SD	n	Days ± SD	n	Days ± SD	n	Days ± SD	n
2			2.3 ± 2.4	10			1.2 ± 0.7	17
3			3.9 ± 4.5	110	12.3 ± 9.0	20	3.7 ± 4.8	76
4	25.9 ± 9.4	15	7.9 ± 6.9	138	11.3 ± 8.5	41	4.7 ± 7.4	45
5	23.8 ± 7.8	81	11.1 ± 8.0	159	11.0 ± 4.7	105	4.9 ± 5.1	44
6	25.2 ± 7.6	262	15.5 ± 8.5	90	10.1 ± 5.5	275	6.8 ± 6.8	31
7	26.7 ± 7.5	233	13.1 ± 8.6	26	9.7 ± 4.4	249	5.8 ± 2.9	6
8	26.6 ± 8.1	108	18.6 ± 7.6	5	9.7 ± 4.2	123	11.0 ± 10.2	3
9	26.5 ± 7.6	48	24.8 ± 15.8	6	9.1 ± 4.5	39	8.0 ± 5.7	4
10–14*	28.5 ± 7.1	108	23.3 ± 4.8	3	10.2 ± 4.7	68		
All†	26.2 ± 7.7	855	9.8 ± 8.6	547	10.1 ± 5.2	920	4.6 ± 5.9	226
r‡	.7762		.9738		.8410		.8861	

*Weighted mean.

†Comparing breeders and nonbreeders, among males t = 37.15, and among females, t = 13.87; P<.05.

‡P<.05.

breeders return earlier than nonbreeders; (5) males return earlier in the spring than females; and (6) younger birds and (7) most nonbreeders spend fewer days at the rookery and leave earlier in the fall than older birds and breeders, respectively. Many of these characteristics have also been reported in studies of other seabird species where marked individuals have been studied over a long period. Taken together they present a profile common to migratory, long-lived seabirds with the exception of point (2), which had not been reported previously, and point (5), the earlier arrival by males. The male and female Black-legged Kittiwake return at the same time (Coulson and White 1958*a*), but the male Royal Penguin returns slightly earlier than the female. Overall, the age-related patterns of arrival and attendance in the Adélie are remarkably similar to those of the Royal Penguin (see Carrick 1972: fig. 16), except that Royals molt ashore at their rookeries. Sedentary species like the Yellow-eyed Penguin exhibit none of the above characteristics.

Delayed return thus has two manifestations, the first being in the number of years spent at sea before revisiting the natal area. Why some species delay longer is not clear (see ch. 9 and 10). Like Adélie Penguins, Royal Penguins (Carrick and Ingham 1967, Carrick 1970), Manx Shearwaters (Harris 1966*a*), gannets (Nelson 1978*a*), and Black-legged Kittiwakes (Wooller and Coulson 1977) return to natal colonies in significant numbers by their second and third years; Black-footed and Laysan albatrosses (*Diomedea nigripes* and *D. immutabilis;* Rice and Kenyon 1962), South Polar Skuas (Wood et al. 1970), and Sooty Terns (*Sterna fuscata;* Harrington 1974) do so by their third and fourth years.

The second manifestation of delayed return appears in the date within a season that a bird first arrives. Like Adélie and Royal penguins, kittiwakes return during the spring in a temporally segregated pattern (Coulson and White 1958*a*): birds with breeding experience come first and are followed in sequence by inexperienced breeders and then nonbreeders. Gannets show a similar pattern of separation: mature males arrive first, followed in order by mature females, young birds in adult plumage, and then immatures. Furthermore, young birds spend only brief periods at the rookery (Nelson 1966*a,* 1978*a*). Harris (1966*a*) and Harrington (1974) reported progressively earlier arrival with greater age in the Manx Shearwater and Sooty Tern, respectively. Harrington, in addition, found the visits of young terns to be quite brief compared to those of older birds.

From a proximate standpoint, the age and date of first return for Adélie Penguins are related to levels of maturity and annual cycles in reproductive physiology (Ainley 1975a) and behavior, including migration (Ainley 1978). From an ultimate standpoint, Ficken and Ficken (1967) suggested that maturation rate is adaptive and evolves in response to intraspecific competition for food, space, and breeding partners. This could be so, but to apply the idea to Adélies requires that we first assess the actual advantages or disadvantages for the individual who delays visits to a rookery or who restricts first visits to short duration. When do the advantages of visiting the rookery outweigh those of staying away? Are there advantages to staying away or not visiting? These are two questions that must be answered.

Amadon (1964) stressed that the skills involved in flight and food capture require time for "maturation and perfection." Ashmole and Tovar (1968) proposed that securing food from the sea was difficult, and Orians (1969), Recher and Recher (1969), Dunn (1972), and Buckley and Buckley (1974) proved that skill in food capture does increase with age (i.e., for the aquatic birds they studied, it is probably perfected through learning). For the Adélie Penguin, the fact that young breeders supply less food to their chicks than do older ones indicates that the ability to capture food increases with age and experience for them as well (Ainley and Schlatter 1972). The fact that experience reduces the degree to which ice conditions affect spring migration indicates that their travel efficiency is improved by practice, too (table 3.5). Practice in feeding can only take place at sea, and the long migration to the rookery and the period of fasting involved can be accomplished successfully only after successful feeding has allowed fat reserves to be established. Being in prime physical condition also increases the chances of avoiding predation by leopard seals that concentrate at the narrow entrances to the rookery (Ainley and DeMaster 1980). Until food capture and swimming skills are perfected, it is advantageous to stay at sea in the pack ice.

Travel to the rookery uses the most time and energy

early in the season when sea ice extends farthest from shore (Stonehouse 1967, Ainley and LeResche 1973) and when migration may cover more than 100 km over broken ice floes (Emlen and Penney 1964). Later in the summer, though significant predation by leopard seals at rookeries still occurs (Penney and Lowry 1967, Müller-Schwarze and Müller-Schwarze 1975), more abundant food (Marr 1962) and less extensive pack ice mean that travel can be much more rapid. The advantages of visiting the rookery then might outweigh the dangers. It is, in fact, during the late summer reoccupation period that young birds concentrate their visits as shown in the arrival peaks of young birds during late December (fig. 5). In contrast, it is interesting that the average departure dates of nonbreeders, especially the youngest ones, correspond fairly closely with the time that parents also discontinue occupation of the rookery (though they make short visits thereafter; table 3.6). The significance of this similarity is not immediately apparent, but the first week of January happens to be the time when the pack ice completely disappears from the southwestern Ross Sea (Ainley et al. 1978). Being animals essentially of the pack ice rather than of the open water (Ainley and O'Connor in press), when the ice retreats its greatest distance from Crozier, Adélies might find it no longer worthwhile to visit the rookery without a substantial purpose (e.g., to feed chicks). Young birds thus cut short their visits and follow the mass exodus of failed breeders and older nonbreeders to the distant and retreating pack ice. There they feed heavily to build up fat reserves used in the long fast of the annual molt.

The advantages of visiting the rookery will be discussed in greater detail later (ch. 9 and 10), although some preliminary comment should be made here. Certainly a bird has to visit the rookery to breed, and breeding is more prevalent among older birds. The short breeding season requires that the older birds (breeders) arrive early to take advantage of the first favorable breeding conditions. Males arrive sooner in order to establish territories (a process in which females do not participate), which means they visit over a longer span of time by the end of the season. At least one or, for some individuals, more visits are apparently necessary for young birds before they breed because few, if any, Adélies

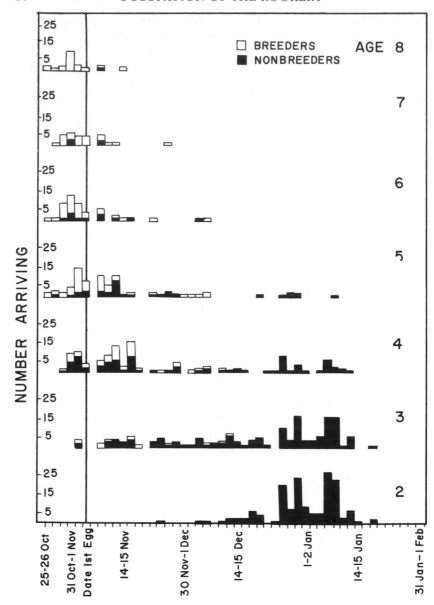

FIGURE 5   **The number of Adélies by age group arriving each day at Cape Crozier, 1969 (from Ainley 1975b).**

breed on their first visit. The advantages of prebreeding visits are the opportunities to learn social skills, to become familiar with the breeding grounds (including how to cope with leopard seals there; ch. 4), and to become attached to a territory (ch. 4) and possibly to a partner (ch. 6). All of these are likely to increase breeding success and survival.

4
THE ACTIVITIES
OF PREBREEDERS

We will eventually show that up to four years elapse from the time young Adélies first visit Cape Crozier until they finally breed there. In this chapter we will describe the activities of these birds during their prebreeding years. Without the benefit of known-age birds, Sladen (1958) characterized this period for individual Adélies as one of "wandering" and immature behavior including "inexperienced" breeding. In support of this, Ainley's (1975*b*) observations on the social interactions of young birds indicated that their behavior was often incomplete or out of context (see chap. 5). Reid et al. (1967), describing a small number of known-age Adélies at Cape Hallett, noted that young birds wandered, occupied usually peripheral nests, and only sometimes bred.

With increasing age, activities ashore progressed from wandering, to lone occupation of territory, to pairing on territory, and finally to breeding (see also LeResche and Sladen 1970). Data from six consecutive years of observation resulting in 4,285 instances of individual birds performing one or more of these activities once during a given season illustrate the progression from the second through the seventh year of life (table 4.1). The percentage of birds wandering decreased gradually from 73 percent of two-year-olds to virtually no six- or seven-year-olds; percentages of birds alone

TABLE 4.1 The activities of Adélie Penguins at the rookery in relation to age and experience; Cape Crozier, 1963 to 1968.

Age (yrs)	EXPERIENCE: year in rookery	Activity								Totals
		Wandering		Alone on nest		Paired, not breeding		Breeding		
		n	%	n	%	n	%	n	%	
2	First	577	73.0	129	16.3	85	10.7	0	0.0	791
3	First	779	51.7	391	25.9	306	20.3	32	2.1	1,508
	Second	117	42.9	77	28.2	67	24.5	12	4.4	273
4	First	144	33.0	162	37.1	96	22.0	35	8.0	437
	Second	134	25.4	165	31.3	130	24.7	98	18.6	527
	Third	18	22.5	22	27.5	16	20.0	24	30.0	80
5	First	21	21.4	32	32.7	23	23.5	22	22.4	98
	Second	33	17.1	64	33.2	45	23.3	51	26.4	193
	Third	22	15.0	42	28.6	35	23.8	48	32.7	147
	Fourth	5	13.9	10	27.8	10	27.8	11	30.5	36
6	First	3	14.3	4	19.0	8	38.1	6	28.6	21
	Second	7	13.7	15	29.4	8	15.7	21	41.2	51
	Third	3	6.1	12	24.5	10	20.4	24	49.0	49
	Fourth	1	2.4	13	31.7	10	24.4	17	41.5	41
	Fifth	0	0.0	1	20.0	2	40.0	2	40.0	5
7	First	0	0.0	2	67.0	1	33.0	0	0.0	3
	Second	0	0.0	1	16.7	0	0.0	5	83.3	6
	Third	0	0.0	0	0.0	1	14.3	6	85.7	7
	Fourth	1	10.0	2	20.0	3	30.0	4	40.0	10
	Fifth	0	0.0	0	0.0	1	50.0	1	50.0	2

TABLE 4.1 (*continued*)

Totals											
First	1,524	53.3	720	25.2	519	18.2	95	3.3	2,858
Second	291	27.7	322	30.7	250	23.8	187	17.8	1,050
Third	43	15.2	76	26.9	62	21.9	102	36.0	283
Fourth	7	8.1	25	28.7	23	26.4	32	36.8	87
Fifth	0	0.0	1	14.3	3	42.9	3	42.9	7
	1,865		1,144		857		419		4,285

at a territory increased from 16 to 33 percent in two- through four-year-olds and then declined to 18 percent in seven-year-olds as more individuals began to pair and breed; percentages of birds paired but not breeding increased from only 11 percent of two-year-olds to about 22 percent (19 to 24 percent) of older birds; and percentages of birds breeding increased from no two-year-olds to 57 percent of seven-year-olds.

While these trends clearly indicate that activities of Adélies at the rookery change with age, activities were also dependent to some degree on experience there (table 4.1). A consistent, small drop in the incidence of wandering occurred between birds' first and second seasons; and a consistent, substantial increase in the incidence of breeding occurred between birds' first, second, and third seasons (significantly different, $P<.05$). One and sometimes two years of previous experience thus affected activity, but more years of experience did not. In the case of breeding, where up to two years of previous experience at the rookery modified its incidence, experience actually modified the age-dependent change. For example, although 30 percent of four-year-olds ($n = 18$) present for the third time bred, only 22 percent and 26 percent of three-year-olds present for the first and second times, respectively, bred. Breeding incidence in five-year-olds did not surpass that of three-times-present four-year-olds until the five-year-olds, too, had visited in two previous seasons. In older age groups the effect of age overcame any experience factors.

Regardless of age, the influence of experience on the progression of behavior in an individual strongly indicated true learning, or the "modification of behavior by previous experience" (Scott 1958). This learning appeared to be necessary as a prelude to breeding: while a few birds did breed during the first year they were sighted (probably they were missed earlier), a large jump in breeding incidence occurred among birds visiting for their second time. Although some individuals did not progress through the entire typical course of development, many did; and time spent at the rookery in any behavior whatsoever appeared eventually to aid breeding efficiency (ch. 7). That prebreeding experience at the rookery exists in the face of its disadvantages (chs. 3, 9, and 10) is indirect evidence for its adaptive significance, and learning is the most obvious advantage that the individual gains from it.

WANDERING

Sladen (1958) originated the term *wanderers* to describe the rather specific group of Adélies present primarily during the reoccupation period and secondarily during peak egg-laying. He characterized them in this way:

> The successful breeders, whether established or unestablished, were concerned solely with establishing territory, building nests, incubating eggs and rearing their chicks. Another group of Adélies, though in adult plumage, behaved differently. Individual birds were seen wandering round the periphery of the colonies closely scrutinizing their surroundings. If they approached too near an occupied nest, they were pecked away vigorously. Sometimes one would walk through a colony as though in quest of something; it might even settle down in a space just out of pecking range, or stand in an empty nest scoop, or come and wander round the periphery again. These birds were, however, essentially unattached, unattached to nest-sites, unattached to any particular colony, or even rookery (1958:26).

The Cape Crozier data confirm each of these facts and further illustrate that the incidence and diffuseness of wandering changes with age (tables 4.2 and 4.3). Sladen's definition rightfully emphasizes that wandering is *peripheral* and that wanderers are unattached to nest site, colony, or even a specific rookery.

With no known-age birds to observe, Sladen (1953, 1958) predicted the age of wanderers as mostly two-year-olds and some three-year-olds. Older birds also wander, but otherwise Sladen's prediction is largely correct. As illustrated in table 4.1, of 1,865 instances of birds wandering recorded on a yearly basis (i.e., an individual is recorded as one wanderer each season even if it is observed wandering many times that season), 577 (31 percent) of these were two-year-olds, and 896 (48 percent) were three-year-olds. The remaining 21 percent were mostly four-year-olds, but a few five- and six-year-olds were included also. Although these figures are biased by the unequal numbers of birds passing through each age group during the study, they prob-

TABLE 4.2 Incidence of wandering in relation to the age of 983 individual Adélie Penguins, Cape Crozier, 1967–1968 and 1968–1969.

Age (yrs)	Individuals observed	Individuals wandering at least once	Percent wandering	Percent never wandering*
2	157	156	99	1
3	403	298	74	26
4	219	105	48	52
5	130	36	28	72
6	39	2	5	95
7	35	2	6	94

*In relation to age, $r = .9555$ ($P<.05$).

ably accurately reflect the proportion of two- and three-year-olds in the wandering group since only small proportions of the older birds present were wandering.

A good reflection of the decline in wandering incidence is the proportion of birds *not* seen wandering during a season. During the 1967–1968 season only 1 percent of two-

TABLE 4.3 Average number of colonies visited by Adélies of different age and sex in the seasons 1967 to 1974.

Age (yrs)	Male		Female	
	$\bar{x} \pm SD$	No. birds	$\bar{x} \pm SD$	No. birds
2	1.5 ± 1.0	82	1.3 ± 0.5	95
3	1.7 ± 1.0	238	1.5 ± 0.9	220
4	1.5 ± 0.9	287	1.2 ± 0.6	220
5	1.1 ± 0.4	443	1.0 ± 0.3	329
6	1.1 ± 0.2	355	1.0 ± 0.2	279
7	1.0 ± 0.2	229	1.0 ± 0.2	198
8	1.0 ± 0.0	60	1.0 ± 0.2	45
9	1.0 ± 0.2	37	1.0 ± 0.0	22
10	1.0 ± 0.0	39	1.0 ± 0.0	19
11	1.0 ± 0.2	33	1.0 ± 0.0	14
12&13	1.0 ± 0.0	16	1.0 ± 0.0	11
All	1.2 ± 0.6	1,819	1.2 ± 0.5	1,452

year-olds were observed *only* at territory; the remaining birds were seen wandering at least once (table 4.2). Among older birds the proportion never seen wandering increased with age. Thus, wandering was an activity for more than 99 percent of the observed two-year-olds and fewer than 5 percent of the six-year-olds. Still another reflection of the decline in wandering with age is seen in the average number of colonies in which birds were seen each season (table 4.3). Almost all two- and three-year-olds visited more than one colony, as did many four-year-olds; but as indicated by the low means and especially the low standard deviations, birds older than five years were rarely seen in more than one colony. If they were seen elsewhere, they were probably walking between the beach and their colony of residence.

The modifying effect of experience on wandering incidence was illustrated in table 4.1 and discussed above. More than 53 percent of all wanderers were birds seen in the rookery for their first time; but of birds observed in additional seasons, only 24 percent wandered. The radius of movements declined as well. As suggested by LeResche and Sladen (1970), initial wandering by a young bird is typically patternless, but in subsequent years a definite pattern emerges—that of decreasing radius of wanderings and apparent "homing in on a spot." Carrick and Ingham (1967) and Carrick (1970) also noted increased attachment to a given area with age in Royal Penguins at Macquarie Island.

Great variation existed in the rate at which individuals attached themselves to a site, as best illustrated in specific examples. One typical case was that of Adélie 419-18431, which at age four wandered from colony to colony (see fig. 2 for localities):

DATE	LOCATION	ACTIVITY
24 Nov. 1967	C10.0	Wandering
26 Nov. 1967	C15.0	Wandering
29 Nov. 1967	B4.0	Wandering
2 Dec. 1967	C15.8	Wandering

In contrast, a bird may reside continuously in a single colony without being attached to a specific territory there.

The record for 519-11078 as a three-year-old was as follows:

DATE	LOCATION	ACTIVITY
19 Dec. 1967	B5.6	Wandering
21 Dec. 1967	B5.5	Wandering
22 Dec. 1967	B5.0	Wandering
25 Dec. 1967	B5.5	Wandering
26 Dec. 1967	B5.2	Wandering
27 Dec. 1967	B5.5	Wandering
30 Dec. 1967	B5.1	Wandering
31 Dec. 1967	B5.1	Paired
1 Jan. 1968	B5.0	Wandering
2 Jan. 1968	B5.2	Wandering

Such attachment to a wandering area may persist for longer than one season, as in the case of 519-17909:

DATE	AGE	LOCATION	ACTIVITY
21 Dec. 1964	2 yrs	M	Wandering
24 Dec. 1965	3 yrs	B5	Wandering
1 Jan. 1966		B5	Wandering
10 Jan. 1966		B5	Wandering
19 Nov. 1966	4 yrs	B5	Wandering
12 Dec. 1966		B5	Wandering
31 Dec. 1966		B5	Wandering

Wandering was sometimes slow and investigative, with shifts from one colony or area to another taking place over a number of days, or rapid and cursory, with movements from area to area occurring within hours. The typical wanderer in the upper reaches of study area C, near the hut we lived in, made a circuit of the hut with five to seven other birds and returned to the upper C colonies within a half hour. A "young" bird (not banded), marked with an orange bib and then observed on 2 December 1967, moved from the place of marking (subcolony B12.1) at 1200 to colony B5, 330 m away, by 1215. At 1500 it was 440 m away in colony C6.0, where it remained until 1830, when the bib was removed; the bird then moved to colony C10.0, 150 m distant (see Sladen and LeResche 1970).

More impressively rapid wanderings were shown by birds seen within days at Crozier and at other rookeries in the Ross Sea. A few examples merit special note. A three-year-old, 519-11046, was observed wandering in area N at Cape Crozier on 27 December 1967. The next day E. B. Spurr (EBS) observed the same bird 74 km away at Cape Bird. Another three-year-old, 519-11049, was wandering in Crozier area E on 17 December 1967, wandering at Cape Bird (EBS) on 2 January 1968, paired on an empty, well-built nest in Crozier colony B3 on 15 January, and wandering in Crozier area M on 20 January. A third three-year-old was wandering at Crozier (colony B2.0) on 24 December 1967 and was wandering and fighting (EBS) at Cape Bird 5 days later. More distant sightings of individuals during the same season were of a two-year-old (519-18171) seen wandering at Cape Royds 17 December 1965 and at Crozier (more than 100 km distant by sea) 11 days later and of a three-year-old (519-17835) wandering at Crozier 22 November 1965 and at Beaufort Island (80 km away) 55 days later. Significantly, all records of birds wandering at localities away from the natal rookery were of two- and three-year-olds. All older Crozier birds found at other rookeries were thought by observers to be attached to territory, having apparently emigrated (Ainley and DeMaster 1980), and are not properly termed youthful wanderers.

While the radius of wandering changed with age, the site of hatching clearly influenced this change. More than 98 percent of all observations of birds two through five years wandering in the 1967–1968 season were within their natal rookery (table 4.4), and over 70 percent were within their natal areas. Among two- through four-year-olds, 50 to 58 percent were within their natal colony group; in fact, 36 percent of all observations of wandering two-year-olds, 26 percent of three-year-olds, and 24 percent of four-year-olds were in the precise colonies where they hatched. Since the number of sightings in a particular place was an index to time spent by a bird in that place, table 4.4 probably presents a fairly accurate time budget of wanderers, as well as an indication of

TABLE 4.4   The number and percentage of observations of wandering Adélie Penguins (n = 596 birds) aged two to five years, in relation to their hatching sites; Cape Crozier, 1967–1968.

WANDERING SITE	CATEGORIES OF NATAL SITES*			
	Rookery	Area	Colony group	Colony
Same as natal	1,017	731	511	254
Different	8	286	220	212
TOTAL OBSERVATIONS	1,025	1,017	731	466†
Percent of total observations:				
Same as natal	99.2	71	50	26
Different	0.8	28	22	22
Percent of observations in this spatial category:				
Same as natal	99.2	72	70	55
Different	0.8	28	30	45

*These spatial categories of rookery, area, colony group, and colony indicate that wandering occurred within a radius of 1 km, 100 m, 30 m, and 10 m of the natal nest, respectively.
†45 natal colonies unknown.

how many birds within a given age-group were wandering and where they were wandering in relation to natal site.

Though clearly influenced by natal site, wandering was also linked to eventual breeding site. By summarizing all years of observation at Crozier and linking natal areas and breeding areas, it is apparent that Adélies do tend to breed near where they were raised as chicks (table 4.5). At least half of all birds bred in their respective natal areas, or within about 100 m of their natal nest, and a large proportion of the remainder bred in areas nearby. It could possibly be that, depending on what it experienced during its wanderings, a bird strengthens or weakens its ties to the natal site in the process of finding its eventual breeding site.

Penney (1968) reasoned that two colonies studied at Wilkes Station increased rapidly in size over a three-year period because of an influx of young birds. Except for colonies reduced by intense disturbance or by having been drifted over (see chap. 8), no spectacular changes in the size of study colonies were noted at Cape Crozier from 1961 through 1969. One colony did form in area B during our ab-

TABLE 4.5 Breeding areas relative to natal areas (banding locations), Cape Crozier, 1963 to 1975; the number and percentage (in parentheses) of Adélies from the four natal (banding) areas that bred in the various study areas and East Rookery(x) are shown.

NATAL AREA	BREEDING AREA														
	B	M	N	C	P	L	E	H	Q	S	D	G	F	X	Total
B	(49) 446	(10) 90	(20) 182	(2) 22	(2) 14	(3) 30	(1) 10	(11) 99	(1) 7	1	1	(1) 6	2	1	911
C	(3) 34	(5) 49	(28) 280	(42) 420	(12) 121	(2) 22	(1) 13	(2) 20	(1) 11	(1) 12	1	(1) 10	2	2	997
E	(1) 9	(1) 7	(2) 15	(1) 6	(1) 8	(10) 65	(57) 385	(21) 145	(2) 14	3	(1) 8	(1) 8	(1) 5	1	679
D	(1) 1	(1) 2	(1) 2	(2) 4	(4) 8	(1) 2	1	(3) 6	(6) 12	(19) 42	(58) 126	(3) 7	(2) 4	1	218
Total	490	148	479	452	151	119	409	270	44	58	136	31	13	5	2,805

sence in 1970 to 1973, however, and several young known-age birds resided in it; and another formed in area N near the border of area C. During our absence between 1975–1976 and 1980–1981, colonies on the outer periphery of areas B and especially C declined in size even more. Regardless of the ultimate reasons for these changes (see chaps. 8 and 9), young Adélies did show preferential movement in their wanderings from some colonies to others. This is illustrated by comparing the number of birds banded as chicks in a colony and later observed wandering anywhere within the rookery, to the number of birds banded elsewhere and seen wandering within the colony (fig. 6). Instances where the latter number was higher than the former appear as negative

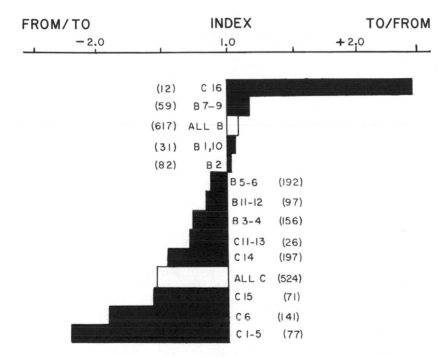

FIGURE 6 **Wandering of two through four-year-old Adélie Penguins in relation to natal area and colony, showing the proportions entering and leaving each colony and area. Values above the horizontal line show net immigration, and those below show net emigration. Numbers in parentheses are the numbers of birds banded in each colony and later observed; 1,141 separate observations are included, Cape Crozier, 1963 to 1968.**

ratios; appearing as positive ratios are those in which more birds were observed within the colony than were banded there and later seen.

Colony C16, abutting the North Hill portion of area N, had the highest rate of influx among the B and C colonies studied. It had 29 banded wanderers recorded and only 12 recovered chicks banded within its boundaries, for an index of 29/12 or +2.42. Rates for all other colonies in area C were lower than those for all colonies in area B, and all other C colonies had negative indices. Colonies or colony groups apparently attractive to wandering birds were B7, 8, and 9; B1 and 10; and B2. Colonies B5 and B6, where the largest numbers of known-age wanderers were seen, had the fifth highest index but "lost" more wanderers than they "gained." They also progressively lost ground to a growing snow field. Colonies C1 through C6 (grouped) had the highest rate of loss with an index of −2.20. The latter colonies were the most disturbed by human activity (chap. 8).

It appeared, therefore, that among those colonies studied, two- through four-year-olds preferentially wandered in area B (an overall index of +1.08) and colony C16. Further, these young wanderers "left" all colonies in area C (overall index: −1.52) except C16. The new colony in area B was overly supplied with nesting stones; this and its exposure (no drifting snow) probably contributed to its initial attractiveness. Once a few youngsters became attached to the site, their high level of social interaction (see chap. 5) probably attracted others, and so on (Nelson 1978b; see chapter summary).

The number of Adélies of known sex observed wandering at various ages, compared with the number of birds of known sex seen in the rookery at those ages (table 4.6), indicates a differential tendency between males and females to wander. During the prime wandering years (two to four years of age), more males were observed wandering per known male present than females wandering per female present (P<.05). Beyond the fourth year, wandering observations per bird decreased for both sexes, as they did for the entire population.

Considering wandering observations per bird to be an estimate of the relative time spent wandering by males and

TABLE 4.6   Wandering: observations of nonbreeding, known-age Adélie Penguins of known sex; Cape Crozier, 1963 to 1969.

Age (yrs)	NUMBER OBSERVED IN ROOKERY		NUMBER "WANDERING" OBSERVATIONS		"WANDERING" OBSERVATION/ BIRD*	
	Males	Females	Males	Females	Males	Females
2	17	30	17	21	1.00	0.70
3	49	95	54	74	1.10	0.78
4	44	47	43	31	0.98	0.66
5	27	33	22	13	0.81	0.39
6 & 7	18	12	2	1	0.11	0.08
Totals	155	217	138	140	0.89	0.65

*Comparing males and females, $X^2 = 87.86$; $P<.05$.

females and further assuming that the ratio of two- to four-year-old nonbreeding males to females is at least one (this is reasonable since females breed at earlier ages than males), it is evident that the majority of wanderers at a given time were males. The combined data in table 4.6 for birds two to four years old indicate that there were 1.12 wandering observations for each male and only 0.78 for each female. Therefore *at least* 59 percent (1.12/1.12 + 0.78) of wanderers in this age group were males. Females at these ages, as seems reasonable in light of their earlier breeding, wander less and keep company more (see below). The data in table 4.3 lend further support to this idea.

PREBREEDING TERRITORY OCCUPATION

Sladen (1958) and Ainley (1957b) described how nonbreeding wanderers sometimes demonstrated attachment to territory and even fought for it but were then likely to wander away (see chap. 5). Thus strong territoriality is not a common characteristic of wanderers. Although there is great variation among individuals, for males, a period of wandering leads to lone occupation of a nest (or nests), to keeping company at a single nest, and finally to breeding; for females, wandering leads to keeping company and then to breeding.

The age at which Adélies were first observed alone at territory was slightly older than their age of first return to the rookery (fig. 7). On the average, birds spent at least part of a season wandering without establishing territory before eventually becoming attached (usually temporarily) to a site. As shown in table 4.7, 13 percent of 892 Adélies were first observed alone at territories at age two, whereas 30 percent of all young birds return to the rookery for the first time at that age (table 3.1). The plurality (50 percent) were first alone at territory as three-year-olds, and almost all birds ever seen alone at territory had been thus observed before the fifth year.

The incidence of lone occupation of a territory increased progressively with age and previous experience at the rookery (fig. 8, appendix 2). Among 694 two-year-olds all at the rookery for the first time, only 16 percent were observed alone at territory. Thirty-five percent of 1,105 inexperienced three-year-olds occupied territory alone, compared with 47 percent of 174 birds the same age seen at Crozier for the second season. Similarly, incidence of lone territoriality increased with experience among four-year-olds from 48 percent of 321 inexperienced birds to 54 percent of 303 birds at the rookery the second season to 69 percent of 32 birds present for the third season. A plateau was

TABLE 4.7   The ages at which Adélie Penguins (n = 892) were first observed alone at territories; Cape Crozier, 1963 to 1969.

Age	Percent observed alone at territory for first time		
(yrs)	Males	Females	Totals*
2	7	13	13
3	49	50	50
4	32	24	29
5	12	8	7
6 & 7	0	5	2
n	59	38	892

*Includes birds of unknown sex.

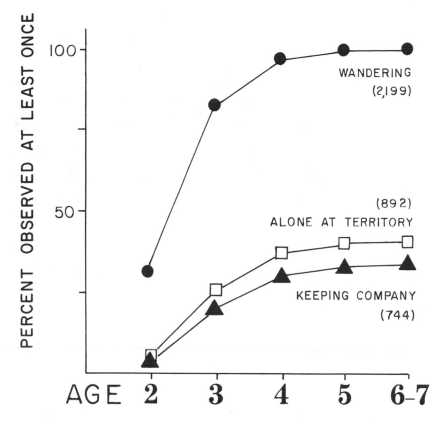

FIGURE 7 **Ages of 2,199 prebreeding Adélie Penguins when observed (1) at the Cape Crozier rookery, (2) alone at territory, and (3) keeping company. The ordinate represents the cumulative proportion of observed birds seen at least once in their lives in each of the behaviors.**

reached by experienced birds in this age group because, thereafter, lone occupation of sites did not increase. Instead, more birds were observed paired at territory than previously.

Although experience did increase the tendency of birds to occupy territories, age had a much greater effect. The number of inexperienced three-year-olds on territory was more than twice that of two-year-olds, and even the number of inexperienced four- and five-year-olds exceeded that of experienced three-year-olds.

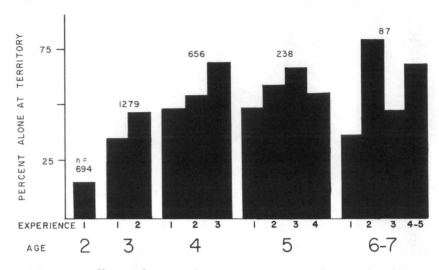

FIGURE 8 **Effects of age and experience on incidence of sightings alone at territory of 2,954 nonbreeding Adélie Penguins ages two to seven years; Cape Crozier, 1963 to 1969.**

More nonbreeding males of all ages were seen alone at territory than females of the same age (fig. 9), a difference that confirms the patriarchal nature of territoriality in this species. Among nonbreeding birds aged two to seven years, 68 percent of males (n = 155) and only 23 percent of females (n = 217) were observed alone at territory at least once during a given season, a difference that is highly significant (P<.05, *t*-test). In many cases, females had definite tread marks and were probably "alone" only temporarily at a male's territory.

Given our schedule of frequent and regular observation, the number of times in a season that birds were observed at least once in a behavior provided a logical index of time spent in that behavior (see Ainley 1978). Time spent alone at territory (fig. 10, appendix 2), as measured by the mean number of sightings alone at territory per bird per season (for birds seen alone at territory at least once), increased with age from two to five years. Having one or two (but no more) years of experience had an additional positive effect.

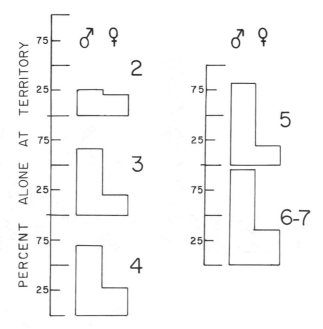

FIGURE 9   The influence of age and sex on the incidence of lone territory occupation by 372 nonbreeding Adélie Penguins ages two to seven years; Cape Crozier, 1963 to 1969.

Not only did more males spend time alone at territory but males of a given age were also observed alone at territory more often in a given season than females the same age ($x^2 = 23.39$, p<.05). Two-year-old males seen alone at territory were observed 1.5 times per individual in that situation compared to 1.0 times for females. Disparity between the sexes in times seen alone at territory increased with age, from 2.8 (males) vs. 1.5 (females) sightings per bird in three-year-olds, to 3.3 vs. 1.2 in four-year-olds, 7.4 vs. 2.2 in five-year-olds, and 7.6 vs. 3.2 in older birds.

The site of lone occupation of territory, as with wandering (cf. table 4.4), was related to natal locality, and the correlation was slightly stronger (table 4.8). Among Adélies two to five years old seen alone at territory, 99 percent were at the Crozier rookery. Of these, 84 percent were seen alone at territory within their natal area. Under the same consid-

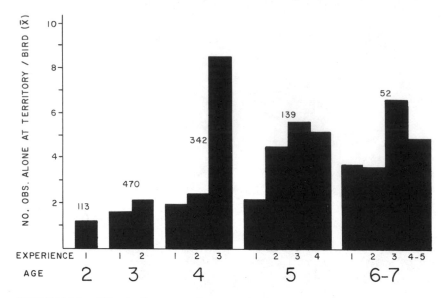

FIGURE 10   The influence of age and experience on the time spent alone at territory by 1,116 nonbreeding Adélie Penguins ages two to seven years; Cape Crozier, 1963 to 1969.

TABLE 4.8   The number and percentage of observations of Adélies "alone at territory" in relation to natal locality; 811 birds aged two to five years; Cape Crozier, 1965 to 1969.

TERRITORY SITE:	CATEGORIES OF NATAL SITES			
	Rookery	Area	Colony group	Colony
Same as natal	1,786	1,507	911	542
Different	26	279	485	364
TOTAL OBSERVATIONS	1,812	1,786	1,396*	906†
Percent of total observations:				
Same as natal	98.6	83	54	32
Different	1.4	15	28	21
Percent of observations in this spatial category:				
Same as natal	98.6	84	65	60
Different	1.4	16	35	40

*111 colony groups of observation unknown.
†5 colonies of observation unknown.

erations, only 72 percent of all wandering observations in the natal rookery were in the natal area ($P<.05$, t-test). Similarly, 54 percent of observations of young Adélies alone at territory in the natal area occurred in the natal colony group, compared to 50 percent of wandering observations ($P<.05$); 60 percent of these observations were in the colony of rearing (vs. 54 percent for wanderers; $P<.05$).

Another good indication of the degree to which a penguin was "attached" to its territory was nest quality. As discussed in chapter 2 (pp. 16–17) and in Ainley (1978), we scored nest quality using four categories: scoop, poor nest, fair nest, and good (or well-built) nest. These categories considered only the number of stones and their arrangement and did not include considerations of location, drainage, and so on. Thus we measured stone-gathering and retaining ability. Figure 11 shows nest quality of prebreeding Adélies occupying territory alone. In general, nest quality improved with age in birds of equivalent experience and with experience in birds the same age. The number of scoops and poor nests observed for two-year-olds differed significantly ($P<.05$, t-test) from that for three-year-olds visiting their first season. Similarly, inexperienced three-year-olds differed in nest quality from inexperienced four-year-olds, which had a greater proportion of fair to good nests than the younger birds. Differences were not significant ($P>.05$) in comparisons between inexperienced birds four vs. five years old and five vs. six and seven years old.

Three-year-olds seen for the second season had a significantly ($P<.05$) lower proportion of fair to good nests than did second-seen four-year-olds. Second-seen four- and five-year-olds had statistically the same nest quality, but both had significantly ($P<.05$) fewer fair to good nests than did second-seen six- and seven-year-olds. Among birds of the same age, then, nest quality increased significantly if a bird had a previous season of experience, but additional seasons of experience did not have an added effect on improving nests.

KEEPING COMPANY

Nonreproductive association among penguins of opposite sex was first described by Richdale (1945, 1951), who

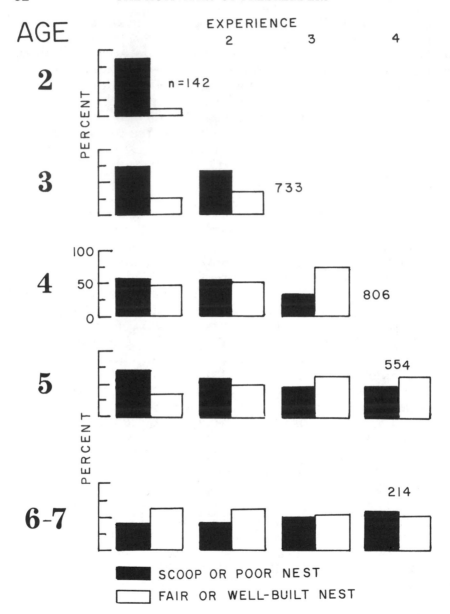

FIGURE 11   The influence of age and experience on nest quality when alone at territory; 2,449 observations of nonbreeding Adélie Penguins ages two to seven years; Cape Crozier, 1963 to 1969.

coined the term "keeping company," which he then defined somewhat nebulously. Sladen (1958:63) was more specific and used the term "to describe the partnership of two birds of opposite sex at a nest-site, which may or may not lead to the establishment of a mated pair." He suggested that the behavior "facilitated the formation of new pair-bonds" (i.e., mated pairs) and that it had value in making nest material easier to secure and retain. Penney (1968) termed the same behavior "trial pairing" but concluded it had little influence on eventual formation of mated pairs.

Keeping company was a common behavior in prebreeding Adélies (table 4.9), and, like lone occupation of territory, its incidence and intensity were related to age, experience, and sex. On the average, young birds would first keep company shortly after they had been alone at territory, which succeeded their first return to the rookery to wander (fig. 7). This progression in the age at which individuals were first seen wandering, alone at territory, and keeping company is further demonstrated in table 4.10. At every age under six years, a significantly greater cumulative proportion of individuals was observed wandering than was seen alone at territory (P<.05, t-test), and in four-year-olds a greater proportion was seen alone at territory than was seen keeping company (P<.05). By six or seven years of age, only 41 percent of all prebreeders observed were seen keeping com-

TABLE 4.9   **The ages at which prebreeding Adélie Penguins (n = 744) were first observed keeping company; Cape Crozier, 1963 to 1969.**

Age (yrs)	Percent keeping company for first time		
	Males	*Females*	*Total**
2	0	8	11
3	24	63	47
4	44	21	29
5	29	6	10
6 & 7	2	2	2
n	45	91	744

*Includes birds of unknown sex.

TABLE 4.10 Progression by age of 2,199 Adélie Penguins sighted wandering, alone at territory, and keeping company; Cape Crozier, 1963 to 1969.

Age (yrs)	Wandering Cumulative no.	%	Alone at territory Cumulative no.	%	Keeping company Cumulative no.	%
2	698	32*	113	13	82	11
3	1,803	82*	556	62	434	58
4	2,124	97*	812	91†	651	88†
5	2,187	99*	877	98	725	97
6 & 7	2,199	100	892	100	744	100

*Differs significantly from AIT and keeping company (P<.05, t-test).
†Differs significantly from keeping company (P<.05).

pany. If breeders were included, 49 percent were observed keeping company. This calculation, while it well illustrates the age-dependent progression to keeping company behavior, unduly weights the larger numbers of two- to four-year-olds in the sample. If we consider only birds seen as five- to seven-year-olds, keeping company at these ages occurred in 75 percent of all those present. Thus by these ages, keeping company had become typical behavior.

The older an Adélie was and the greater number of previous seasons of experience it had had at the rookery, the more likely it was to keep company (fig. 12, appendix 3). Among nonbreeders during their first season at the rookery, only 11 percent of two-year-olds were observed keeping company, as contrasted to 24 percent of three-year-olds, 31 percent of four-year-olds, 30 percent of five-year-olds, and 56 percent of six- and seven-year-olds. These differences between birds two, three, and four years old were significant statistically (P<.05, t-test), but those between birds four, five, and six and seven years old were not (P>.05).

Experience also increased the incidence of keeping company in Adélies of the same age. Of three-year-olds with one previous year of experience at the rookery, 32 percent kept company as contrasted to only 24 percent of inexperienced three-year-olds (P<.05, t-test). Among four-year-olds, incidence also increased significantly between inexperienced and once-experienced birds (P<.05), but among

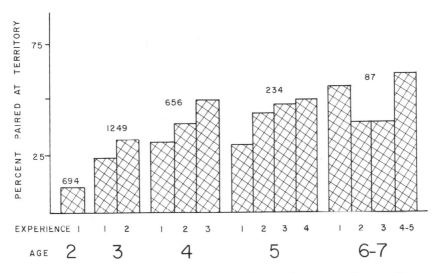

**FIGURE 12   The influence of age and experience on the tendency
of Adélie Penguins to keep company; 2,920 observations of nonbreeding Adélie Penguins ages two to seven years; Cape Crozier,
1963 to 1969.**

older birds no significant increases occurred as a result of
more experience.

In contrast to the pattern observed in wandering and
lone territoriality, a higher proportion of females than males
was observed keeping company (fig. 13, appendix 3). Of
nonbreeding two-year-old females observed, 13 percent
were keeping company, but no two-year-old males were so
observed. Similar comparison for birds three and four years
of age was statistically significant ($P<.05$, t-test), but comparison for still older birds was not ($P>.05$).

As with the duration of lone occupation of territory, the
amount of time spent keeping company (as measured by the
number of observations per bird seen keeping company per
year) generally increased with age (fig. 14, appendix 3). The
trend, however, was not as marked as in territory occupation. Two-year-olds (all inexperienced) observed keeping
company at least once were each so observed a mean of 1.1
times per year (86 observations of 76 individuals), significantly less often than three-year-olds present for the first

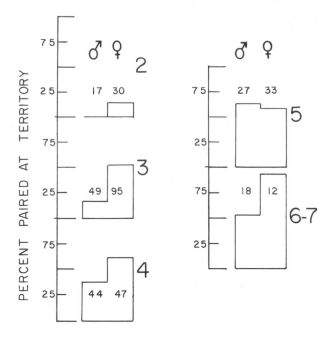

FIGURE 13   The influence of age and sex on the incidence of being paired at a territory in 372 nonbreeding Adélie Penguins ages two to seven years; Cape Crozier, 1963 to 1969.

time (P<.05, *t*-test). The mean number of observations per season of inexperienced Adélies keeping company increased from 1.7 for three-year-olds to 1.8 for four-year-olds, 1.9 for five-year-olds, and 2.9 for six- and seven-year-olds; but none of these differences was statistically significant (P>.05, *t*-test).

In individuals the same age, added experience increased the number of times a bird was seen keeping company in a season. Thus, among three-year-olds, inexperienced birds were observed keeping company an average of 1.7 times per season, and birds present at the rookery for the second time were so observed 1.9 times per season (P<.05, *t*-test). Similar and statistically significant differences (P<.05) occurred with greater experience in older birds as follows (appendix 3): second- vs. third-seen four-

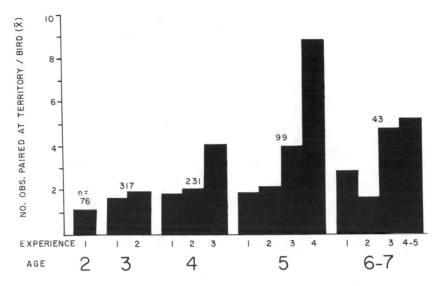

FIGURE 14 **The influence of age and experience on the time spent paired at a territory by 766 nonbreeding Adélie Penguins ages two to seven years; Cape Crozier, 1963 to 1969.**

year-olds; second- vs. third- vs. fourth-seen five-year-olds; and first- plus second-seen (lumped) vs. third- plus fourth-seen six- and seven-year-olds. Thus, similar to other behaviors, one or two years of previous experience, but no more, affected the tendency of Adélies to display this behavior. In the duration of keeping company, differences among individuals of different sex but the same age, however, were not evident (P>.05; *t*-test; n = 159 birds) even though the proportion of females keeping company was significantly higher.

Since paired birds could guard nests more efficiently than could single ones, keeping company affected nest construction. Figure 15 summarizes the factors of age, experience, and pairing as they affect nest quality. Median behavior for age-experience classes, indicated by arrows in the figure, generally increased from lone occupation of poor nests (two-year-olds, inexperienced) to alone at good nests (all four-year-olds) to paired at poor or fair nests (fourth-

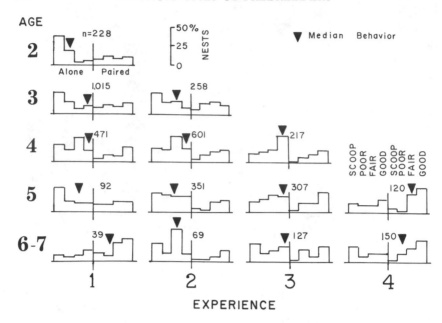

FIGURE 15　The influence of age and experience on nest quality and pairing; 4,045 observations of nonbreeding Adélie Penguins ages two to seven years, Cape Crozier, 1963 to 1969.

seen five-year-olds and first- and fourth-seen six- plus seven-year-olds). The patterns did not change greatly with added experience.

While nest building (and nest quality), a reproductive behavior, did not increase with previous rookery experience by birds keeping company, keeping company itself did offer the opportunity for young birds to experience interactions with a bird of the opposite sex in a nesting situation. Beyond that, the role of keeping company has heretofore been unclear for young birds. As stated above, Sladen (1958) suggested that keeping company "facilitated" future mating; but Penney (1968), even though terming it "trial pairing," concluded that previous association had little influence on future choice of mate.

LeResche and Sladen (1970), based on observations in 1966–1967 and 1967–1968, concluded that "there is as yet no evidence to suggest that [choice of mate] depends upon anything other than the exigencies of a given season." Their statement was based on 13 birds banded after keeping company with young known-age Adélies for five days during 1966–1967 and 1967–1968. In only two cases (15 percent) did these nonbreeding partners mate the following season. It still is not clear, however, whether in the 11 other cases both birds returned the next year. In 1968–1969 a much larger sample of birds was banded after keeping company with known-age birds late in the season. The next year, in 12 of 14 instances where both birds returned, they paired and bred. In all 14 cases, keeping company had lasted for two to three weeks, instead of for five days, the criterion used by LeResche and Sladen (1970). Three of the 12 known-age birds were four-year-olds in 1968–1969 and had never bred before; of the remainder, all were five to seven years old, two had never bred, five were nonbreeders that had bred previously, and four were failed breeders. These results indeed indicate that keeping company can lead to establishment of a pair bond in the season preceding reproduction. This is to say nothing of the many pairs that fail to breed successfully, maintain their pair bond by keeping company for the remainder of that season, and then pair together again in breeding the next season (Spurr 1977; see ch. 8).

CHAPTER SUMMARY/SYNTHESIS: THE SIGNIFICANCE OF PREBREEDING ACTIVITIES

During prebreeding years the behavior of a young male progresses from wandering to lone occupation of territory to keeping company. With the latter two activities, it learns about building and maintaining a nest. The behavior of a female progresses in a similar direction except that she usually does not remain for long, if at all, on a territory without being paired. These progressions in activity are important in maintaining a breeding population and in introducing an individual to breeding activities as discussed below.

Four major aspects of wandering are significant in the behavioral development of the individual Adélie and in structuring the breeding population. First, it was the least mature behavior of the four major ones observed. It occurred often in the youngest and most inexperienced birds and virtually disappeared by the sixth year of life. Second, it was localized, with natal site and eventual breeding site as focal points; wanderings began near the hatching site and become progressively localized around the site of first breeding. Initial occupation of territory was even more localized than wandering. Third, males wandered more than females because females more often became paired at territories. Fourth, there was demonstrable movement by wandering from some colonies to others. Individuals showed differences in the time spent wandering and the extent of their travels, some becoming immediately localized and others wandering ashore farther than the boundaries of their natal rookery.

Young "unemployed" birds are a common social unit at the breeding grounds of many seabird species. Lockley (1942) and Serventy (1956) called such birds "prospectors" in the shearwater populations they studied. Such birds in many seabird species form what Tinbergen (1960) called "clubs" in his study of Herring Gulls (*Larus argentatus*), where the unemployed individuals actually gather at traditional sites for long periods. Other examples of club behavior occur in such diverse species as gannets and boobies (Nelson 1978*a, b*), South Polar Skuas (Schlatter and Sladen 1971), and Cassin's Auklets (*Ptychoramphus aleuticus;* Manuwal 1974). Like Adélie Penguins, young unemployed Royal Penguins (Carrick 1972) and Sooty Terns (Harrington 1974) move about in the rookeries rather than form clubs; the young terns, in fact, rarely land but fly above the breeders on the ground. Richdale (1957) viewed the short period of wandering in Yellow-eyed Penguins as a passing phase leading immediately to breeding. Their prebreeding period, in his expanding population, was so short that wandering seemed a rather unimportant stage in development though necessary for dispersal and arrival at the breeding site.

Wandering and initial territory occupation are important to the individual Adélie Penguin because during these activities it learns skills useful in breeding. Primary learning may be of the physiographic features of the rookery and of areas suited—perhaps individually suited?—for breeding.

"Prospecting" in this sense is an aid to future breeding success. Further learning of the social behavior necessary for successful breeding, especially while keeping company (ch. 5), must occur. In addition to previously experienced social interactions at sea (where Adélies usually occur in small flocks; Ainley 1972, Ainley and O'Connor in press), young birds experience the unfamiliar interactions of the breeding ground as they move about, including, for instance, the territorial distances of breeding individuals and how to travel expeditiously through dense breeding groups. They gain additional experience in such matters as they occupy territories, however briefly. By the time they keep company they may be learning the characteristics of potential mates.

A prime result of wandering and the progression to other activities is the maintenance of traditionality, a characteristic probably important to individuals in populations with delineated feeding and breeding ranges that do not change rapidly. In contrast, Coulson and White (1956, 1960) and Nelson (1978*a, b*), for the rapidly expanding populations they studied, stressed the function of young nonbreeding kittiwakes and gannets as explorers and founders of new colonies. Penney (1968) suggested that young wanderers colonized new areas in the Adélie Penguin rookery where he studied. Wandering, while serving this "prospecting" or dispersal function, is mainly the link between the hatching site and eventual breeding site: youngsters characteristically wander near their natal site and breed near the area where they have wandered. This maintains the physical and, to an extent, the social structure of areas and colony groups (and, to a lesser degree, of colonies).

The social structure of breeding groups is further kept intact by the prebreeding experience the new breeder has had *in that group.* Lone occupation of territory and keeping company are perhaps more important in this respect, but a wanderer has often learned the routes of travel and the colony and territory spacing of his eventual breeding colony. This and the progression to territory occupation and keeping company allow the bird to enter the breeding group in a more orderly manner.

Perhaps the most important function of prebreeding activities in terms of the population is the provision of a flexible reservoir for breeding. This is a function necessarily shared with nonbreeding territoriality and keeping company (LeResche and Sladen 1970). The reservoir concept is here considered in the spatial and social sense (i.e., of maintaining physiognomic and social coherence in the rookery) rather than in the population sense (i.e., of maintaining production).

The reservoir of wanderers within a single rookery can be conceptualized as a point source of emigration to various sites within that rookery (another, smaller group provides emigrants to other rookeries; see below). These wanderers are each "trained" in the organization of a particular, large area (usually near the natal site) but are unattached to specific sites. Certain factors influence their movements within the wandering areas: traditional factors (i.e., the familiarity of the natal area), vacuum factors (i.e., deserted nest sites with many nest stones about, a physical gap; a lack of dominant breeders, a social gap), or social factors (i.e., individual compatibility with an individual or a group of breeders). With increased maturity and familiarity with rookery activities, these movements localize, the exact site depending upon the interactions of these factors. Further maturing leads to territoriality, pairing, and eventual breeding in a physical and social location to which the bird is suited and with which it is familiar.

This model seems to fit the characteristics of the "average" young bird. It is further supported by the fact that males, the eventual establishers of territory, wander more than females. In addition, the "attractiveness" of certain colonies (fig. 6), while far from specifically explainable, demonstrates that differential forces and experiences of some kind are affecting the localization of young birds. For gannets, Nelson (1978b) suggested that a concentration of young birds in a certain colony and particularly the high level of displaying and social activity they generate tend to draw even more young individuals there to establish territories. This phenomenon may also apply for Adélies, but formation of the initial group of young birds must have to do with the factors discussed above.

Ainley and DeMaster (1980) reported extremely low emigration rates for Crozier Adélies. In some situations, though, the trait must be adaptive. Allowing the colonization of new rookeries (new colony formation in the natal rookery is considered a reservoir function), emigration seems of minor importance to Adélies today, but this has not always been the case. The species has bred on Ross Island for only the last 6,000 years and conceivably did so even earlier, during the several interglacial periods preceding the present one (reviewed by Young 1981). During periods when Antarctic ice sheets advanced in the southern Ross Sea, areas on Ross Island would have been inaccessible to Adélies; the last advance reached maximum extent about 10,000 years ago. In addition, Sladen (1964) hypothesized an apparent range extension in the closely related Chinstrap Penguin (*Pygoscelis antarctica*) during the previous 20 to 25 years, attributing it to increased food supply resulting from depletion of the large krill-eating whales (see ch. 10). Trivelpiece and Volkman (1979) offered the same explanation for a remarkable invasion of an Adélie Penguin rookery by adult Chinstraps early in the spring. After evicting the Adélies, they quickly paired and bred. The phenomenon so totally contradicts the characteristics of wandering in young birds (absent in older ones) as a means of colony establishment and the high degree of philopatry displayed by adult pygoscelid penguins, however, that another explanation seems likely. Perhaps the Chinstraps' original colony site was destroyed by a cataclysmic event, such as a snow slide, forcing the mass movement of breeding adults to an alternate site. Obviously more information is needed to explain this observation.

Given the possibility of such changing conditions, retention (or evolution) of an emigratory potential is functional. Most penguin species, however, tend to be traditional rather than exploitative and to favor tradition-preserving behavior (e.g., faithfulness to mate and site, return to natal colony, and so on). Atlantic Gannets also have a tendency for tradition-preserving behavior, but since the mid-1800s when their population was reduced to a mere vestige of its former size, "pioneering" individuals have brought about a relatively rapid reoccupation of their range and recovery of their numbers (Nelson 1978b). Thus vacuum or social factors may become important to seabirds in circumstances when resources are abundantly available. The emigrants, or "pioneers" as Nelson calls them, need not be forced away from a population by limited resources, but their traditional tendencies can be overcome by abundant resources elsewhere. Nevertheless, regardless of resource availability, some small portion of a seabird population will disperse elsewhere.

The disruptive effects young Adélies have on breeding birds has been stressed to the point of dubbing them "hooligans" (Levick 1914, Sladen 1958). Contrary to these reports, young birds at Cape Crozier caused very little disruption. The timing of their presence to coincide with the periods when they were least disruptive of breeding (ch. 3) reduced disturbance. While they did on occasion molest a chick or drive one from the crêche, wanderers were more characteristically shy, and when they occupied a territory it was usually peripheral. They were observers more often than participants in overt social interactions, kept to the edges of colonies, and were subordinate when challenged by territorial birds. Their behavior stressed aspects positive or neutral to adult breeders, while providing learning experiences to themselves and reservoir and expansion capabilities to the population.

5
BREEDING BEHAVIOR

 The present study is concerned with breeding biology; and because successful breeding requires an Adélie to be expert in social interactions, we would like to review here the social behavior of the Adélie Penguin. This will provide background for later discussions and may also provide the reader with a feeling for the living bird, who is confronted with real situations in the breeding effort. Emphasis in this chapter is on differences in display usage by birds of different age and breeding status.

Several major studies have been published on the social behavior of the Adélie Penguin: Levick (1914), Sladen (1958), Sapin-Jaloustre (1960), Penney (1968), Spurr (1975a), and Ainley (1975b). Supplementary work has been contributed by Penney (1962), Thompson (1974), Ainley (1978), and Müller-Schwarze and Müller-Schwarze (1980). Almost all of these were studies in animal behavior, their prime purpose being to describe displays and their social functions. Only Ainley (1975b), who was primarily interested in how display behavior determined whether a bird paired and bred, and to some degree Spurr (1974), related the use of displays directly to breeding success. No new data are presented here, but with the detailed information on breeding biology now available (in other chapters) we will revise interpretations of previous data on display behavior. (Refer to the references above for detailed descriptions of displays.)

To breed successfully, an Adélie Penguin must accomplish three major social tasks: secure and maintain a territory upon which to build a nest, develop a pair bond with an individual of the opposite sex so that eggs are laid in that nest, and with its mate coordinate the care of eggs and chicks. All of these tasks are accomplished by the exchange of information between the Adélie and its neighbors, mate, and offspring.

Through evolution, information about an Adélie's intent has been encoded in visual and vocal displays; and depending on contextual information, the recipient decodes the meaning contained in the transmitted message. A limited number of display messages exists, but their use in a wide variety of situations is possible because meanings can change based on context (Smith 1965, 1969a, 1977). Not only does an Adélie acquire information through communication but, in supplying information to others, it "manages" social interactions by leading the recipient to perform appropriately (Smith 1969b).

It appears that behaving appropriately in response to the displays of others and even following its own displays are abilities that develop with practice in Adélie Penguins as age and experience increase (Ainley 1978). Thus the chances of breeding and of doing so successfully are increased as Adélies learn to manage their social interactions. Interestingly, young Adélies, and older ones that have difficulty acquiring mates, display much more often in given situations than do older, successful individuals. The latter act more directly. For example, when another Adélie comes too close, instead of prefacing Attack with elaborate displays as an inexperienced bird would, they indicate their aroused antagonism merely by raising their crest (Ainley 1975b) and then Pecking or Attacking only if the intruder moves closer. The individual differences in aggressiveness detected by Spurr (1974) are certainly manifestations of age-related differences in these birds.

ESTABLISHMENT AND MAINTENANCE OF TERRITORY

In this species, the male establishes the territory. The relationship to natal site and the experience during wanderings as a juvenile determine the approximate location (see ch. 4), but exact location in a colony is probably a matter of the timing of arrival and the availability of sites. Older birds usually occupy their territory of previous years regardless of colony configuration. After the large majority of older, experienced males arrive, the younger ones appear and fill in the several vacant interior spaces or, more likely, establish territories on the periphery (ch. 8).

Upon arrival an older bird usually proclaims itself with Locomotory Hesitance Vocalization [(LHV), the Loud Mutual Display (LMD) of most authors (fig. 16). Since it is not always mutual, as in this and other cases, Ainley (1975*b*) renamed it after the analogous display described by Smith (1966) for other species.] Then the bird gives forth the "song" of the species, Ecstatic Vocalization (EV; all authors). Both these displays are highly individualistic and are

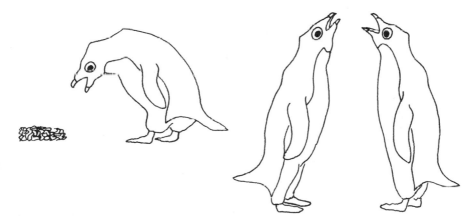

FIGURE 16 An Adélie calling a Locomotory Hesitance Vocalization (LHV) as it approaches its nest (left); and a pair in LHV (right) (from Ainley 1975*b*).

largely proclamations of self: "This is me, Adélie Penguin X, and I am approaching [LHV] or occupying [EV] my space, my territory." The emphasis on territory is much stronger in the EV than the LHV; EV also emphasizes in particular the male-ness and breeding condition of the caller. Males already present give rebuttals by uttering the same calls in return, mostly EV, and also perform Bill-to-Axilla Displays (BAx; all authors; fig. 17), which are defensive, territorial calls of low intensity (Ainley 1975*b*, Spurr 1975*a*). Between calls the newly arrived, older bird occasionally lies down in the old nest depression and Scratches, a behavior that indicates ownership of a specific site (Ainley 1975*b*, Spurr 1975*a*). Eventually the bird begins to build a pile of nest stones.

The younger, less established, but physiologically ma-ture male is usually less emphatic about his arrival. He finds a nest scoop (these depressions last for decades) at or near the site he occupied the previous season, perhaps mainly during the reoccupation period. Once there, he performs EV in response to the same calls given by other lone males. Soon he is engaged in a "battle of words," using EV and BAx, with several neighbors.

The youngest males, all of which are nonbreeders and most of which are physiologically immature, begin to oc-cupy territories during or after their wandering phase (see ch. 4). They, too, utter EV and perform BAx but then often wander away soon afterward. Thus, though they do proclaim their territoriality, it is really without any "conviction." On occasion young males also utter an EV on snow slopes or ice floes near the rookery. Such a performance is obviously well out of context. Frequency of use of the EV decreases with increased age (Ainley 1975*b*).

FIGURE 17
Adélie Penguin expressing annoyance at the presence of an intruder through Bill-to-Axilla (from Ainley 1975*b*).

The territory is maintained by both the male and his mate. He continues to collect the majority of stones for the nest, but she also collects them just before departing to sea after being relieved of incubation. We observed (ch. 4) that older birds built better nests than younger ones.

A female will help defend the territory almost immediately after a male has accepted her on his territory. Young females, however, may wander away not long after a defensive engagement against intruders or nearby pairs. Thus she may also display without much "conviction" in the messages she transmits.

A number of displays are used by Adélies to defend a territory. The most extreme is the Attack (all authors), which occurs relatively rarely and usually when one male arrives to find another occupying his former territory. Other displays used to defend territory, in order of decreasing hesitance to Attack and increasing proximity to the intruder, are Crest Erect and head shake (Ainley 1974, 1975*b*), Bill-to-Axilla, Sideways (Spurr 1975*a*) or One-sided Stare (Ainley 1975*b*; fig. 18), Alternate Stare (all authors; fig. 19), Point (Spurr 1975*a*) or Direct Stare (all other authors), and Gape and Peck (Ainley 1975*b*, Spurr 1975*a*; fig. 20). All of these are defensive because the signaler is hesitant both to leave its territory and to come into physical contact with the intruder. Spurr (1974) found that the frequency of Pecks at intruders increased at egg hatching. Thus the presence of chicks decreased a parent's hesitance to physically engage an opponent.

In response to intruders actually on their territories, young birds are more likely to display than Attack. Of dis-

FIGURE 18
Sideways (or One-sided) Stare (from Ainley 1975*b*).

FIGURE 19
Alternate Stare (from Ainley 1975*b***).**

FIGURE 20   Two Adélies Gaping at each other (from Ainley
1975*b***).**

plays given, young Adélies, compared to older experienced individuals, tend to give the more defensive ones (Ainley 1978). Spurr (1974) found that birds nesting at the periphery of colonies tend to Peck intruders less frequently than those nesting more centrally. As shown in chapter 8, the majority of peripheral nesters are young birds.

Defense of territory also involves repelling predators, namely skuas. The same displays used against penguin intruders are used against predators (Ainley 1975*b*, Müller-Schwarze and Müller-Schwarze 1977).

DEVELOPMENT AND MAINTENANCE OF
THE PAIR BOND

A singing male is not only proclaiming his territoriality and sex but is also announcing that he is not paired and is ready to become so. Evidence for this is Penney's (1968) observation that the frequency of EV in unpaired males is much higher than in males with mates. A paired male that begins to sing in response to the territorial element of EV in neighboring males is inhibited from further song by the Headwaving (Ainley 1975*b*; the Quiet Mutual Display of other authors) of his mate.

To a large extent, pairing is a matter of timing and location. Led by affinities to her natal site, experiences during wanderings as a younger bird (ch. 4), or experience as a previous breeder (ch. 8), a female will encounter a limited number of unpaired males in the colony to which she returns. Her arrival there as an unpaired female stimulates unpaired males to go into EV. She must then choose among the several singing males. Upon what she initially bases her choice is unknown, but certainly recognition of a mate with whom she bred or kept company in a previous season and perhaps nest location and quality are involved (ch. 4; Ainley 1978). If her partner of the previous season is not among the unpaired males present she will approach another.

When a female finally approaches an unpaired, singing male, a sequence of male/female interactive displays is begun (Ainley 1975*b*, Spurr 1975*a*). The rate at which one display follows another is a function of several factors, including whether the two birds recognize each other as previous partners, their previous experience as breeders, and their inherent aggressiveness. The sequence is as follows: the female approaches slowly with feathers Sleeked and head down; the male maintains the Crest Erect of his EV and, as she approaches closer, watches in a Sideways Stare; she reaches his side by Bowing and by maintaining her ground if he Pecks lightly once or twice (fig. 21); he Bows and then lies down in his nest and Scratches; she moves around by his scratching foot and Bows; he rises from the nest, walks around behind her, and she steps into the nest; if she lies down, they copulate, and the pair bonding has begun. After copulation the male often gathers more nest stones. Between this time and the laying of the first egg, a minimum of about seven days later (ch. 7), they will copulate many times, and the male will gather more stones. By scratching and moving stones about with her bill, the female forms a nest bowl. After laying her eggs she, too, gathers a number of stones just before leaving to feed at sea.

If a female approaches the EV of her previous mate, the

FIGURE 21
The initial meeting of potential
mates on a male's territory; the
female is to the left (from Ainley
1975*b*).

above sequence—to copulation—will be completed immediately. Between strangers it may be several hours or even
several days before initial copulation. If after the female has
made the initial choice of a new mate, her former mate returns—announcing his arrival with LHV and EV—she is
likely to approach the latter if only a few days have passed
between her arrival and his. Arrivals far out of synchrony,
however, are the most common cause for "divorce" when
both members of a pair return the next spring (ch. 8). If a
male returns to find his former nest site occupied, a fight
may ensue. If his former mate happens to be paired with the
new male, her choice of the one to support will probably
depend on how long she has been paired with the new
mate.

Many young males and males who are habitually nonbreeders are sometimes too aggressive toward a female approaching their EV (Ainley 1975*b*, 1978; Spurr 1974). The
female then flees. Males and females often terminate the
pairing sequence at some premature point, which, at the
least, results in more time being spent between arrival and
egg laying (ch. 6) or, at the most, results in no pair bond
being formed. For example, at the point at which lying in
the nest is supposed to occur, females often refuse to do so
initially or they even walk away; this is more characteristic of
young females (Ainley 1975*b*). If a male "finds" a female
lying in his nest, he is more likely to display defensively toward her if he is young and is more likely to copulate if he is
older and more experienced (Ainley 1978).

During the several days between initial pairing and egg
laying, both members of a pair become completely familiar
with the location of their nest in the colony and probably

learn to recognize each other by sight, and the female probably learns to recognize her mate's voice through his occasional song in response to the EV of neighbors. In response to intense disturbance (e.g., a full fight on a nearby nest), members of a pair will learn each other's voices by calling LHVs in duet (the LMD of other authors). The members of many new pairs, however, have probably never heard the LHV of their partners until their first nest relief when the female returns from feeding at sea two weeks after laying the eggs (see below).

COORDINATION OF CARE FOR EGGS AND CHICKS

Soon after laying her eggs, the female leaves to feed at sea, and from then on the two members of an Adélie pair spend little time together. While eggs are being incubated, they are together for about an hour during only four to six nest reliefs; when young chicks are being guarded, parents relieve each other on ten to twenty occasions. For the three to four weeks when the chick is in the crêche, the two parents may see each other briefly on only a few occasions (Taylor 1962, Spurr 1977). The chicks see their parents, mostly one at a time, during brief feeding visits (an hour or so) every two to three days.

The relative rarity of being together once eggs are laid and the shortness of the breeding season place a premium on the pair's synchrony, which came about through their coincident arrivals and was strengthened during pair bonding. After egg laying, the coordination of their breeding efforts is then mediated by their synchrony of activity and by individual recognition. The degree of synchrony between mated birds, which is manifested in the timing of nest reliefs, is critical to the successful fledging of young (Davis 1982).

One important display, the LHV, is the major vehicle used to reestablish contact between mates and between parents and their chicks. Following establishment of the pair bond and egg laying, regardless of whether its mate, eggs, or chicks are still present, an Adélie will begin to call LHVs when approaching its nest, beginning a few meters away (in fact, even older birds that failed to pair during the occupation or egg-laying period usually call LHVs upon returning to their nests at the beginning of the reoccupation period). Instantly recognizing the caller by voice, the mate and/or chicks will call LHV in response (Penney 1962). Sometimes the approaching caller is slightly off in its "choice" of nest, but LHVs from the mate change its direction immediately. Shortly after identity has been established, a nest relief takes place and/or chicks are fed (Thompson 1974). The arriving bird stops calling once the mate has stepped from the eggs or tiny chicks; the departing bird continues to call as it steps off the eggs and moves from the nest as the mate takes its place. After nest relief, the relieved partner collects stones for about an hour and then leaves for the sea. Müller-Schwarze and Müller-Schwarze (1980) discovered that LHV repetition rate communicated readiness to relieve in the arriving mate and readiness to allow the partner to take over nest duties in the incubating mate. This is a good example of how an Adélie can "manage" its social interactions.

During the crèche stage, the LHV calls of a parent at the nest bring its chick(s) running from the crèche. Sometimes other chicks approach as well, but by recognizing its own chick through the chick's LHV voice, the parent feeds only its own offspring (Thompson 1974). Soon after feeding the chick(s), the parent departs, often to avoid persistent begging by its offspring.

Once eggs are successfully laid, overall reproductive success is a function of several factors, some of which are affected by pair synchrony, tardy return by the partner feeding at sea, inattentiveness by the incubating partner, poor choice of nest location (peripheral nest or nest subject to drifting snow), poorly constructed nest (reducing incubation efficiency or allowing melt water to contact eggs), insufficient amounts of food brought to chicks, and predation at sea. All of these factors are affected by the age and experience of an Adélie, as we shall reveal in following chapters. No information is available on whether age and experience determine the ease by which partners adjust synchrony or establish recognition. Younger, less experienced birds, however, do require more time between arrival, pair formation, and egg laying (ch. 6). Besides indicating more difficulty in establishing a pair bond, this may also indirectly indicate less facility in adjusting synchrony.

The above has been a brief summary of the display behavior in Adélie Penguins. Emphasis on behavior sequences used in the breeding process revealed how older Adélies interact more successfully in social situations.

6
INITIAL PAIRING AND BREEDING

 We have seen how various factors affect the arrivals and visits of Adélie Penguins at a rookery and what the youngest birds do once there. Their activities were viewed as an age- and experience-related progression that eventually leads to breeding. During their pre-breeding years they learn to interact socially among themselves and with older birds in activities related to breeding. Several factors then operate to determine whether an individual does or does not breed: physiologically mature males compete among themselves for fewer mature females, and success in this depends on how efficient or capable they are in social interactions. Physiologically mature females rarely fail to breed and then only if their nutritional well-being is inadequate (Ainley 1975*a, b,* 1978).

The present chapter introduces the subject of breeding, to be investigated in more detail in the following chapters, by exploring how age, experience, and other factors affect breeding incidence and by investigating the factors that determine where a bird first breeds. We also relate spring arrival to pairing and egg laying.

AGE AT FIRST BREEDING

The modal age of first breeding in a sample of 337 birds, 1964 to 1969, was four years; the second most common age

TABLE 6.1 Age and experience of 337 first-time breeding Adélie Penguins; Cape Crozier, 1964 to 1969.

Age (yrs)	Year in rookery	Males	Females	Total*
3	First	0	22	34
	Second	0	6	10
	Total	0	28	44
4	First	0	17	34
	Second	12	49	90
	Third	6	9	22
	Total	18	75	146
5	First	6	3	24
	Second	11	17	44
	Third	9	6	24
	Fourth	3	2	6
	Total	29	28	98
6	First	0	2	6
	Second	5	7	19
	Third	6	2	9
	Fourth	5	1	7
	Fifth	1	0	1
	Total	17	12	42
7	First	0	0	0
	Second	0	1	4
	Third	0	0	2
	Fourth	0	0	0
	Fifth	0	0	1
	Sixth	0	0	0
	Total	0	1	7
Totals		64	144	337

*Includes birds of unknown sex.

was five (table 6.1). Since more banded cohorts passed through ages younger than six years than had reached six years or older, the absolute numbers of penguins first breeding at these younger ages provide inflated estimates of proportions, although they probably accurately reflect modal values.

A weighting of values in table 6.1 and additional data on eight-year-olds reflect this discrepancy. To correct for it, ab-

TABLE 6.2 Age at first breeding by Adélie Penguins at Cape Crozier, 1964 to 1969; corrected for mortality and cohort size for birds banded in areas B and C.

Age (yrs)	A No. first breeders observed	B No. originally banded in cohorts	C Proportion surviving*	D Corrected cohort size, B × C	E No. first breeders (corrected) A ÷ D × 1000	F Percent first breeding
3	44	21,479	0.20	4,296	10	3.0
4	146	16,420	0.14	2,299	64	19.2
5	98	11,420	0.09	1,028	95	28.4
6	42	6,420	0.07	449	94	28.1
7	7	2,310	0.05	116	60	18.0
8	1	2,308	0.04	92	11	3.3

*From Ainley and DeMaster (1980: fig. 4).

solute numbers first breeding at each age were divided by the number of birds passing through each age (table 6.2); the latter was derived by correcting the number originally banded by the proportion surviving to each age. The modal age for first breeding then becomes ages five and six, with seven-year-olds becoming more heavily represented. If we consider Adélies through eight years of age, that is, the age at which all have bred at least once, and if we correct for cohort size, 3 percent of first-time breeders were three years old; 19 percent were four; 28 percent, five; 28 percent, six; 18 percent, seven; and 3 percent, eight.

The average age of first breeding by males (6.2) was delayed more than a year past that of females (fig. 22, table 6.3). Using a different method of calculation, Ainley and De-Master (1980) estimated the average ages of first reproduc-

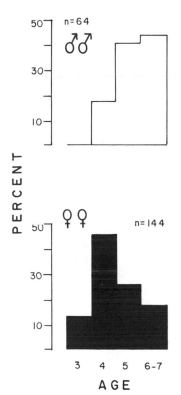

FIGURE 22
The age distribution of 64 male and 144 female first-time-breeding Adélie Penguins, corrected for cohort size; Cape Crozier, 1964 to 1969.

TABLE 6.3   Age of first breeding in Adélie Penguins of known sex; Cape Crozier, 1964 to 1969.

Age	MALE			FEMALE		
	Observed	Corrected*	Corrected	Observed	Corrected*	Corrected
(yrs)	n	n	%	n	n	%
3	0	0	0.0	28	7	7.1
4	35	15	3.9	75	33	33.3
5	72	70	18.2	28	27	25.3
6	56	125	32.5	12	27	25.3
7	19	164	42.6	1	9	9.1
8	1	11	2.9	0	0	0
Totals	183	385	100.1	144	99	100.1
$\bar{x} \pm SD$	5.3 ± 0.9	6.2 ± 0.9†		4.6 ± 1.0	5.0 ± 1.2†	

*Corrected by dividing the number observed by the corrected cohort size shown in table 6.2.
†$t = 10.99$, P<.05.

tion to be 4.7 for females and 6.8 for males, which agree closely with the figures in table 6.3. No males bred at three years of age, whereas 7 percent of all female first-breeders were of that age. Assuming an equal sex ratio among eventual breeders (and therefore at first breeding; Ainley and De-Master 1980) and correcting for cohort size, we find that 4 percent of first-breeding females were three years old and 7 percent of first-breeding males were four years old. Only 34 percent of females breed first after the fifth year, whereas 60 percent of males breed first at ages six years or older.

Most first-time breeders were in the rookery for their second year, fewer for the first, and progressively fewer for the third, fourth, and fifth years. Table 6.4, in which known-sex and unknown-sex first-time breeders were combined, shows that half of all first breeders were at the rookery for their second year, 29 percent for the first, and 17 percent for the third and that fewer than 5 percent had been present (i.e., observed) more than three seasons previous to first breeding. As suggested by their greater delay in breeding compared to females, males generally had more experience at the rookery before first breeding than had females (fig. 23). Whereas 31 percent of 144 female first-breeders were at

TABLE 6.4 **Experience of 337 first-time-breeding Adélie Penguins; Cape Crozier, 1964 to 1969.**

Age (yrs)	Percent with X years in rookery				
	First	*Second*	*Third*	*Fourth*	*Fifth*
3	77	33			
4	23	62	15		
5	25	45	25	5	
6	14	46	21	17	2
7	0	57	29	0	14
All Ages	29	50	17	4	1

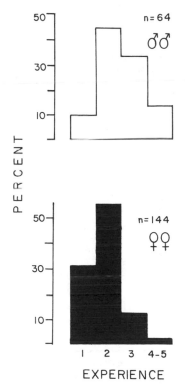

FIGURE 23
Experience at first breeding of 64 male and 144 female Adélie Penguins; Cape Crozier, 1964 to 1969.

the rookery for their first summer, only 10 percent of 64 first-breeding males were equally inexperienced. It is likely that many birds breeding in their "first" seasons at the rookery visited in previous years but for such short periods that they were missed by us. Fully 86 percent of females were present at Cape Crozier for their first or second season when they first bred; 46 percent of males were present for the third, fourth, or fifth season at initial breeding. The greater delay in breeding for males is related to an unequal sex ratio among older Adélies (Ainley and DeMaster 1980). The greater number of males increases the competition for a smaller number of available mates, and younger males more often lose in the contest (see ch. 10).

The incidence of breeding increased with age (table 6.5). None of 219 two-year-olds observed from 1967 through 1975 bred, and only 9 percent of three-year-olds did so. Large increases in the proportion of birds breeding continued successively until the sixth year, and then the trend

TABLE 6.5   The incidence of breeding in Adélies of known age and sex;* Cape Crozier, 1967 to 1975.

Age	MALE			FEMALE			TOTAL	
	Breed	Total	%	Breed	Total	%		%
(yrs)	n	n	Breed	n	n	Breed	n	Breed
2		104	0		115	0	219	0
3		244	0	39	228	17	452	9
4	33	256	13	110	226	49	482	30
5	179	449	40	227	333	68	782	52
6	347	527	66	338	414	82	941	73
7	315	391	81	301	333	90	724	85
8	165	198	83	149	164	91	362	87
9	62	78	79	40	46	87	124	82
10	57	64	89	32	36	89	100	89
11	45	59	76	27	33	82	92	78
12	31	38	82	20	24	83	62	82
13	14	16	88	8	8	100	24	92
14	4	4	100				4	100

*A regression of age (three years and older) against incidence of breeding resulted in the following values of r: males .8509, females .7640, and totals .8298 (P<.05).

TABLE 6.6   Breeding incidence as related to age and experience: 422 breedings by Adélie Penguins ages three to eight years; Cape Crozier, 1963 to 1969.

Age	YEARS IN ROOKERY									
	First		Second		Third		Fourth and Fifth		Total	
(yrs)	%	n	%	n	%	n	%	n	%	n
3	3	(1,147)	5	(184)					3	(1,331)
4	10	(355)	25	(402)	43	(56)			20	(813)
5	28	(87)	34	(145)	43	(111)	41	(27)	35	(370)
6–8	27	(22)	57	(46)	5	(55)	48	(50)	50	(173)
3–8	6	(1,611)	24	(777)	46	(222)	45	(77)	16	(1,287)
r*	.8613		.9889		.9449		1.000		.9783	

*Regression from age three through six to eight years against breeding incidence; all significant (P<.05).

leveled off. Similar increases in incidence with age occurred in birds with an equal number of years of experience in the rookery (table 6.6). For example, of 777 Adélies present at Crozier for the second time, incidence increased from 5 percent of three-year-olds to 83 percent of eleven-year-olds. Among birds of the same age, breeding incidence increased with experience at the rookery. This was more evident in young birds because with increased age, the effect of added experience decreased. For example, among 813 four-year-olds, overall breeding incidence was 20 percent; but within this group, breeding increased from 10 percent of those individuals present for the first time to 20 percent of those present for their second season and 43 percent of birds at the rookery for the third season. Among five-year-olds, breeding incidence increased with two or three years of additional experience but not with a fourth, and among six-year-olds only one additional year of experience had an effect. Among older birds, however, experience did not increase breeding incidence (P<.05, t-test).

Breeding incidence increased more rapidly with prior *breeding* experience (table 6.7) vs. mere presence in the rookery as just discussed. For example, 18 percent of 793 previously inexperienced (at breeding) four-year-olds bred, whereas 55 percent of the 20 four-year-olds that had pre-

TABLE 6.7   Breeding incidence related to age and previous breeding experience: 422 breedings by 388 Adélie Penguins age three to seven years; Cape Crozier, 1964 to 1969.

Age	PREVIOUS YEARS OF BREEDING							
	None		One		Two and three		Total	
(yrs)	%	(n)	%	(n)	%	(n)	%	(n)
3	3	(1,331)					3	(1,331)
4	18	(793)	55	(20)			20	(813)
5	32	(308)	53	(60)	100	(5)	36	(373)
6&7	42	(129)	45	(29)	60	(15)	50	(173)
5–7	35	(437)	51	(88)	70	(20)		

viously bred once did so again (P<.05, t-test). After the first year of previous breeding experience, additional experience did not increase breeding incidence. This is revealed in the combined data for five- to seven-year-olds where there were no statistically significant differences in birds having one or two years of breeding experience (P<.05; t-test). There was also no effect of breeding experience on breeding incidence after five years of age because in six- and seven-year-olds (combined), breeding incidence was the same regardless of experience (P<.05). It appears, then, that a year of previous experience speeds the rate of maturation in younger Adélies, at least with regard to increasing their tendency to breed.

With few exceptions, incidence of breeding was higher among three- through seven-year-old females than among males of the same age, experience in the rookery, and breeding experience (tables 6.8 and 6.9). Thus, of 22 age-experience cells in the tables where comparison is possible, females showed the higher breeding incidence 19 times and males only twice (in one case, incidence was equal at 0 percent for both sexes). Combining all experience classes, more females of ages three through seven years bred than did males of the same ages.

A discrepancy between incidences of breeding among known-sex individuals (tables 6.8 and 6.9) and those of all known-age birds observed (tables 6.6 and 6.7) resulted from

TABLE 6.8 Breeding incidence (percent of birds) by age and experience among male and female Adélie Penguins of known age; Cape Crozier, 1963 to 1969.

| Age (yrs) | YEARS IN ROOKERY | | | | | | | | Total Number | | BREEDING Incidence | |
| | First | | Second | | Third | | Fourth & fifth | | | | | |
	Males	Females	Males	Females	Males	Females	Males	Females	Males	Females	Males	Females
2	0	0							17	30	0	0
3	0	23	0	0					49	180	0	16
4	0	47	33	70	55	85			62	133	29	71
5	50	60	61	64	60	67	40	56	60	90	52	72
6&7	0	67	50	85	70	67	50	80	39	43	54	72
Totals									227	476		

TABLE 6.9 Breeding incidence (percent of birds) in relation to age and previous breeding experience among male and female Adélie Penguins of known age; Cape Crozier, 1964 to 1969.

Age (yrs)	BREEDING EXPERIENCE—NUMBER OF PREVIOUS BREEDINGS								Total number		BREEDING Incidence	
	None		One		Two		Three					
	Males	Females	Males	Females	Males	Females	Males	Females	Males	Females	Males	Females
3	0	16							49	180		
4	29	54		61					62	133	29	65
5	56	67	50	55		100			60	90	52	64
6	77	80	0	75	50	38		100	32	34	56	71
7	0	100	40	83	100			50	7	9	43	78
Totals									210	446		

the fact that most birds positively sexed were breeders. Therefore, incidences in the first two tables were inflated, and the latter two represented incidence by age more accurately. The ranges of difference between sexes in the first two tables, however, were real, since there was no bias in sexing either males or females except that inherent in their differential incidence of breeding. In fact, even in the oldest age groups, a greater proportion of females bred than did males (Ainley and DeMaster 1980; see ch. 9).

FACTORS AFFECTING THE SITE OF FIRST BREEDING

Chapter 4 showed that the locality where wandering and occupation of territory were most likely to occur was directly related to the locality where a bird hatched, and in light of this it is not surprising that the site where an Adélie first bred was also positively correlated with birthplace. Ninety-six percent of all recorded first breedings by known-age birds (337) occurred in the rookery where the breeder was hatched (table 6.10). The remaining 4 percent occurred in the adjoining East Rookery. Among those breeding in the natal rookery, 77 percent (or 185/239) bred in the area (see Definitions in ch. 2 and footnote in table 4.4) of their birth; 58 percent of these young Adélies bred in the colony group of their hatching; and 56 percent of these bred in the very colony where they were hatched. Comparison of these proportions with those relating natal site to wandering and territory-occupying locales (tables 4.4 and 4.8) shows that patterns and absolute percentages were similar (see also table 4.5).

Sexual differences in the importance of the natal site relative to the eventual breeding site were evident but slight. Chapter 4 showed that males spent more time wandering than did females and were thus the primary "prospectors" within the population. As a result, more females bred within the areas, colony group (both significantly greater; P<.05, t-test), and colonies (P<.05) of their hatching than did males.

Wandering locale was similarly but more strongly re-

TABLE 6.10 **Site of first breeding in relation to natal site for 337 Adélie Penguins; Cape Crozier, 1964 to 1969.**

| | BREEDING SITE | | | |
	Rookery	Area	Colony group	Colony
Number of breedings:				
Same	325	185	66	32
Different	12	54*	48†	25‡
Percent of total breedings:				
Same	96	55	19	9
Different	4	16	14	7
Percent of total breeding observations in this spatial category:				
Same	96	77	58	56
Different	4	23	42	44

*86 sightings, natal area unknown.
†71 sightings, natal colony group unknown.
‡ 9 sightings, natal colony unknown.

lated to first breeding site (table 6.11). In 260 observations of wandering birds, 97 percent occurred in the rookery where first breeding later occurred (vs. 96 percent of first breedings occurring in the natal rookery; $P<.05$, t-test). Eighty percent of these occurred in the area of eventual breeding (vs. 55 percent of breedings occurring in natal areas; $P<.05$), 53 percent (vs. 19 percent; $P<.05$) were in colony groups eventually used for breeding, and 38 percent (vs. 9 percent; $P<.05$) were in eventual breeding colonies. In all but the first case, percent coincidence of wandering and breeding locales was significantly greater than coincidence of hatching and breeding sites.

Among birds of known sex, no consistent difference in wandering/breeding site correlation was evident. As with the breeding/natal site correlation, however, females showed a significantly greater tendency to breed in an area of previous wandering than did males ($P<.05$, t-test; fig. 24). The sexes did not differ significantly at the colony or colony group levels.

The site of breeding corresponded much more closely to the territorial site occupied during previous seasons than

TABLE 6.11 **Locality of wandering by prebreeding Adélie Penguins in relation to their eventual site of first breeding; 260 total observations.**

	Rookery	Area	Colony group	Colony
		BREEDING SITE		
Number of observations wandering:				
Same	253	207	138	98
Different	7	44*	37†	35‡
Percent of total observations:				
Same	97	80	53	38
Different	3	17	14	13
Percent of observations in this spatial category:				
Same	97	82	79	74
Different	3	18	21	26

* 2 sightings, area unknown.
†32 sightings, colony group unknown.
‡ 5 sightings, colony unknown.

did breeding site and wandering locale of the previous season or breeding site and natal site. Correlations between previous territorial occupation and breeding were 99 percent within the same rookery (vs. 97 percent of wanderings occurring within the breeding rookery and 96 percent of breedings within the natal rookery), 97 percent within the same area (vs. 80 percent and 55 percent), 88 percent within the same colony group (vs. 53 percent and 19 percent), and fully 78 percent of territorial occupation occurring within the colony of eventual first breeding (vs. 38 percent of wandering observations and 9 percent of breedings within the colony of hatching). All differences between correlations were statistically significant (P<.05, t-test; table 6.12). Together, they illustrate well the progressive spatial restriction with age as discussed in chapter 4.

Sexual differences in correlations between previous territorial and eventual breeding sites were not evident (fig. 24). Both sexes tended to breed first in the locality where they first began to occupy territory.

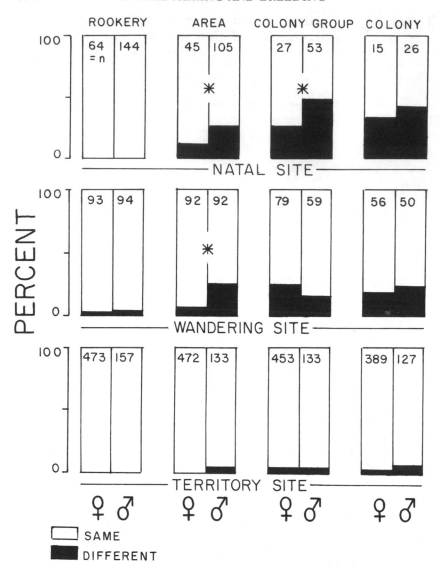

FIGURE 24   The sites of hatching, wandering, and territorial occupation of known-age Adélie Penguins in relation to site of subsequent first breeding; 1,025 observations of Adélies ages two to
seven years, Cape Crozier, 1963 to 1968. Shaded areas are observations at a site different from that at first breeding; unshaded areas
are sightings at the same site. Male-female differences marked with
an asterisk (*) are statistically significant (P<.05; t-test).

TABLE 6.12   Previous observations of territorial occupation at the site of first breeding.

	BREEDING SITE			
	Rookery	Area	Colony group	Colony
Number of observations at territory:				
Same	730	714	645	571
Different	5	16	28*	25†
Percent of total observations:				
Same	99	97	88	78
Different	1	2	4	3
Percent of observations in this spatial category:				
Same	99	98	96	96
Different	1	2	4	4

*41 colony groups, observations unknown.
†49 colonies, observations unknown.

THE TIMING OF PAIRING

The behaviors comprising the pairing process were discussed in the preceding chapter. Established breeders performed few displays and instead acted quite directly during pair formation, whereas young, unestablished birds acted indirectly by displaying a great deal. Younger birds were also less active socially. Prior breeders, through their direct approach and greater social activity, paired shortly after arrival, the females more so than males, and there was no discernible relationship to age (table 6.13). Those birds whose previous breeding experience was unknown remained unpaired for a much longer time. In this group many of the birds through six years probably had no previous breeding experience.

One might expect that the time between arrival and egg laying would show a pattern similar to the time between arrival and pairing, only slightly longer, when Adélies of different ages are compared. This, however, was not so (table 6.14). In females, egg laying was delayed six to ten days after arrival; females had to be present during the courtship

TABLE 6.13 Average number of days between arrival and pairing for males and females known or unknown to have bred previously;* Cape Crozier, 1967 to 1974.

Age (yrs)	MALE Prior breeders $\bar{x} \pm SD$	n	History unknown† $\bar{x} \pm SD$	n	FEMALE Prior breeders $\bar{x} \pm SD$	n	History unknown† $\bar{x} \pm SD$	n
2			4.9 ± 6.8	9			4.7 ± 6.4	40
3			18.6 ± 18.1	64			7.4 ± 11.3	142
4			1.6 ± 1.6	9			3.9 ± 8.3	128
5	3.7 ± 3.3	7	15.0 ± 17.6	207	1.2 ± 0.7	32	2.5 ± 6.2	135
6	5.4 ± 4.9	22	10.3 ± 15.2	173	1.3 ± 1.5	38	3.8 ± 9.3	113
7	4.6 ± 7.1	14	7.8 ± 9.8	103	1.2 ± 0.5	17		
8–9	2.2 ± 1.3	8			1.3 ± 0.9	14		
10–13	4.7 ± 4.6	32			1.0 ± 0.0	12		
Total	4.5 ± 4.7	83	12.3 ± 15.1	565	1.2 ± 0.9	113	4.5 ± 8.6	558

*Statistical comparisons: males vs. females, prior breeders $t = 7.290$ and history unknown $t = 10.619$; prior breeders vs. history unknown, males $t = 4.072$ and females $t = 4.670$. All are significantly different ($P < .05$).

†Includes a high proportion of first-time breeders.

TABLE 6.14 Average number of days between arrival and egg laying for males and females known or unknown to have bred previously;* Cape Crozier, 1967 to 1974.

Age (yrs)	MALE Prior breeders Days ± SD	n	MALE History unknown† Days ± SD	n	FEMALE Prior breeders Days ± SD	n	FEMALE History unknown† Days ± SD	n
4			9.7 ± 2.6	18	8.6 ± 2.8	8	9.3 ± 8.6	31
5	12.3 ± 2.8	6	12.4 ± 6.2	101	10.2 ± 2.8	22	7.7 ± 4.1	93
6	13.0 ± 4.6	21	12.0 ± 6.4	172	9.4 ± 3.3	30	7.0 ± 3.3	140
7	12.9 ± 4.2	15	13.5 ± 5.7	144	9.4 ± 2.8	20	7.2 ± 3.4	128
8	13.9 ± 3.6	8	13.6 ± 5.5	36	7.2 ± 3.4	34		
9	16.0 ± 9.1	19			5.3 ± 3.6	18		
10	14.1 ± 5.0	27			5.9 ± 2.0	15		
11	10.8 ± 5.8	18			7.5 ± 3.2	6		
12	16.9 ± 5.9	10			6.7 ± 1.6	9		
13	11.3 ± 3.4	3						
All	13.1 ± 5.1	127	12.7 ± 6.2	472	8.4 ± 3.2	162	7.3 ± 4.2	392

*Statistical comparisons: males *vs.* females, prior breeders $t = 9.572$ and history unknown $t = 14.673$; prior breeders *vs.* history unknown, males $t = .669$ and females $t = 2.993$. All are significantly different, P<.05, except for the one between males of known and unknown history.

†Includes a high proportion of first-time breeders.

(pre-egg-laying) period for at least seven days to insure production of viable eggs (Ainley 1978). Older females apparently timed their arrival, pairing, and egg laying very precisely, with little variation around this seven-day period, but younger ones had a day or two more leeway. In contrast, males showed quite a different pattern. Males younger than seven years found eggs in their nests ten to thirteen days after arrival, but in older birds the delay was fourteen to seventeen days. Since younger males arrived later than older ones, this indicates that later-arriving females were in more of a rush to lay their eggs than earlier-arriving ones. Grau and Wilson (1980) recently found that yolk formation requires twelve to thirteen days in Adélie Penguins; and Ainley (1975b) found in Adélies that yolk formation was further along in mature females arriving later in spring than in those arriving earlier. The latter may account for the greater urgency to pair and lay eggs in these birds. Such urgency might be to the advantage of young, inexperienced males because the later-arriving females might be less selective. In contrast, late in the November egg-laying period the number of unpaired, territorial males reaches maximum, and competition for mates among males would then be rather intense. That pairing occurs more rapidly later is indicated by the fact that the number of unpaired males present reaches a peak in the third week of November (egg laying occurs 2 November to 2 December), but at that time their proportion to total males declines with increasing rapidity compared to a "plateau" during the first half of egg laying (fig. 25).

CHAPTER SUMMARY

Adélie Penguins, like other seabirds, defer their first attempts at breeding until they are at least a few years old, much as they defer their first visits to the rookery. The average of first breeding in females was 4.7 to 5.0 years and in males was 6.2 to 6.8 years, depending on which of two methods of estimation is used. Few Adélies breed with no previous rookery experience. The incidence of breeding increases with age, and it increases more rapidly with prior

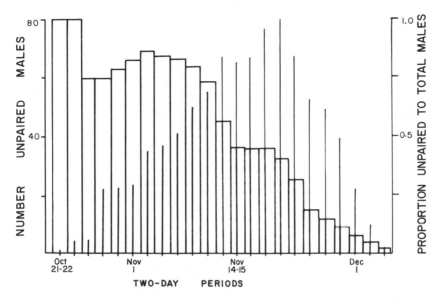

FIGURE 25   The number of unpaired male Adélie Penguins (vertical lines) and their proportion to total males present (vertical bars) in area C during successive two-day periods throughout egg laying; Cape Crozier, 1974.

breeding and not just rookery experience. Adélies first breed close to where they hatched, closer to where they wandered, and closer yet to where they occupied territory as pre-breeders.

Adélies with previous breeding experience paired more rapidly after arrival in the spring than did individuals without the initial experience. Females paired more rapidly than males. Younger, later-arriving males paired more rapidly than older, earlier-arriving ones. This indicates that late-arriving females may be less selective in choosing mates than the earlier ones, as dictated by physiological needs. But there is also a proportionately larger pool of unpaired males available later in the pair-formation period than earlier, and thus females may have relatively more good choices available then.

The advantages of deferring maturity have been discussed briefly already (see summaries of chs. 3 and 4), and the Adélie Penguin data should help to elucidate them further. Since the topic is complex and factors relating to breeding success must be considered, however, we will not attempt to synthesize the various components of this topic until the information in the next chapters is presented (see summary of ch. 7 and ch. 10).

7
ACTIVITIES OF BREEDING WITH RESPECT TO AGE AND EXPERIENCE

 Richdale (1949*a*, 1957), studying a group of Yellow-Eyed Penguins, their ages known by banding, was able to document with certainty age-associated differences in breeding biology, including changes in egg size, incubation period, mate's age, clutch size, fertility, chick survival, breeder survival, strength of pair bond, and possible laying date. Owing to the time period covered during his study (eighteen years), he was able to show not only changes in maturing birds but also changes in birds aging beyond their prime years. Some of the same factors have been since found to vary with age in other seabirds; for example, kittiwakes (Coulson 1963, 1966) and Royal Penguins (Carrick and Ingham 1967, Carrick 1972).

Sladen (1958) suspected that age influenced the breeding biology of the Adélie Penguin also, but breeding birds of known age were not available to him. He hypothesized approximate age groups relative to breeding as follows:

   i. Established (experienced) breeders three to five years old and over; mostly four years old and over.
  ii. Unestablished (inexperienced) breeders two to four years; mostly three years (p. 25).

He characterized these groups (p. 77) as differing in several ways, including quality of nest construction and protectiveness shown for eggs. (It should be noted that Sladen's use of *experienced* and *inexperienced,* being roughly equivalent to *expert* and *novice,* differs from our use, which refers to whether or not a specific behavior has been observed in an individual previously—see ch. 2.) Sladen further stressed that age was only one of three major causes of variation in breeding biology; the others were individual variation and "intensity of behavior."

Cape Crozier data show Sladen's "suggested differences" between young and old breeders to be correct, but they show many additional differences and prove that unestablished breeders may be as old as five and that no two-year-olds and few three-year-olds breed. They also establish similarities in the maturation process between Adélie, Royal, and Yellow-eyed penguins but illustrate that the Adélie matures somewhat more slowly than the Yellow-eyed, and that the Royal matures more slowly still.

In our analyses of factors that obviously depend upon the two members of a pair (e.g., pairing-egg interval, nest-relief routine, egg loss, chick mortality, faithfulness, and so on) or upon the female partner when the known-age Adélie is a male (e.g., laying date, clutch size), we have usually considered *pairs* consisting of one known-age bird and an unknown-age mate as distinct known-age entities. Fortunately, the contribution of the unknown-age partner (perhaps either reinforcing or diluting the behavior being analyzed) can be assessed generally. This will be discussed more fully in chapter 8, where mates of young known-age birds and pairs of known-age birds are considered.

LAYING DATE

An Adélie's age is definitely correlated with the date it returns to the rookery (ch. 3) and with the interval between pairing and laying of the first egg (ch. 6). The combination of these two factors results in the actual laying date, which turns out to be slightly later in November for younger females and which varies little, on the average, for males regardless of age (table 7.1). Richdale (1957) suggested that the male Yellow-eyed Penguin does not affect the ovulation

TABLE 7.1   Average laying date in November for the first egg relative to a parent's age and sex; Cape Crozier, 1963 to 1975.

Age (yrs)	Male Date ± SD	n	Female Date ± SD	n	Total* Date ± SD	n
3			20 ± 3.4	14	20 ± 3.4	14
4	18 ± 4.4	18	20 ± 9.4	42	19 ± 7.9	60
5	19 ± 5.4	107	18 ± 4.4	116	18 ± 4.9	223
6	18 ± 5.2	310	18 ± 4.9	281	18 ± 5.1	591
7	18 ± 4.7	284	18 ± 4.5	266	18 ± 4.6	550
8	18 ± 4.7	152	17 ± 3.9	134	18 ± 4.3	286
9	18 ± 5.0	47	17 ± 3.1	38	18 ± 4.2	85
10	17 ± 5.5	47	17 ± 3.8	30	17 ± 4.8	77
11	15 ± 4.2	32	17 ± 3.3	20	16 ± 3.8	52
12–14	17 ± 3.5	34	18 ± 3.5	24	17 ± 3.5	58
All	18 ± 5.0	1,031	18 ± 4.7	965	18 ± 4.9	1,996

*In a regression of laying date vs. age, $r = -.8837$ ($P < .05$).

date of his mate. Based on our discussion in the previous chapter, this is probably so for Adélies, too, and the later laying dates for young females provide further evidence of this.

Prior breeding experience had an insignificant effect on laying date when age factors were eliminated (table 7.2). On the average, pairs containing a bird four, six, or seven years old that was experienced laid the first egg earlier than pairs with an inexperienced bird of the same ages. In the sample of five-year-olds, however, pairs with an experienced bird laid their first eggs later than pairs with an inexperienced five-year-old. None of these differences was statistically significant ($P > .05$, t-test), which, with the data in table 7.1, indicates that laying date is more a function of physiological condition or maturity than of experience.

It is evident from this and earlier discussions that within several days, the laying date of an Adélie pair is dependent upon the age of the female member. Richdale (1957) reported a similar relationship in Yellow-eyed Penguins but also concluded (p. 21) that "individual mean differences in laying dates ... have a genetic basis"—some

TABLE 7.2　Date in November that the first egg was laid in 271 breedings by Adélie Penguins three to seven years old, 44 by former mates of 3- to 6-year-olds, and 94 by adult controls (sample sizes in parentheses); Cape Crozier, 1967-1968.

Age (yrs)	SEX OF KNOWN-AGE PARTNER		All birds
	Females	*Males*	All birds
3			
Inexperienced	20.7 (20)		20.9 (26)
4			
Inexperienced	19.2 (59)	19.6 (16)	19.3 (88)
Experienced	14.9 (7)		14.9 (7)
Total	18.7 (66)	19.6 (16)	18.9 (95)
5			
Inexperienced	16.2 (24)	18.6 (26)	17.3 (60)
Experienced	18.5 (24)	17.5 (4)	18.4 (29)
Total	17.3 (48)	18.4 (30)	17.6 (89)
6			
Inexperienced	16.9 (11)	17.1 (14)	17.3 (30)
Experienced	15.8 (16)	20.0 (5)	17.0 (21)
Total	16.2 (27)	17.9 (19)	17.2 (51)
7			
Inexperienced	17.0 (1)		17.0 (1)
Experienced	16.2 (6)	16.3 (3)	16.3 (9)
Total	16.3 (7)	16.3 (3)	16.4 (10)
Former mates*	15.0 (8)	16.5 (35)	14.7 (44)
Adult controls†			11.4 (94)

* All experienced, ages unknown.
† All presumed experienced, ages unknown.

females lay consistently early and others consistently late compared to the average laying date of the population. Spurr (1975*b*) came to the same conclusion for Adélie Penguins at Cape Bird, as did Serventy (1963) for Short-tailed Shearwaters. Harris (1966*b*) reported a similar phenomenon in Manx Shearwaters but did not test his results statistically.

　　Rather surprisingly, we could find no such relationship at Cape Crozier in 18 females whose laying dates were

TABLE 7.3 Laying dates of individual female Adélie Penguins.

Female	Age first year	DEVIATION (DAYS) FROM MEAN LAYING DATE					Mean ± SD*
		1967	1968	1969	1974	1975	
18536	5	+3	+1		+6	+3	+3.2 ± 2.1
09844	5			0	+6	+3	+3.0 ± 3.0
11514	4		+3	+5	0	+3	+2.8 ± 2.1
18025	7			+4	+1	+3	+2.7 ± 1.5
11482	5			+2	0	+4	+2.0 ± 2.0
18493	5		+3	0	+2	+3	+2.0 ± 1.4
17987	6		+2	+4	+3	−3	+1.5 ± 3.1
17409	6	−4	+1	+4			+0.3 ± 4.0
14393	3	+4	−3	+1	−6	+3	−0.2 ± 4.2
17817	6		+2	−1	−1	−1	−0.2 ± 1.5
13115	5			+3	0	−4	−0.3 ± 3.5
18408	5		−3	−2	+4	−2	−0.8 ± 3.2
18496	6			−5	+1	+1	−1.0 ± 3.5
18350	6			+1	−4	−3	−2.0 ± 2.6
18217	4			−4	−2	−1	−2.3 ± 1.5
17931	7	−2	0	−3	−4	−3	−2.4 ± 1.5
17516	6	−2	−3	−5			−3.3 ± 1.5
17894	6		−1	−6	−3		−3.3 ± 2.5

* No differences statistically significant (Student-Newman-Keuls multiple range test; P> .05).

known for three or more years (table 7.3). Some females did appear to lay earlier or later, but differences were not statistically significant (P> .05; Student-Newman-Keuls test). Using the same statistical test, Spurr (1975*b*) found differences among 28 females (studied for three seasons) whose laying-date deviations spanned those of birds in the Crozier sample, +3.2 to −3.3. The difference between Spurr's data and ours, other than a slight one in sample size (28 vs. 18, respectively), was that all Cape Crozier females were similar in age and experience; records began with their first year of breeding in almost all cases, and in that year most (n = 13 of 18) were five or six years of age, whereas the ages and previous experience of Cape Bird Adélies were unknown. Spurr could have been comparing groups of birds of different age and experience; those younger would lay later and those older would lay earlier than the average for the population. We conclude that the question of whether some Adélies lay consistently earlier or some later remains unresolved; the answer requires a study of females of known history for four or more seasons. Because of the short season and the high degree of breeding synchrony in Adélies at Ross Island (see below and ch. 3), however, this phenomenon might not become apparent except in large samples of females studied at rookeries in lower latitudes.

Richdale (1957) emphasized the restricted synchrony of egg laying in different species of penguins including the Adélie. Table 7.1 indicates a high degree of synchrony within the Crozier rookery. Half of all eggs at Crozier were usually laid in a six-day period, approximately 15 to 21 November! The earliest egg ever recorded at Cape Crozier (1965) was seen 30 October (table 3.2), but it was out of the ordinary, and the latest was laid by the mate of a five-year-old on 2 December (1967). The widest range of egg production within one season (1967) was 3 November to 2 December, or 29 days. During 1968 the range was only 23 days, from 4 to 27 November.

CLUTCH SIZE

The normal clutch size in this species is two eggs; sometimes a female will lay only one egg, and sometimes a female will lay a third if the first is lost before the second is laid. Mean clutch size was slightly lower in pairs having a four-year-old male or, in particular, a three-year-old female, where it was 1.7 and 1.5 eggs, respectively (table 7.4). Among older breeders there was no difference in clutch size, which for them averaged 1.8 eggs. If only birds of known history were considered, the only truly different clutch size was that of three-year-old females (table 7.5). Thus, breeding experience apparently does not affect clutch size. Taylor (1962) reported a mean clutch size of 1.8 for 100 pairs of Adélies at Cape Royds; Reid (1965) reported 1.9

TABLE 7.4 **Average number of eggs laid in pairs where at least one Adélie Penguin was of known age; Cape Crozier, 1963 to 1975.**

Age	Male		Female		Total*	
(yrs)	$\bar{x} \pm SD$	n	$\bar{x} \pm SD$	n	$\bar{x} \pm SD$	n
3			1.5 ± 0.5	31	1.5 ± 0.5	31
4	1.7 ± 0.5	26	1.8 ± 0.4	92	1.8 ± 0.4	136
5	1.8 ± 0.4	138	1.8 ± 0.4	170	1.8 ± 0.4	349
6	1.8 ± 0.4	321	1.8 ± 0.4	309	1.8 ± 0.4	653
7	1.9 ± 0.4	304	1.9 ± 0.4	287	1.9 ± 0.4	603
8	1.8 ± 0.4	162	1.9 ± 0.3	147	1.8 ± 0.4	313
9	1.8 ± 0.4	52	1.9 ± 0.3	39	1.8 ± 0.4	92
10	2.0 ± 0.3	50	1.8 ± 0.4	31	1.9 ± 0.4	86
11	2.0 ± 0.2	40	1.9 ± 0.3	25	1.9 ± 0.3	66
12	1.8 ± 0.4	31	2.0 ± 0.2	20	1.9 ± 0.3	51
13	1.8 ± 0.4	13	1.5 ± 0.5	8	1.7 ± 0.5	21
14	2.0 ± 0.0	2			2.0 ± 0.0	2
All	1.8 ± 0.4	1,139	1.8 ± 0.4	1,159	1.8 ± 0.4	2,403

*Also includes individuals of unknown sex.

eggs per pair (n = 213) at Cape Hallett; and Spurr (1975*b*) reported 1.9 eggs in central nests and 1.8 eggs in peripheral nests at Cape Bird. The overall average (± SD) in our data for 2,403 clutches was 1.8 ± 0.4 eggs.

INCUBATION ROUTINE

Sladen (1958) was the first to quantify the fasting periods of Adélie Penguins during incubation. He found that first fasts at Signy Island (i.e., from initial arrival at the rookery until next return to sea) averaged 40 days and 21 days for 14 males and 14 females, respectively. We found first fasts at Cape Crozier to average about 27 and 10 days for males and females, respectively. Sladen was impressed by the great length of the fasts and recorded male weight losses of 40 percent or more during the period. Because of the male's ability to fast, he concluded that although females occasionally did take the first incubation watch, Adélies "could not

TABLE 7.5 Average number of eggs laid in pairs where at least one parent was of known age and experience; Cape Crozier, 1963 to 1975.

	FIRST-OBSERVED BREEDERS				PRIOR BREEDERS			
	Male		Female		Male		Female	
Age (yrs)	$\bar{x} \pm SD$	n	$\bar{x} \pm SD$	n	$\bar{x} \pm SD$	n	$\bar{x} \pm SD$	n
3			1.5 ± 0.5	31				
4	1.7 ± 0.5	26	1.8 ± 0.4	86			2.0 ± 0.0	6
5	1.7 ± 0.5	52	1.9 ± 0.3	59	1.7 ± 0.5	6	1.7 ± 0.5	30
6	1.9 ± 0.3	54	1.9 ± 0.2	30	1.8 ± 0.4	13	1.9 ± 0.4	27
7	1.9 ± 0.3	23	1.9 ± 0.3	8	1.9 ± 0.3	100	1.9 ± 0.4	103
8	2.0 ± 0.0	2			1.7 ± 0.5	96	1.9 ± 0.4	105
9					1.7 ± 0.4	26	1.9 ± 0.3	22
10					1.9 ± 0.3	23	1.9 ± 0.3	23
11					1.9 ± 0.2	33	1.9 ± 0.3	19
12					1.9 ± 0.3	21	1.9 ± 0.2	15
13					1.8 ± 0.4	12	1.5 ± 0.5	8
All	1.8 ± 0.4	157	1.8 ± 0.4	214	1.8 ± 0.4	330	1.8 ± 0.4	358

breed successfully unless the male remained behind to incubate eggs as soon as they were laid" (p. 55). Sapin-Jaloustre and Boulière (1951) noted that in two of nine cases in Adélie Land during 1950, the male left for sea first. As Sladen (1958) commented, however, those authors did not mention their criteria for sexing birds. Taylor (1962), sexing his unknown-age birds "by a combination of behavior patterns" (p. 189) at Cape Royds in 1960, recorded 6 (of 35) pairs in which "reversed incubation routines" (Ainley and LeResche 1973) occurred. In three of his cases chicks were eventually raised. Yeates (1968), who recorded lengths of first incubation watches at Cape Royds for 154 pairs over two seasons, concluded that all first watches were by male birds, although he did not state his sexing criteria either. Spurr (1975*b*), who sexed his birds by behavior, reported females incubating first in 8.5 percent of 59 nests at Cape Bird during 1969-1970. Ainley and LeResche (1973) found that sea conditions did not affect the proportion of pairs attempting reversed incubation routines but that such conditions did strongly alter their success by affecting the amount of time required for males to forage at sea and return (see ch. 8).

At Cape Crozier, percentages of breedings involving reversed incubation routines varied little in relation to age (of one known-age partner), except for those pairs including a three-year-old female (table 7.6). The latter incubated first in six of sixteen instances. Otherwise males usually (about 88 percent of instances) incubated first. The high proportion of three-year-old females taking first incubation duties probably resulted from their late arrival date, which increased their chances of encountering unpaired males that had been present for an appreciable period already. Among known males who left first, this was the case in almost all instances; that is, these males had arrived early and paired late. By the time they paired and courted, their fat reserves were low enough that they left prematurely, usually just as their mate laid the first egg.

The Crozier data support Sladen's (1958) contention that a normal (male first) incubation routine is necessary for successful breeding, as a general rule (table 7.7). In 73 percent of reversed incubation routines (16/22), the female deserted before the male returned. In only 18 percent of the cases (4/22) was at least one chick raised to fledging; in two

TABLE 7.6 **The proportion of birds incubating eggs first (vs. his/her mate); Cape Crozier, 1963 to 1975.**

Age	Male		Female	
(yrs)	Percent	n	Percent	n
3			37.5†	16
4	94.1*	17	17.1	35
5	87.8	82	15.0	100
6	89.1	313	12.3	284
7	87.4	286	15.1	265
8	84.7	157	14.0	143
9	86.5	52	22.5	40
10	87.5	48	25.0	28
11	97.3	37	8.7	23
12	93.1	29	10.5	19
13	81.8	11	14.3	7
14	100.0	2		
Total	88.1	1,034	14.9	960

*Not statistically different from the combined percentages for all other age groups (87.8%; $t = .911$, P> .05).

†Statistically different from the combined percentages of all other age groups (14.5%; $t = 2.211$, P< .05).

TABLE 7.7 **The histories of 22 instances in which the female took first incubation watch.**

AGE OF FEMALE	AGE OF MALE	DAYS FEMALE REMAINED	OUTCOME
4	?	1–3	Female deserted nest; male not seen again.
?	4	14	Female deserted nest; male returned 18 days later.
3	?	14	Female deserted nest; male not seen again.
6	?	8	Female deserted nest; male not seen again.
6	?	13	Female deserted nest: male not seen again.
5	?	8+	Female deserted nest; male not seen again.
?	6	4	Female deserted nest; male not seen again.

PLATE 1   The Adélie Penguin *Pygoscelis adeliae*, about 60 cm tall and 3 to 6 kg in weight, depending on sex and time of year.

PLATE 2   One of the 4,485 banded Adélies upon which this study was based.

PLATE 3   David Ainley about to capture a young Adélie in order to adjust its band.

PLATE 4   Incubating eggs nestled atop its rock pile of a nest, an Adélie contemplates a zoom lens.

PLATE 5   Pack ice is by no means an easy surface to move across, especially when one's legs are only a few centimeters long.

PLATE 6 A leopard seal lunges futilely toward a flock of Adélies on an ice floe; the dark specks against the sky are skuas.

PLATE 7 Adélies huddle down on their nests to protect eggs from the wind and blowing snow.

PLATE 8   The beach at Cape Crozier during early spring; flocks of Adélies parade back and forth waiting for the right conditions under which to make a departure.

PLATE 9   An Adélie on its nest "suggests" to a neighbor that it should seek nest stones elsewhere.

PLATE 10   Life can be rather intense within an Adélie Penguin colony, where closely spaced territories are guarded vigorously.

PLATE 11   A group of youngsters, unsoiled by the duties of nesting, pauses in its wanderings about the rookery.

PLATE 12 A view from Post Office Hill, about 1 km from the beach, showing most of the West Rookery at Cape Crozier.

PLATE 13 A parent and its two-week-old offspring.

PLATE 14   A chick just about ready to leave Cape Crozier for the greater unknowns of the sea.

PLATE 15   A South Polar Skua feeds on the remains of a penguin that escaped a leopard seal, though mortally wounded in the attempt (photo by R. J. Boekelheide).

TABLE 7.7   (*continued*)

?	6	4	Female deserted nest; male returned three days later.
5	?	18	Female deserted nest; male not seen again.
5	?	8	Female deserted nest; male not seen again.
5	?	2	Male returned in time to relieve female; he deserted 17 days later.
5	?	10	Male returned in time; two chicks hatched, one fledged.
7	?	8	Female deserted nest; male not seen again.
5	?	6	Male returned in time to relieve female; one chick fledged, one egg addled.
4	?	4–5	Female deserted nest; male not seen again.
5	?	5	Male returned in time to relieve female; two chicks hatched, one fledged.
?	4	5	Female deserted nest; male returned three days later.
4	?	9	Female deserted nest; male not seen again.
6	?	5–8	Male returned in time to relieve female; both eggs later lost.
?	6	3–5	Female deserted nest; male not seen again.
6	?	2–3	Female deserted nest; male not seen again.
4	?	4	Male returned in time to relieve female; two chicks fledged.

other cases the males returned to relieve the female, eggs were eventually hatched, but no chicks were fledged. Females remained alone on their nests from 2 to 14 days before deserting, the mean being 7.9 days for those deserting before their mate returned and 5.6 days for those relieved before desertion. Taylor (1962) recorded a mean of 6.5 days (range: 3 to 14 days) for four similar cases. The mean of 7.9 days appears to be a good estimate of the average physiological reserves available to a female after egg laying, although some endure as long as 10 to 18 days. Of course, the difference partially depends upon (1) nutritional reserves upon arrival at the rookery, (2) energy expended in pairing and egg laying, and (3) length of time at the rookery before egg laying. Since most females (at least, experienced ones) tend to pair within a day upon arrival at the rookery (table 6.13) and since mean arrival to first-egg interval is seven days (table 6.14), the average female who lays two eggs can apparently remain at the rookery something over two weeks (7.0 plus 7.9 days). Ainley and LeResche (1973) showed that only in years of light pack ice were an appreciable portion of pairs who reversed incubation routine successful in incubating eggs to hatching. In those years, the male could feed and return to relieve his mate in a relatively short time.

In three nests from which Sladen (1958: table IX) removed males, females remained 10, 12, and 14 days after the disturbance. In Sladen's nest 35, the female laid two eggs 4.5 days after the male was killed and incubated them for 8 days before deserting (weight = 3.3 kg). Another female dissected by Sladen had laid two eggs and weighed 2.8 kg when still on her nest. At Cape Crozier in 1969, a female (=23; age unknown) was paired on a well-built nest on 4 November. She laid one egg on 11 November, was left alone on the twelfth, and produced a second egg on the thirteenth. She incubated the eggs very lightly (notes: "nervous," "poor attention to eggs") until 17 November when she left the nest and headed toward the beach. She was collected: weight = 2.85 kg; two 14 mm regressing follicles (14 mm diameter), ruptured follicles (11 and 13 mm); *bursa fabricalis* 12 mm × 20 mm (a young bird); fat 10 mm thick at center of incubation patch and 25 mm thick just ventral and posterior to the axilla. This condition represents the very point at which this female, at her minimal nutritional reserves, left her eggs and headed for sea.

LENGTH OF INCUBATION WATCHES

Sladen (1958), Taylor (1962), Stonehouse (1963), Yeates (1968), and Spurr (1975*b*) all recorded lengths of incubation watches for marked birds (table 7.8). For one season (1948) at Hope Bay, Sladen recorded the following as the average incubation schedule: males incubated first for 13 days, were relieved by the female for 15 days; and then returned to incubate for the last 8 days until hatching. Yeates summarized his own, Taylor's, Stonehouse's, and Sutherland's (pers. comm.) information from five years of study at Cape Royds and showed that duration of incubation shifts at that rookery depended upon ice conditions and their effect on the length of travel to feeding grounds. His data, Sladen's, and Spurr's are summarized in table 7.8 along with Cape Crozier data for all birds during the 1967 to 1969 seasons. Crozier data were combined because no significant difference in mean watch length was demonstrable for any watch by age or year (P> .05; *t*-test; see tables 7.9 and 7.10). It is obvious that at Ross Island each member of a pair incubated for shorter but more frequent periods during the 35 days of incubation than his/her counterpart at Hope Bay in 1948. Either 1948 was an unusual season at Hope Bay or some factor of geography (e.g., distance to feeding areas) or latitude caused the differences in incubation schedules between the two areas.

The effect of age and sex on the total number of days spent incubating eggs was investigated in the 1967 and 1968 seasons. Table 7.10 compares by sex the total number of days spent incubating eggs by known-age birds, their mates, and adult controls. Since males normally incubated for more days than females (see controls, in which males incubated 61 percent of the total days), only comparisons of birds of the same sex could be made. Results were as follows:

1. young (three- to seven-year-old) males spent significantly more days incubating eggs than control (adult) males (P<.05; *t*-test);

2. young males spent significantly more days incubating eggs than did male mates of young (three- to seven-

TABLE 7.8 Mean lengths of incubation watches at Cape Crozier compared with those at Hope Bay, Cape Royds, and Cape Bird.

YEAR	WATCH	MEAN DAYS	RANGE	SAMPLE SIZE AND COMMENTS
Cape Crozier				
1967–68	First	13.8	3–20	104
and	Second	10.2	2–20	132
1968–69	Third	4.6	1–13	119
Cape Royds (from Yeates 1968)				
1961–62	First	7.5		Never more than one meter from open water.
	Second	1.8		Same as above.
1959–60	First	11	7–18	29. Never more than a few meters to open water. Pack ice break-out in mid-December.
	Second	9		26
1964–65	First	9	1–15	39. Same as above.
	Second	8	1–19	62. Same as above.
	Third	4	1–15	44. Same as above.
1965–66	First	12.7	1–26	155. Same as above.
	Second	11.2	1–18	103. Same as above.
	Third	4.9	1–16	85. Same as above.
1962–63	First	13.7		Open water 72 km distant in early December. Pack ice break-out in mid-January.
	Second	12.5		
Cape Bird (from Spurr 1975b)				
1969–70	First	14.8	7–23	54. Pack ice break-out by early November.
	Second	11.1	9–15	50
Hope Bay (from Sladen 1958)				
1948–50	First	13	11–19	21
	Second	15	12–17	17
	Third	8	2–12	14

TABLE 7.9 Lengths of the first three incubation watches in days for pairs including one known-age Adélie and for 40 "adults" in control pairs; Cape Crozier, 1967–1968 and 1968–1969. Figures in bold type are watches by the mates of known-age birds.

Age (yrs)	Watch	Male $\bar{x}$	range	n	Female $\bar{x}$	range	n	Totals* $\bar{x}$	range	n
3	First				**13.0**	**13**	**2**	13.0	13	2
	Second				5.0	5	1	5.0	5	1
	Third				**4.0**	**4**	**1**	4.0	4	1
4	First	15.5	13–17	6	**13.7**	**10–17**	**19**	14.0	13–17	27
	Second	**9.7**	**9–11**	6	10.9	8–15	17	10.7	8–15	24
	Third	4.3	3–7	6	**4.4**	**1–7**	**17**	4.4	1–7	23
5	First	12.7	3–17	9	**13.9**	**10–20**	**19**	13.3	5–20	34
	Second	**8.6**	**2–12**	9	12.3	8–20	18	11.0	2–20	32
	Third	5.6	1–13	8	**4.4**	**1–8**	**16**	4.7	1–13	28
6 & 7	First	13.0	9–19	11	**13.3**	**3–18**	**14**	13.2	3–19	27
	Second	**10.9**	**8–13**	10	10.4	9–16	13	10.8	8–16	26
	Third	4.1	1–5	10	**4.3**	**3–8**	**13**	4.4	3–8	26
Controls 1–50										
1968–69	First							14.2	8–18	40
	Second							11.4	8–14	38
	Third							4.7	2–8	38

*Includes individuals whose sex and age were unknown.

TABLE 7.10 Percentage of total incubation days (number of days in parentheses) contributed by males and females of known age and their mates* and by adult "control"* Adélie Penguins; Cape Crozier, 1967–1968 and 1968–1969.

	FEMALES†		MALES‡	
Three-year-olds	39	(56)		
Four-year-olds	42	(473)	71	(161)
Five-year-olds	42	(369)	71	(384)
Six-year-olds	40	(173)	65	(275)
Seven-year-olds	44	(76)	79	(49)
All three- to seven-year-olds	41	(1,147)	69	(869)
All mates*	31	(385)	59	(1,619)
Adult "controls"*	39	(496)	61	(790)

* Ages unknown.

† Known-age females incubated more days ($t = 3.55$, $P < .05$) than the female mates of known-age males but not more than the females in control pairs ($t = .760$).

‡ Known-age males incubated more days than the male mates of known-age females and the males in control pairs ($t = 3.42$, $P < .05$).

year-old) females ($P < .05$). Consequently, young females spent significantly more days incubating eggs than did female mates of young males ($P < .05$); but

3. young females spent about the same number of days incubating eggs as did control females ($P < .05$).

Young males, then, differed from their older counterparts in that they were left on the nest longer during incubation. This could have been because (a) the young males themselves completed feeding trips to sea more rapidly than the average control male or mate of a young female or (b) their mates required a longer time for feeding trips than the average control female (and, in fact, than the average young female). A comparison of the amount of time that breeding birds of different ages spent at sea after their first incubation watch reveals that younger birds took more time to return, but little difference existed after five years of age (table 7.11). Thus, since Adélies probably do pair most often with birds of the same age (ch. 8), choice (b) above seems to be the more accurate interpretation.

TABLE 7.11 Average number of days between first departure and second arrival; Cape Crozier, 1967 to 1974.

Age (yrs)	MALE				FEMALE			
	Breeders		Nonbreeders		Breeders		Nonbreeders	
	Days ± SD	n	Days ± SD	n	Days ± SD	n	Days ± SD	n
2			16.9 ± 5.8	10			18.4 ± 8.6	17
3			24.9 ± 8.4	109	15.4 ± 6.8	16	24.8 ± 8.9	76
4	19.6 ± 9.3	14	32.3 ± 11.4	139	18.6 ± 6.6	36	29.3 ± 10.2	44
5	16.1 ± 6.6	77	31.4 ± 10.7	159	17.9 ± 7.0	102	30.1 ± 11.3	44
6	15.4 ± 4.0	207	27.3 ± 8.9	89	16.8 ± 4.6	237	27.5 ± 13.7	31
7	15.5 ± 4.3	177	28.0 ± 7.5	26	16.8 ± 3.7	218	29.0 ± 5.2	5
8	14.3 ± 4.1	61	24.0 ± 6.5	5	17.0 ± 3.1	98	28.3 ± 11.3	3
9	15.1 ± 3.9	25	21.0 ± 9.3	6	16.6 ± 4.6	31	27.5 ± 7.4	4
10	14.6 ± 3.0	31	0.0 ± 0.0	0	16.6 ± 3.9	24		
11	14.9 ± 7.1	20	20.3 ± 0.9	3	16.6 ± 3.0	14		
12&13	14.1 ± 3.3	16			16.1 ± 2.0	24		
All	15.3 ± 4.8	628	29.0 ± 10.5	546	16.8 ± 4.7	800	26.8 ± 10.8	224
r_{4-12}	−.7612*		−.9630*		−.8598*		−.6630	

*P < .05.

SURVIVAL OF EGGS

Sladen (1958: table XIX) estimated egg and chick mortality merely by assuming that 1,791 nests began with two eggs and by later counting the chicks in nests after hatching. He observed an average overall mortality of eggs and small chicks of 82 percent at Hope Bay during the 1948–1949 season. Taylor (1962) split mortality into segments by time or stage of breeding (i.e., eggs, guarded chicks, crèche chicks) and estimated 36 percent mortality of eggs (including 10 percent addled eggs) during the 1959–1960 season at Cape Royds. Yeates (1968) found 32.5 percent and 43 to 52.5 percent overall egg-to-fledging mortality at Cape Royds for 1964–1965 and 1965–1966, respectively. Egg mortality was at least 9 percent during the first year and approximately 43.5 percent the second. Spurr (1975b) treated the subject in great detail. He found at Cape Bird over a four-year period that 27.7 percent of all eggs laid failed to hatch: 6.7 percent were infertile, 7.6 percent were lost through nest desertion, 0.7 percent were poorly incubated, 0.4 percent were lost during fights, 2.6 percent were taken by skuas, and 9.7 percent could not be accounted for. The majority of eggs lost (49 percent) disappeared during the first twenty days of incubation. During a later season at Cape Bird (1977–1978), Davis (1982) reported failure to hatch in 38.9 percent of eggs laid; 18.5 percent failed because of nest desertion. All birds in these studies were of unknown age, though Taylor classified birds by "experience," as deduced from nest site and time of laying. Egg mortality for Taylor's groups varied from about 35 percent in early-laying nests situated in the interior of colonies to about 45 percent in 33 interior and 43 peripheral nests with late-laid eggs. Tenaza (1971) and Spurr (1975b) also considered the factor of nest locality but only in terms of overall "breeding success" rather than by components of egg and chick survival (see ch. 8).

The above review points out the difficulty in comparing mortality estimates by different workers: (1) each author had his own criteria for establishing a base number of eggs laid from which to calculate mortality (cf. Sladen's assumption of two eggs per nest vs. Taylor's daily observations of nests); (2) few accurately separated mortality into the component parts of egg mortality, nestling mortality, guard stage mortality, and crêche stage mortality; and (3) there was no way to compare the effects of the various investigators.

At Cape Crozier, egg mortality decreased with increased age of breeders but varied from year to year as greatly as it did because of age-related differences. The average number of eggs hatched was lowest among pairs containing a four- or five-year-old male (1.5 eggs) or, in particular, a three- or four-year-old female (1.2 to 1.5 eggs; table 7.12). In pairs where the known-age male or female was older than five years, an average of 1.7 eggs hatched per nest. These figures, when compared with those on number of eggs laid (table 7.4), indicate egg mortalities of 11 percent in pairs where the known-age Adélie was five years of age and older, about 14 percent where males were four years old, and about 20 percent where females were three or four years old.

Year-to-year trends in age-related egg loss were obscured by combining data from different cohorts and especially by combining data from five breeding seasons. To determine yearly differences, egg losses were separated by year and cohort, and loss was figured by Mayfield's (1961) method where egg-days is the basic unit of measure (table 7.13). During the 1968–1969 season, all ages and every co-

TABLE 7.12 **Average number of eggs hatched by Adélie Penguins of known age; Cape Crozier, 1963 to 1974.**

Age	Male			Female			Total*		
(yrs)	$\bar{x} \pm SD$	n		$\bar{x} \pm SD$	n		$\bar{x} \pm SD$	n	
3				1.2 ± 0.4	29		1.2 ± 0.4	29	
4	1.5 ± 0.5	11		1.4 ± 0.5	85		1.4 ± 0.5	108	
5	1.5 ± 0.5	86		1.5 ± 0.5	146		1.6 ± 0.5	252	
6	1.6 ± 0.5	161		1.6 ± 0.5	169		1.6 ± 0.5	340	
7	1.7 ± 0.5	143		1.6 ± 0.5	139		1.7 ± 0.5	285	
8	1.6 ± 0.5	36		1.6 ± 0.5	34		1.6 ± 0.5	72	
9	1.8 ± 0.4	13		1.7 ± 0.5	16		1.8 ± 0.4	30	
10–13	1.8 ± 0.5	54		1.7 ± 0.4	26		1.7 ± 0.4	81	
All	1.6 ± 0.5	504		1.6 ± 0.5	644		1.6 ± 0.5	1,197	
r †	.9006			.8933			.8202		

*Includes individuals of unknown age.
†All significant (P< .05).

TABLE 7.13 Percent egg loss by parental age and cohort, Adélie Penguins; Cape Crozier, 1964 to 1969.

Age (yrs)	COHORT					
	1961–62	1962–63	1963–64	1964–65	1965–66	Total
3	51 (145)*	0 (12)	0 (156)	49 (304)	81 (125)†	50 (742)
4	18 (167)	18 (823)	40 (1,384)	58 (1,113)†		40 (3,487)
5	41 (262)	36 (1,765)	50 (1,428)†			42 (3,455)
6	38 (369)	63 (1,110)†				56 (1,479)
7	42 (518)†					42 (518)

* In parentheses, $\sum$ (egg × no. days present) for all eggs laid.
† 1968-1969 breeding season.

hort lost a greater percentage of eggs than during any other year. Four-year-olds, for example, had a 58 percent egg loss rate (1,113 eggs times x days) compared to 40 percent, 18 percent, and 18 percent by four-year-olds during the preceding three seasons. Similarly, during 1968–1969, birds hatched in 1962–1963 (six-year-olds) lost eggs at a rate of 63 percent as compared to only 36 percent, 18 percent, and 0 percent by the same cohort when they were five, four, and three years old. Cohort-related differences in egg loss were patternless, although cohorts did differ in overall egg-fledgling mortality (see below). Thus, no cohort group of known-age Adélies was consistently more successful than any other in retaining eggs. The high loss of eggs in 1968–1969 was attributable to the persistent pack ice cover that year and to a consequent high nest desertion rate (Ainley and LeResche 1973). Previous breeding experience did have an effect on the number of eggs hatched or, conversely, the number lost (table 7.14 compared with tables 7.4 and 7.5). On the average, first-time breeders lost 0.3 to 0.4 eggs per nest, but birds with at least one year of previous experience lost only 0.1 to 0.2 eggs per nest ($P<.05$, t-test).

CHRONOLOGY OF EGG LOSS

No significant difference emerged between age/experience groups of birds in the chronology of egg loss (table 7.15). By the tenth day of incubation, three- to seven-year-olds had

TABLE 7.14 Average number of eggs hatched relative to parent's age and experience; Cape Crozier, 1963 to 1974.

| | FIRST-OBSERVED BREEDERS | | | | PRIOR BREEDERS | | | |
| | Male | | Female | | Male | | Female | |
Age (yrs)	$\bar{x} \pm SD$	n	$\bar{x} \pm SD$	n	$\bar{x} \pm SD$	n	$\bar{x} \pm SD$	n
3			1.2 ± 0.4	29				
4	1.5 ± 0.5	11	1.4 ± 0.5	77			1.5 ± 0.5	8
5	1.5 ± 0.5	36	1.5 ± 0.5	49	1.4 ± 0.5	7	1.5 ± 0.5	28
6	1.5 ± 0.5	34	1.3 ± 0.5	21	1.8 ± 0.4	14	1.6 ± 0.5	29
7	1.7 ± 0.4	16	1.6 ± 0.5	7	1.8 ± 0.4	12	1.6 ± 0.5	16
8					1.4 ± 0.5	8	1.9 ± 0.4	11
9					0.0 ± 0.0	0	1.8 ± 0.4	6
10					1.8 ± 0.4	10	1.9 ± 0.3	8
11					1.8 ± 0.4	12	1.8 ± 0.4	4
12&13					1.7 ± 0.5	8	1.4 ± 0.5	9
All*	1.5 ± 0.5	97	1.4 ± 0.5	183	1.7 ± 0.5	71	1.6 ± 0.5	119

* The average for *all* first-observed breeders was 1.43 ± 0.50 eggs and for *all* prior breeders was 1.64 ± 0.50 ($t = 4.20$, P > .05).

TABLE 7.15   Mean number of days between the laying and loss (excluding infertile eggs) of the eggs of known-age parents, adult controls, and former mates of young Adélie Penguins; Cape Crozier, 1967 to 1969.

Age (yrs)	Eggs lost	Mean laying-loss interval (days)*
3	9	14.8
4	54	18.7
5	53	18.1
6	41	15.3
7	11	11.5
All 3- to 7-year-olds	168	17.1
Adult controls	63	14.7
Former mates of young birds	20	17.9

* No statistical difference between any of these groups (P> .05, t-test).

lost 47 percent of the 168 eggs eventually lost (fig. 26), adult controls had lost 48 percent of 58 eggs, and former mates had lost 57 percent of the 14 eggs eventually lost. Ninety percent of eventual losses occurred by the twenty-second day of incubation among three- to seven-year-olds, by the twenty-fourth day by controls, and by the eighteenth by the small sample of former mates. These observations agree with those of Spurr (1975b) and Davis (1982). In all groups, loss rate remained fairly constant at 4 to 5 percent per day through the time of 90 percent loss. The remaining 10 percent were lost in the last twelve to sixteen days, which flattened the curve.

The reason eggs were lost could seldom be ascertained. The event was rarely observed, and only once in a while did circumstances indicate the cause of loss. For example, if a bird remained alone at the nest for longer than the normal incubation shift, attended the egg(s) less closely, and then the nest was found deserted, we concluded that the partner's failure to return was responsible for the loss. If the Adélie in question never appeared again, the egg was probably lost because of his or her death (or, as in one substantiated case,

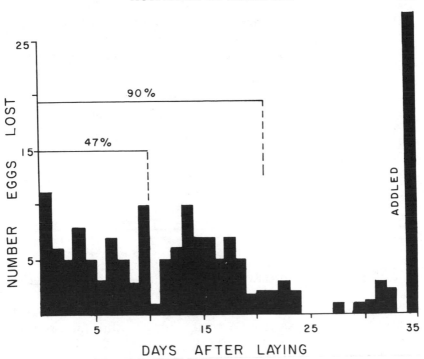

FIGURE 26   The chronology of loss for 168 eggs of Adélie Penguins ages three to seven years; Cape Crozier, 1964 to 1968. Addled eggs are shown as being lost on day 34.

emigration). If he or she returned to the nest site later, tardiness caused desertion by the mate. In contrast, if a bird attended the nest alone for significantly less time than the average incubation watch and we then found an empty nest, "blame" for loss of eggs probably rested with that bird, although exact circumstances (e.g., skua predation, attack by another Adélie, or simple desertion) were unknown. In some cases, eggshell fragments, a bloody Adélie, or other such clues added further evidence.

In a number of cases, reasonable evidence for the cause of egg loss was available (table 7.16). Nine percent of egg loss resulted from disappearance of either a known-age bird (2 percent) or its mate (7 percent) during a trip to sea. The four other causes of egg mortality (tardy return from sea,

TABLE 7.16   Reasons for loss of 150 eggs (excluding addled eggs) by three- to seven-year-old Adélie Penguins and their mates; Cape Crozier, 1964 to 1968.

CIRCUMSTANCES	PROPORTION OF TOTAL LOSS
Mate failed to return	0.09
Mate returned tardily	0.24
Incubating bird deserted prematurely	0.23
Bird in attendance when egg lost	0.23
Female in first incubation watch	0.21
Total	1.00

desertion of nest, predation or other causes while an Adélie was present, and improper incubation routine) each accounted for 21 to 24 percent of eggs lost. Davis (1982) studied only nest desertion among the several factors that contribute to the failure of eggs to hatch, and his findings agree with ours.

ANOMALIES AND BEHAVIORAL IRREGULARITIES RELATING TO EGG LOSS

Close observation of individually marked birds showed that one cannot assume that a bird involved in incubating an egg or rearing a chick is genetically responsible for it. Some birds incubated others' eggs, either on the original nest or when eggs had rolled from nest to nest; a young male took two egg-producing mates within two days; and birds were in several instances observed copulating at one nest before laying eggs in another. The following is a rather complex example of such irregularity.

Female 519-17485 bred with one male (A) as a three-year-old, kept company with a second male as a four-year-old, and bred with a third male (B) as a five-year-old. As a six-year-old in 1967–1968 this female's activities were as follows:

31 Oct.: On nest (site 1), one meter from 1966–1967 site, with male C through 5 Nov.

6 Nov.: Alone and asleep at site 2; male C with unbanded bird on nest (site 1).

7 Nov.: With male D at site 3; male C with unbanded bird on nest (site 1).

8 Nov.: On nest (site 1) with male C and one egg; nest-relief ceremony completed.

9–10 Nov.: No observations because of a severe storm.

11 Nov.: With male C on nest (site 1); no eggs (destroyed during storm).

12 Nov.: With male C on nest; no eggs.

13 Nov.: Not seen; male C with unbanded bird on nest (site 1).

14 Nov.: Not seen; male C alone on nest with no eggs; male B alone on nest nearby (mated, one egg produced 17 Nov.).

15 Nov.: Not seen; male C with unbanded bird on nest with one egg.

18–24 Nov.: Not seen; male C alone incubating two eggs on nest.

27 Nov.: Alone on male C's nest (site 1); incubating two eggs. She and male C subsequently hatched both eggs and raised one chick to fledging.

Thus this young female (with two years of previous breeding experience) during one season (1) kept company with two males; (2) bred with one, laying and losing one egg; (3) went to sea for fourteen days; (4) returned to incubate two eggs laid by another female; and (5) successfully hatched both eggs, raising one chick. All the while, this female's mate from the previous year bred one meter away. In 1968–1969, 519-17485 (then seven years old) did not return to Cape Crozier until 4 December, a month after male C. By mid-November he had produced two eggs with a new mate. She did not breed.

A few other exceptional cases demonstrate specifically the impossibility of always taking even daily observations at face value when considering egg or chick loss. These examples show that (1) eggs sometimes move from nest to nest—eggs that are eventually "lost" may not have belonged to that nest at all or eggs actually lost may be replaced by others, thus obscuring the loss—and (2) eggs deserted by both birds of the pair producing them may hatch under the care of other Adélies. In these cases, of course, the birds and their eggs were marked.

Examples from three different nests during 1968 illustrating (1) above were as follows:

Nest A. 23 Dec.:   519-19151 (male mate of known-age bird) alone, two chicks;

24 Dec.:   519-19151 alone, two chicks plus one egg;

25 Dec.:   519-18051R (known-age bird) alone, two chicks.

Nest B. 23 Nov.:   519-11477 (male) alone, one egg (marked);

28 Nov.:   519-11477 alone, two eggs (one marked);

2 Dec.:   marked mate alone, one egg (unmarked).

Nest C. 8 Dec.:   519-18113Y (male) alone, one egg (marked);

9–11 Dec.:   519-18113Y alone, two eggs (one marked);

12 Dec.:   519-18113Y alone, one egg (marked).

Another example, illustrating (2) above, is the case of four-year-old female 519-18217. After twelve days keeping company with an unmarked male, she paired at the nest of a different male, 519-19028, and laid one egg the next day (obviously not fertilized by the second male). Following the normal procedure, she then went to sea, only to have her place in the incubation routine taken by 519-19096 (female), who was present when the egg hatched and together with 519-19028 (male) when the chick disappeared.

INCUBATION PERIOD

The incubation period of Adélie Penguin eggs is somewhat longer than that predicted by egg volume (cf. Worth 1940, Reid 1965), but the difference is not as extreme as that of Emperor Penguins. The best published incubation periods for Adélie eggs are tabulated in table 7.17. These range from 33.3 to 39.2 days, depending variously on whether the eggs considered are first or second eggs of a clutch and on the location and season of the observation. Sladen (1958) reported a mean of 3.2 days between the laying of the first and

TABLE 7.17 **Published incubation periods ($\pm$ 1 day) for Adélie Penguins.**

INCUBATION PERIOD			
Days	(Range)	SAMPLE	SOURCE AND REMARKS
36	(36–38)	13 first eggs	
34	(33–36)	7 second eggs	Sladen (1958), marked eggs;
35	(33–38)	20 eggs (total)	Hope Bay and Signy Islands
33.3	(32–35)	7 single eggs	
34.8	(33–39)	63 first eggs	Taylor (1962), Cape Royds
33.3	(30–37)	59 second eggs	
34.1	(30–39)	150 eggs (total*)	
35.5	(33–38)	100 first eggs	
34.1	(32–37)	100 second eggs	Reid (1965), Cape Hallett
34.8	(32–38)	200 eggs (total)	
39.4	(38–40)	4 single eggs	
39.2	(36–43)	20 first eggs	Yeates (1968), Cape Royds
37.9	(33–42)	20 second eggs	
38.6	(33–43)	44 eggs (total)	
33.8	(32–35)	7 single eggs	
34.7	(32–38)	42 first eggs	Spurr (1975b), Cape Bird
33.2	(31–35)	42 second eggs	

*Includes the clutches above, as well as those in which three eggs were laid.

second eggs in 25 clutches. Taylor (1962), Reid (1965), and Spurr (1975b) reported this interval as 3.0, 3.2, and 3.0 days for 105, 91, and 61 clutches, respectively. Using hatching interval, Taylor (1962) calculated that an equivalent of only 34 hours of continuous incubation occurred during the 72+ hours between the laying of the two eggs. Thus the first egg is not fully incubated until the second is laid, which lengthens the apparent incubation period of the first egg.

No previously published records of incubation period in relation to the age of parents are available. We compared the incubation periods of eggs attended by known-age birds (three to seven years old) and those incubated by controls (table 7.18). The data for known-age birds were from two seasons, 1967–1968 and 1968–1969, but years were combined in each age group because no statistically significant differences occurred (P>.05, t-test). Furthermore, although mean incubation period for birds four, five, and six years old was 33.6 days (n = 37) in 1968–1969, no statistical difference between seasons was demonstrable (P>.05, t-test). Thus we compared both seasons of known-age bird data with control data from 1968–1969 only. No significant or consistent differences in incubation period occurred between known-age birds of different ages, all known-age

TABLE 7.18   **Incubation periods in days for Adélie Penguin eggs laid and incubated by known-age parents; Cape Crozier, 1967–1968 and 1968–1969.**

Age (yrs)	$\bar{x}$*	Range	SD	n (eggs)
3	34.0	33–35	0.8	3
4	33.9	31–37	1.6	23
5	34.0	32–36	1.4	47
6	33.7	32–35	1.0	15
7	35.0	34–37	1.1	6
All 3- to 7-year-olds	34.0	31–37	1.4	94
Adult controls†	34.9	31–37	1.3	66
Total	34.0	31–38	1.4	160

* All statistically equivalent (P>.05, t-test).
† Ages unknown

birds, and adult controls. Variation within groups was great but was individual rather than age related.

ADDLED EGGS

Addled eggs, eggs that are not lost but never hatch, result from any of several causes. Fertilization may never occur because of lack of or improperly timed copulation, infertile spermatozoa or ova, or immotile or otherwise disabled spermatozoa. Fertilized eggs may cease developing because of freezing, fluctuating temperatures of incubation, or inherent abnormalities in the zygote. Any of these factors could result from behavioral or physiological insufficiencies related to the age of parent birds. For example, Bahshawe (1938) described incomplete copulations in Gentoo Penguins (*Pygoscelis papua*); Sladen (1958) suggested and Ainley (1975*b*, 1978) confirmed that among Adélies incomplete sex acts were more prevalent in young birds.

Taylor (1962) and Spurr (1975*b*) reported that 10 and 6.7 percent, respectively, of eggs in the nests they studied failed to hatch, although they were incubated to full term. Richdale (1954, 1957) found that youth affected egg size and reported a marked increase in the fertility of eggs laid by females as their age increased. He also reported decreased fertility in very old females.

In our study, the age of at least one parent significantly affected the proportion of eggs lost because of addling (table 7.19; r = $-.9608$, P<.05). The eggs of three- and four-year-olds showed the highest percentages of infertility (25 percent), but only 13 percent of eggs laid by six- and seven-year-olds were infertile, a percentage similar to that of the adult controls. The figures for young Adélies are comparable to those for three-year-old Yellow-eyed Penguins (Richdale 1957), in which 30 percent of the eggs they laid were infertile. Incredibly, though, 68 percent of eggs laid by *two-year-old* Yellow-eyed Penguins failed to hatch because of infertility! Owing to the dangers inherent in breeding, especially among young Adélies, such a low fertility would quickly select against breeding that young in the Adélie Penguin (see chs. 9 and 10).

TABLE 7.19 **Proportion of addled eggs among eggs lost by known-age and adult control Adélie Penguins, 1967 and 1968.**

Age (yrs)	Number of eggs lost	Number of addled eggs	Percent addled
3 & 4	63	16	25*
5	53	12	22
6 & 7	52	7	13*
All 3- to 7-year-olds	168	35	21†
Adult controls‡	63	5	8†

*Difference not statistically significant ($t = 1.80$, P>.05).
† Difference statistically significant ($t = 2.72$, P<.05).
‡ Age unknown.

PARENTAL ATTENDANCE DURING THE GUARD STAGE

Variations in the lengths of trips to sea to gather food for chicks or, conversely, in nest attendance are ambiguous indicators of age-related differences in breeding success. Were young breeders to spend longer at sea (and hence less time in nest attendance) than older ones, the behavior could be construed as either (a) inefficiency in feeding at sea or (b) low intensity care for young. In this section we attempt to separate the effects on nest attendance of these two possible factors.

Chicks usually hatch after three major incubation watches plus a few shorter ones. Following hatching, a chick's physiological need for food increases tremendously (Emison 1968, LeResche and Boyd 1969). In normal years, disappearance of sea ice at about hatching time allows faster foraging trips. During guard and crèche stages, parents visit the rookery approximately on alternate days or every two days, depending upon rookery and ice conditions (Sladen 1958, Taylor 1962, Emison 1968).

We made 2,454 observations of three- to seven-year-old Adélies and their mates with their chicks during guard and crèche stages. Comparisons were made of the number of observations of known-age birds and of their mates as an indi-

TABLE 7.20   Proportion of time spent in nest attendance by Adélie Penguins during guard and crèche stage; Cape Crozier, 1966 to 1969.

Age (yrs)	Male		Female	
	Percent of days	Number of days	Percent of days	Number of days
3			47	199
4	56	90	46	740
5	53	186	45	610
6	57	132	46	396
7	52	25	49	76
Total	55	433	45	2,021

Summary	
Category	Percent of days at nest
4- to 7-year-old males	55
Male mates of 3- to 7-year-old females	55
3- to 7-year-old females	45
Female mates of 4- to 7-year-old males	45

cation of nest attendance (table 7.20). This method seems the best way both to eliminate bias as to year, ice conditions, and time of season and to avoid the possibility of mistaking the sexes of observed birds. In table 7.20 we summarize the proportion of observations at the nest of known age males, mates of known-age females, known-age females, and mates of known-age males.

Apparently, age has no measurable effect on the proportion of brooding and guarding duties undertaken by Adélie Penguins. All known-age males and male mates of known-age females were present during 55 percent of observations at their nests. Adult males were present a statistically equivalent 52 percent of (446) observations by Taylor (1962; calculated from his table 11). Similarly, known-age females and mates of known-age males were present 45 percent of the time ($P > .05$, t-test); and Taylor's adult females were present 48 percent (n = 446) of the time. Thus no trend in attendance was evident as young Adélies matured from three through seven years.

Having established that the youngest breeders incubate for the same number of days as their older counterparts (choice [b] above), we next investigated the amount of time required for their chicks to enter crêches (table 7.21). This we felt was a measure of (a) above: feeding efficiency at sea by parents. We assumed that crêche entry at first depends on the chick wandering from the nest and that only if a chick was extremely reluctant to join the crêche would the parent "desert" it. In other words, when the chick reaches a certain level of development and vigor, it begins to wander from the nest, and field observations tend to support this assumption. Results indicated that chicks of the youngest parents enter crêches at ages a few days older than those of older parents (P<.05). Our conclusions are that less well fed chicks, being less vigorous, enter crêches at older ages and that the chicks of younger breeders are less well fed than those of older parents. Additional information lends support to this idea (e.g., Ainley and Schlatter 1972).

We also investigated the fledging age for chicks of differently aged parents during 1967–1968 and 1969–1970, but our sample sizes were not large compared with other analyses. Accurate measures of fledging age with adequate samples have not often been published. Taylor (1962) reported an age at fledging of 50.6 days (range 41–56; n = 113), and Ainley and Schlatter (1972) reported that the majority of chicks at Crozier fledged at 50 to 53 days (range 42–57 days; see ch. 3). We found the average age at fledging to be 48.8 days (table 7.22). Youngest fledging ages were exhibited by the chicks of breeders three (♀) and four (♂) years old, but they were not statistically distinct from those of the chicks of older parents. Taylor (1962) observed, though, that chicks hatching later in the season (i.e., mostly those of the youngest and least-experienced breeders because they laid eggs later) fledged at a younger age. Thus there is a discrepancy between the two studies. Nevertheless, if all chicks fledged at about the same age and considering the above analysis on crêche-entry ages, we see that the chicks of youngest parents spent the least amount of time in crêches. We again conclude, therefore, that based on this indirect evidence, the chicks of youngest parents are less well fed than those of older ones.

TABLE 7.21 Average age (in days) for Adélie Penguin chicks to enter crèche, by age and sex of parent; Cape Crozier, 1967 to 1974.

PARENT'S AGE (yrs)	MALE PARENT		FEMALE PARENT		TOTAL*	
	Days to crèche ± SD	n chicks	Days to crèche ± SD	n chicks	Days to crèche ± SD	n chicks
3–4	26.1 ± 4.3	7	25.9 ± 5.7	45	25.8 ± 5.4	54
5	23.8 ± 4.5	49	22.8 ± 4.9	91	23.2 ± 4.7	144
6	22.4 ± 5.7	131	23.6 ± 5.1	137	23.0 ± 5.4	270
7	22.6 ± 4.3	120	22.5 ± 4.1	116	22.6 ± 4.2	236
8	23.8 ± 5.2	28	24.6 ± 5.7	32	22.9 ± 4.1	155
9	21.3 ± 2.5	10	21.3 ± 3.0	15	21.3 ± 2.7	25
10	21.6 ± 2.6	25	20.7 ± 2.7	9	21.4 ± 2.6	34
11–13	23.3 ± 4.7	22	22.9 ± 5.9	14	23.1 ± 4.3	36
All	22.8 ± 4.9	392	23.3 ± 5.1	459	23.1 ± 5.0	954
3–5	24.1 ± 4.5	56	23.9 ± 5.2	136	23.9† ± 5.1	198
6–13	22.5 ± 4.8	336	23.1 ± 4.7	323	22.8† ± 4.7	756

*Includes birds of unknown sex.
† Differences are statistically significant ($t = 2.832$, $P < .05$).

TABLE 7.22 Average number of days from hatching to fledging by age and sex of parent; Cape Crozier, 1967 and 1969.

PARENT'S AGE (yrs)	MALE PARENT		FEMALE PARENT		TOTAL	
	Days ± SD	n chicks	Days ± SD	n chicks	Days ± SD	n chicks
3			45.5 ± 4.0	6	45.5 ± 4.0	6
4	44.8 ± 6.2	4	48.2 ± 9.6	19	47.6 ± 9.0	23
5	49.4 ± 3.4	13	50.3 ± 3.1	28	50.0 ± 3.2	41
6	50.0 ± 6.1	30	49.3 ± 3.8	28	49.7 ± 4.8	58
7	47.3 ± 5.8	16	46.7 ± 4.8	11	47.1 ± 5.3	27
8	46.8 ± 6.0	6	49.5 ± 2.8	8	48.3 ± 4.2	14
All	48.7 ± 5.8	69	48.8 ± 5.5	100	48.8 ± 5.6	169
3 & 4*	44.8 ± 6.2	4	47.6 ± 8.2	25	47.2 ± 8.0	29
5–8*	48.9 ± 5.5	65	49.3 ± 3.4	75	49.1 ± 4.4	140

*Difference not quite significant ($t = 1.797$, $P > .05$).

NESTLING SURVIVAL

As already noted (p. 124) many workers have lumped survivorship-mortality estimates for eggs and for chicks of the nestling and crêche stages. Furthermore, different workers have used different criteria for establishing the base number of eggs or chicks from which to compute survival. Taylor (1962) reported the fate of 150 chicks, and from his data we calculate 24.7 percent mortality after hatching (i.e., guard and crêche stages combined). Yeates (1968) reported 69 percent and 6 percent mortalities after hatching in two years at Cape Royds. Spurr (1975b) reported 20.9 percent mortality through the guard stage over four years at Cape Bird: 9.4 percent disappeared through predation, 6.3 percent through the loss of a parent, 1.0 percent from fighting among adults, and 4.2 percent through reasons unknown. In a later season (1977–1978), Davis (1982) found that 18.4 percent of chicks died of starvation (owing ultimately to loss of a parent).

On the average, Adélie Penguins that hatched eggs at Cape Crozier raised 1.6±0.5 chicks to the crêche stage (table 7.23). Such a high figure indicates that chick mortality was relatively low, an observation also made by Taylor (1962) at Cape Royds. Except for late nests at colony edges, he found that there was a nestling mortality of 25 percent in chicks that hatched and that 76 percent of the chick mortality occurred before chicks reached crêches. Few chicks died once they reached the crêche.

The number of chicks raised to the crêche increased with a parent's age up to eight years (table 7.23). The chicks of older parents also weighed more than those of younger parents, thus assuring them greater chances of survival once they fledged (Ainley and Schlatter 1972). Previous breeding experience was a factor as well: parents that had bred before raised more chicks to crêche than those observed breeding for the first time (table 7.23).

As with egg loss, nestling mortality varied by year, and we studied this phenomenon also by using Mayfield's (1961) method (table 7.24). The same year that all ages and all cohorts had the highest egg loss (1968–1969; see table 7.11), all ages and all cohorts had the lowest nestling loss. Four-year-olds, for example, lost nestlings at a rate of 17 per-

TABLE 7.23 Average number of chicks raised to crèche for Adélies hatching eggs relative to a parent's age and breeding experience; Cape Crozier, 1967 to 1974.

Age (yrs)	FIRST-OBSERVED BREEDERS Male $\bar{x} \pm SD$	n	Female $\bar{x} \pm SD$	n	PRIOR BREEDERS Male $\bar{x} \pm SD$	n	Female $\bar{x} \pm SD$	n	TOTAL* $\bar{x} \pm SD$	n
3		3	1.3 ± 0.5	13					1.3 ± 0.5	13
4	1.6 ± 0.5	7	1.3 ± 0.5	42			2.0 ± 0.0	3	1.4 ± 0.5	52
5	1.6 ± 0.5	24	1.5 ± 0.5	37	1.5 ± 0.5	2	1.4 ± 0.5	17	1.5 ± 0.5	80
6	1.6 ± 0.5	23	1.4 ± 0.5	17	1.8 ± 0.4	12	1.6 ± 0.5	21	1.6 ± 0.5	73
7	1.8 ± 0.4	13	2.0 ± 0.0	3	1.7 ± 0.5	10	1.7 ± 0.5	12	1.7 ± 0.5	38
8–13					1.8 ± 0.4	33	1.7 ± 0.5	33	1.8 ± 0.5	66
Total†	1.6 ± 0.5	67	1.4 ± 0.5	112	1.7 ± 0.5	57	1.6 ± 0.5	86	1.6 ± 0.5	322

* Regression between age and number of chicks ($r = .9568, P < .05$).

† The difference between first-observed breeders (1.48 ± 0.5 chicks) and prior breeders (1.64 ± 0.5 chicks) is statistically distinct ($t = 2.853, P < .05$).

TABLE 7.24 Percent nestling loss by parental age and cohort for Adélie Penguins; Cape Crozier, 1964 to 1969.

Age (yrs)	COHORT (YEAR OF HATCHING)					
	1961–62	1962–63	1963–64	1964–65	1965–66	Total
3	64 (53)*	no data	32 (46)	37 (158)	0 (79)†	34 (336)
4	89 (43)	61 (338)	36 (573)	17 (493)†		42 (1,447)
5	41 (172)	46 (773)	32 (632)†			39 (1,577)
6	40 (364)	37 (369)†				38 (733)
7	31 (290)†					31 (290)

*Nestling × days in parentheses.
† 1968–1969 breeding season.

cent in 1968–1969, less than the 36 percent, 61 percent, and 89 percent loss by four-year-olds in the previous three seasons. That same year, four-year-olds lost eggs at a rate of 58 percent which is *more* than the 40 percent, 18 percent, and 18 percent loss by four-year-olds in previous years. The high negative correlation between proportional egg loss and nestling loss by cohort and season ($r = -.593$; $P < .05$) indicates that with fewer chicks at the start, it was easier for parents to care for them. It further indicates that two chicks are the maximum that Adélies can raise on Ross Island.

OVERALL EGG-CHICK MORTALITY

The overall pattern in the mortality of eggs, nestlings, and crèche chicks by age of parent is similar to that of egg loss since egg loss accounted for 58 to 76 percent of total loss by birds of all ages (tables 7.25 and 7.26).

Trends in egg-to-fledgling survival (table 7.25) were confused in three- through six-year-olds because of differences in years and cohorts (table 7.26). By the time breeders were seven years old, however, they fledged a significantly higher proportion of young than did younger parents. Seven-year-olds fledged 40 percent of eggs laid, compared to 29 percent by all younger birds and 45 percent by adult controls (i.e., established breeders of unknown age). Former mates of younger parents fledged an equivalent 47 percent of eggs laid.

TABLE 7.25 Total egg-chick loss by Adélie Penguins, analyzed by Mayfield's (1961) method; Cape Crozier, 1964 to 1969.

Age of Parent (yrs)	Number (egg, nestling, chick × days)	Percent egg-chick loss
3	1,255	75
4	5,784	69
5	6,013	71
6	3,004	74
7	979	60*
All 3- to 6-year-olds	16,056	71
Former mates of 3- to 6-year-olds	1,473	53
Controls	10,667	55*

* Significantly lower (P<.05, *t*-test) than three- through six-year-olds combined.

Egg survivorship curves, based again on Mayfield's method (fig. 27), comparing eggs cared for by three-through six-year-olds (and their mates; n = 16,056 egg, nestling, and chick × days), those cared for by seven-year-olds and their mates (n = 979), and those cared for by established adults (n = 10,667), indicate that the greater losses by younger birds were incurred during all three stages of development. In this sample, older breeders (i.e., seven-year-olds and adults) have eliminated the loss of chicks in crêches and have also reduced losses during incubation and the guard stage.

Experience also affects overall chick production, mostly by increasing the proportion of birds fledging one or two chicks (table 7.27). Since experience has no effect on clutch size and less of an effect on the proportion of birds hatching eggs, added experience increases fledging rates more by reducing the mortality of chicks rather than of eggs.

CHAPTERS 6 AND 7 SYNTHESIS: THE INTERPLAY OF AGE AND EXPERIENCE IN BREEDING BIOLOGY

We have now discussed the basic breeding biology of Adélie Penguins and, in the process, have determined whether in-

TABLE 7.26 Percent egg-chick loss by parental age and cohort for Adélie Penguins; Cape Crozier, 1964 to 1969.

Age (yrs)	COHORT (YEAR OF HATCHING)					Total
	1961–62	1962–63	1963–64	1964–65	1965–66	
3	85 (198)*	0 (36)	32 (202)	78 (593)	81 (226)	75 (1,255)
4	91 (247)	68 (1,217)	66 (2,482)	68 (1,838)		69 (5,784)
5	65 (437)	73 (3,122)	70 (2,454)			71 (6,013)
6	62 (1,355)	80 (1,649)				74 (3,004)
7	60 (979)					71 (17,035)

*Number of egg, nestling, chick × days in parentheses.

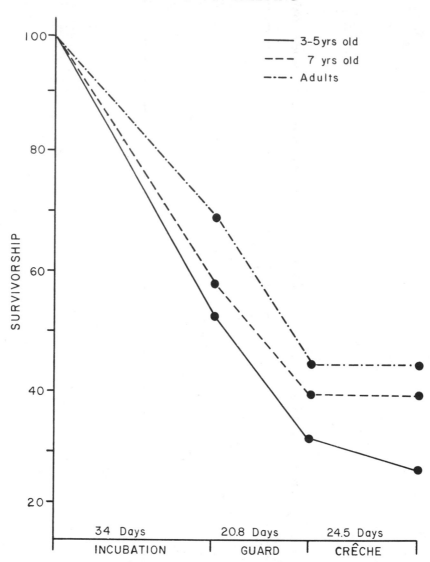

FIGURE 27 **Survivorship curves for eggs, nestlings, and crêche-age chicks.**

creased age or rookery experience of the birds could change the values measured. So complex is the interplay of age and experience in changing breeding biology that a summary proves helpful in understanding their relative roles (table

TABLE 7.27 The number and percent of Adélie Penguins laying, hatching, and fledging eggs and chicks relative to their prior breeding experience; Cape Crozier, 1963 to 1974. Data are from appendix 5.

PRIOR SEASONS BRED		EGGS LAID*			EGGS HATCHED			CHICKS FLEDGED		
		1	2	3	0	1	2	0	1	2
0	n	77	281	2	108	111	141	175	144	41
	%	21.4	78.1	0.6	30.0	30.8	39.2	48.6	40.0	11.4
1	n	20	111	1	40	30	62	58	49	25
	%	15.2	84.1	0.8	30.3	22.7	47.0	43.9	37.1	18.9
2+	n	6	32	0	10	8	20	17	12	9
	%	15.8	84.2	0.0	26.3	21.0	52.5	44.7	31.6	23.7
Totals	n	103	424	3	158	149	223	250	205	75
	%	19.4	80.0	0.6	29.8	28.1	42.1	47.2	38.7	14.2
	r	−.8188	.8731	−.7206	−.8304	−.9357	−.9951†	−.7755	−.9844	−.9921†

*No statistical differences in relation to number of previous breeding seasons.
†P<.05.

TABLE 7.28 **A summary of how age and experience affect productivity in Adélie Penguins; the numbers refer to tables detailing the indicated absence or presence of effects.**

	AGE		EXPERIENCE	
	Yes	*No*	*Yes*	*No*
Age of first breeding			6.4	
Breeding incidence	6.5		6.6 & 6.7	
Laying date	7.1			7.2
Clutch size	7.4			7.5 & 7.7
Incubation routine	7.6 & 7.10			
Incubation period		7.18		
Egg fertility	7.19			
No. eggs lost	7.4/7.12		7.5/7.12 & 7.14	
No. eggs hatched	7.12		7.14 & 7.27	
Parental attendance		7.20		
Chick age at crèching	7.21			
Chick age at fledging		7.22		
No. chicks to crèche/fledge	7.23 & 7.27		7.23 & 7.27	

7.28). The most obvious fact that appears from this is that only age can change laying date, clutch size, incubation routine, or egg fertility. This means that physiological maturity or experience at sea that ultimately increases fat reserves (but that, unlike rookery experience, we cannot quantify) is more important than social experience at the rookery in changing factors that are concerned with the laying of eggs. Once viable eggs are laid, however, both age and rookery/breeding experience affect the number of eggs and chicks lost and the number of chicks ultimately fledged.

In the absence of direct observation we can only guess that older, more experienced birds reduce the losses of eggs and young chicks by being more attentive to them, more aggressive toward nest predators, or more successful at finding food quickly. It is obvious that experience could increase effectiveness in dealing with nest predators, and it is equally obvious that having larger fat reserves (related to physiological maturity and experience at sea) can help to increase a bird's attentiveness and reduce its likelihood of deserting the nest. From several facts reviewed previously we know that older birds more efficiently travel at sea and find food. Any other factors involved are less obvious though no less important, and some work indirectly through age and experience. Some of these we will discuss in the following chapter; for instance, the effect of nest location—which is age/experience related—on productivity.

An important fact that emerged from this chapter and previous chapters in regard to experience was that usually only one or sometimes two additional seasons at the rookery increased proficiency in breeding activity. This is important when viewed against the relatively few breeding years that an Adélie has available to it (ch. 9) and the rather short time available each summer to reproduce. Adélie Penguins just do not have the time to "experiment" and thereby increase breeding proficiency; their responses to many situations must to a large degree be genetically programmed through natural selection.

Another fact that has emerged in regard to experience is that experience at sea is just as important in determining breeding success as experience at the rookery. The number of years spent dealing with marine factors can affect such things as arrival date, the length of feeding trips during incubation, and, as Ainley and Schlatter (1972) demonstrated, the fledging weight of chicks. All of these factors point to increased feeding ability with greater age/experience. Carrick and Ingham (1967) and Carrick (1972) felt that social dominance at sea was more important than feeding proficiency in determining the amount of food captured by Royal Penguins breeding at Macquarie Island. Spurr (1974) felt that this could also be true for Adélies. Such a theory is probably not testable for any penguin species nor has it ever been reported with supporting data for any seabird, whereas several studies on marine birds have reported age-related differences in success at food capture (e.g., Orians 1969, Dunn 1972, and Buckley and Buckley 1974). The fact that one- and two-year-old Adélies leave large areas of seemingly suitable marine habitat vacant and actually concentrate within or close to the areas where breeding adults are feeding (Ainley and O'Connor in press) is inconsistent with the hypothesis that older birds have direct, negative effects on

the feeding success of younger ones. Royal Penguins are remarkably similar to Adélies in many aspects of their breeding regimes and ecology, but we believe it unlikely that
Carrick and Ingham's theory applies to Adélie Penguins.
The exclusion of young, inexperienced birds by established
ones has been ruled out by Nelson (1978*b*) as a possibility
for gannets.

8
FACTORS OTHER THAN AGE AND EXPERIENCE THAT AFFECT PRODUCTIVITY

 Chapters 3 through 7 were concerned with describing Adélie Penguin breeding biology and the way it is affected by age and experience. Both experience at sea and in the rookery were found to have effects. In virtually all factors studied, increased age or experience increased breeding success in some way. Other factors also influenced Adélies in their breeding activities, and some of these we shall now consider. In some cases, age and experience play indirect roles in the pressures that these factors exert.

THE EFFECT OF NEST LOCATION

Several authors have noted differences in the productivity of birds nesting at the periphery of colonies compared to those nesting more centrally (i.e., with at least one nest between theirs and the periphery). Patterson (1965) discussed this for Black-headed Gulls *Larus ridibundus,* Nelson (1966*b*, 1978*a, b*) for gannets, Coulson (1968) and Wooller and Coulson (1977) for kittiwakes, and Carrick (1972), briefly, for Royal Penguins. For Adélie Penguins this phenomenon has been studied by Penney (1968), Tenaza (1971), and Spurr (1974, 1975*b*). Most of these authors concluded that centrally nesting individuals were qualitatively better breeders and, being of better quality, were better able to compete successfully with other individuals for central territories. Only Nelson (1978a) totally disagreed. He concluded that young birds predominate among peripherally nesting gannets as a result of arriving later than older birds and that the lower reproductive success of peripheral birds results from age-related factors rather than from qualitative differences per se between central and peripheral birds—young birds merely exhibit lower breeding success. Nelson came to this conclusion because (1) he could recognize age classes of breeders by virtue of plumage differences and (2) he noticed that older birds tended to nest at their site of previous years rather than moving to more central positions left vacant because of the former owner's death. Such vacancies were filled by young gannets who returned early enough to find them unoccupied. Penney (1968) and Spurr (1974, 1975b) were unable to age the Adélie Penguins they studied but did consider the possibility that young birds might tend to nest at colony peripheries. They, along with others, agreed that a bird nesting at a colony edge was subjected to more disturbance by other penguins and to a greater risk of predation by skuas.

Our data support the observations of others that Adélie Penguins occupying peripheral nests exhibit lower reproductive success than those occupying central nests (table 8.1). Overall the difference was very small, about 0.1 chicks, but nonetheless significant and no doubt the result of the especially great differences exhibited between the peripheral and central breeders of the youngest ages. In table 8.1 some age classes were combined so that sample sizes were at least thirty birds. In five of the seven year/age classes compared, higher nesting success (chicks per pair) occurred among birds having central nests; but within individual age-classes, only among three- and four-year-olds combined was the difference statistically significant. For birds eight years of age and older, nesting success between central and peripheral nesters was quite similar. We conclude that the poorer average reproductive performance of Adélies nesting at colony edges results from the especially low success of young birds in such circumstances. In addi-

TABLE 8.1 Reproductive success of known-age birds relative to their nest location in colonies at Cape Crozier; success is measured in two ways: percentage of breeders raising at least one chick to crèche and the mean number ($\pm$SD) of chicks raised to crèche.

Age (yrs)	PERIPHERAL NEST			CENTRAL NEST		
	Successful, %	Chicks per nest, $\bar{x}$	n	Successful, %	Chicks per nest, $\bar{x}$	n
			1967 & 1968			
3 & 4*	41.3*	0.5 $\pm$ 0.7†	46	63.4*	0.8 $\pm$ 0.8†	41
5	50.0	0.7 $\pm$ 0.8	54	52.2	0.8 $\pm$ 0.8	46
6 & 7	52.4	0.7 $\pm$ 0.7	42	48.5	0.7 $\pm$ 0.8	33
			1974			
5	60.4	0.8 $\pm$ 0.7	53	65.2	1.0 $\pm$ 0.8	46
6 & 7	65.2	0.8 $\pm$ 0.7	141	74.1	1.0 $\pm$ 0.7	139
8	70.6	1.0 $\pm$ 0.8	34	72.7	0.9 $\pm$ 0.7	33
9–13	69.2	1.0 $\pm$ 0.8	65	75.7	1.1 $\pm$ 0.8	70
Total†	60.0*	0.8 $\pm$ 0.7†	435	67.6*	0.9 $\pm$ 0.8†	408

*Difference between peripheral and central nests is statistically significant (P<.05); for percent successful $t = 2.08$, and for chicks per nest $t = 1.87$.

†Difference between peripheral and central nests is statistically significant (P<.05); for percent successful $t = 2.29$, and for chicks per nest $t = 1.93$.

tion, greater age or another year of experience apparently allows Adélies to overcome the disadvantages of a peripheral nest. This is important because colony shape and size are rather dynamic; a bird occupying an inner site one season may find itself on the periphery in the next year or two without having switched sites.

We have explored only part of this phenomenon for Adélie Penguins. Still to be answered is the question, Do young Adélies tend to nest more at colony edges than within colonies? Circumstantial evidence indicates the answer to be yes. First, LeResche and Sladen (1970) showed that the youngest breeders tended to switch nest sites after breeding at one site the first year; they thus substantiated Sladen's (1958) and Penney's (1968) hypothesis that "established" breeders were very faithful to a nest site in contrast to "un-established" breeders. Second, our data show that arrival time during spring advances with age (ch. 3) and thus central nest sites would probably be occupied when younger breeders arrived. Fortunately, we also have direct evidence that young Adélies nest more at colony edges than within colony interiors: 53.5 percent of three- to five-year-olds compared to 47.2 percent of birds seven and older nested at the peripheries of Cape Crozier colonies (P<.05; *t*-test; table 8.2). Three-year-olds, all females, were actually exceptional, but the sample was too small to change the outcome for three- to five-year-olds as a group; their tendency not to nest at peripheries would be logical, however, because they had to have paired with older males.

Equally interesting were the facts that no Adélie older than seven years (n = 221) nested more than five nests in from a colony edge and that only three (1.4 percent) of these birds occupied the fifth nest in. A significantly larger proportion of younger birds (3.8 percent, n = 822; P<.05, *t*-test) occupied nests that were four or more sites in from the periphery. In contrast, disregarding three-year-olds (all females nesting with older birds), more birds eight and older nested within one or two sites of the colony periphery than did younger birds—47.1 percent (n = 221) vs. 38.2 percent (n = 822; P<.05), respectively. Older Adélies thus avoided the most central nests, probably because those were too difficult and painful to reach. Since an Adélie must trespass on every territory along its path into a colony, the chances of suffering an outright Attack (Ainley 1975*b*, Spurr 1975*a*) instead of a "mere" Peck (Ainley 1975*b*, Spurr 1975*a*) are increased relative to the number of territory boundaries violated (see Penney 1968:106).

Imagine the situation of an Adélie establishing a central territory and faced with the prospect of traveling to the outside of the colony to collect the hundreds of stones for its nest. No wonder thievery has developed in this species! The frequency of agonistic encounters is high in the center of a colony, and thus also of little wonder is the fact that the centrally nesting Adélies tend to be less tolerant of one another (more aggressive? Spurr 1974) than their peripheral counterparts. Because of the deleterious qualities of the central

TABLE 8.2 Nest location within colonies for Adélies of known age; Cape Crozier, 1968 to 1974.

NUMBER OF NESTS TO PERIPHERY OF COLONY

Age (yrs)	0		1		2		3		4+		Total
	n	%	n	%	n	%	n	%	n	%	
3	6	37.5	5	31.3	2	12.5	1	6.3	2	12.5	16
4	45	58.4	14	18.2	10	13.0	6	7.8	2	2.6	77
5	48	52.2	25	27.2	9	9.8	5	5.4	5	5.5	92
6	197	55.6	89	25.1	42	11.9	15	4.2	11	3.1	354
7	142	50.2	74	26.1	44	15.5	12	4.2	11	3.9	283
8	31	55.4	16	28.6	9	16.1	3	5.4			59
9+	65	40.1	55	34.0	24	14.8	15	9.3	3	1.9	162
7–9	238	47.2*	145	28.8	77	15.3	30	6.0	14	2.8	504
3–5	99	53.5*	44	23.8	21	11.4	12	6.5	9	4.9	185

* Difference between these categories for birds 7 to 9+ and 3 to 5 years of age is significant; $P < .05$, t-test.

area, older, more experienced birds tend to avoid nests deep within large colonies; and it might also be that younger, less experienced birds are more attracted to the increased activity and greater social stimulation in colony centers (see also Wooller and Coulson 1977).

The fact that older Adélies avoided both peripheral nest sites and sites more than three nests from the periphery is particularly important in regard to the methods of study employed by researchers who compared nesting success between "central" and peripheral nesters. Tenaza (1971) explored the problem in greatest detail and, in fact, stated that "most central nests evaluated were actually near colony edges (to minimize observer disturbance)" (p. 81). His motives were exemplary but resulted in a comparison between one sample with the highest possible proportion of young birds (i.e., peripheral birds) and another sample with the highest possible proportion of oldest birds (i.e., birds nesting one or two sites away from the periphery). Little wonder that he discovered major differences in nesting behavior and success between his two samples. Penney (1968) and Spurr (1975b) did not define "central" nest in their respective samples. Knowing them to be researchers sensitive to disturbance, we think it likely, though, that they, too, studied samples similar to Tenaza's.

It appears that the Adélie Penguin and the North Atlantic Gannet are largely similar with regard to the relative significance of peripheral and central nest sites. Both species are conservative in their tendency to switch from one nest to a more central one, and large numbers of old birds do nest at colony peripheries. There are also some parallels with the kittiwake, as discussed by Wooller and Coulson (1977). Neither these authors nor Nelson (1978a), however, described an avoidance of centralmost nests in large colonies of kittiwakes or gannets. Since these birds fly to their territory they do not have the problem of trespassing on other territories to reach it. The fact that Adélies avoid nests in the center of large colonies may be another reason certain colonies were avoided by young birds (ch. 3). About 50 percent of colonies at Crozier were composed of fewer than 50 nests (ch. 2), and in such colonies few nests would be more than four from the periphery.

THE EFFECT OF MATE'S AGE

Many of the manifest characteristics of Adélies discussed in this monograph were dependent not only on an individual but on its mate as well. Almost all breeding factors and productivity estimates depend upon both partners of the pair. Keeping-company behavior and nest quality are similarly altered by the performance of the known-age bird's partner. If a young bird mates with an older, more experienced Adélie, its youthful ineptitude will be diluted and its expertise enhanced. Conversely, if a youngster's mate is itself a young or inept bird, youthful behavior will be reinforced, and defects in performance will be even more obvious.

It is difficult to separate an individual's influence on the performance of a pair. Therefore in previous chapters we sometimes reported observations on mates of young Adélies by following them in years after their breeding associations with the young birds had finished. In the preceding chapters these birds were known as *former mates*. The difficulty of dual influence on some activities of paired birds remained, however, for at least two reasons: (1) perhaps a bird inclined to breed with a young bird one year will do so again, and (2) with an added year of experience the mate's performance will improve the next year. Thus it is invalid to compare the performance of a mate one year with its performance the previous year when it was younger, less experienced, and paired with a younger, less experienced partner.

LeResche and Sladen (1970), citing data later presented in LeResche (1971), concluded that mates of young Adélies "are probably among the less fit individuals in the population.... Perhaps they are also youngsters or older, senescent birds." Ainley and Schlatter (1972) thought that young Adélies pair with other youngsters, citing dates of return and rapid pairing as supportive evidence. At the time of these reports, however, there had been only three cases in which the ages of both partners in a pair were known, and only young birds were available.

Richdale (1957) presented very extensive data on mates of known-age Yellow-eyed Penguins. He found that young females mate predominantly with older males because of, he surmised, the latter's attractiveness in terms of dominance, whereas older females mate with younger males because of their greater availability. The situation for Yellow-eyed Penguins, however, might be different because their sedentary nature would result in young and old birds being present simultaneously before the egg-laying period. For Adélies the staggered dates of migration and the rapidity of pairing, as Ainley and Schlatter (1972) hypothesized and as shown in previous chapters here, reduce the chances for old birds and young birds to pair. It would also be advantageous for an old bird to avoid pairing with a young bird, as we shall see below.

We encountered 103 pairings of known-age birds that resulted in the production of eggs, 1968 to 1975. To investigate the degree to which birds of one age paired with those of other ages, we divided the actual number of observed pair combinations by the maximum number of such combinations possible. The latter we took to be the lesser number of breeding males or females available for pairing (table 8.3). The results of these "weighted" combinations are shown in table 8.4. The highest number of pair combinations runs diagonally down the table, indicating that Adélies of a given age tended to pair with others of or close to their age. The classes five through eight were particularly instructive in this because all age combinations were possible; yet five-year-olds paired only with birds younger than eight, and eight-year-olds paired only with birds older than six. Six-year-olds were at somewhat of a pivotal age and showed the widest array of pair combinations.

The following are comparisons between young Adélies (three to seven years of age), former mates, and adult controls that were made in the seasons 1967 and 1968 and in the next season after "former" mates were paired with young birds. The reproductive performance of these mates confirms the observation that young birds paired with young birds (see comments at the end of the second paragraph in this discussion). These data were summarized from previous chapters. Controls were selected on 4 November so they undoubtedly included the oldest, most experienced Adélies.

TABLE 8.3 The number of pairings between two birds both of known age (in years); and (separated by /) the number of breeding males or females, whichever is less, available for respective age combinations. Read the table left to right.

AGE OF BIRD	AGE OF MATE								
	3	4	5	6	7	8	9	10	11+
3		2/37	1/93	1/104	0/57	0/13			
4	2/37	1/37	2/130	0/165	0/94	0/31			
5	1/93	2/130	4/164	3/406	3/356	0/181	0/109	0/118	0/128
6	1/104	0/165	3/406	9/310	6/590	3/415	1/256	1/250	1/284
7	0/57	0/94	3/356	6/590	9/280	4/409	4/273	1/267	0/300
8	0/13	0/31	0/181	3/415	4/409	0/144	1/182	1/176	0/209
9			0/109	1/256	4/273	1/182	0/49	2/92	0/125
10			0/118	1/250	1/267	1/176	2/92	0/43	3/119
11+			0/128	1/284	0/300	0/209	0/125,	3/119	0/76

TABLE 8.4 **The weighted* number of pairings for possible age combinations among pairs where both members are of known age (in years). Read the table left to right; a space = no age combination possible and bold type = the two highest numbers of pairings. Data are from table 8.3.**

AGE OF BIRD	AGE OF MATE								
	3	4	5	6	7	8	9	10	11+
3		**5.4**	1.1	1.0	0	0			
4	**5.4**	2.7	1.5	0	0	0			
5	1.1	**1.5**	2.4	0.7	0.8	0	0	0	0
6	**1.0**	0	0.7	**2.9**	1.0	0.7	0.4	0.4	0.4
7	0	0	0.8	1.0	**3.2**	1.0	**1.5**	0.4	0
8	0	0	0	**0.7**	1.0	0	0.5	0.6	0
9			0	0.4	**1.5**	0.5	0	**2.2**	0
10			0	0.4	0.4	0.6	**2.2**	0	**2.5**
11+			0	0.4	0	0	0	**2.5**	0

*The observed number of pairs for each combination divided by the number of breeding males or females, whichever was less, available for respective age combinations times 100.

1. Mean laying date of pairs involving one former mate was earlier (14.7 Nov.) than that of young birds (16.4 to 20.9 Nov.) but later than that of controls (11.4 Nov.).

2. Clutch size of former mates when breeding with unbanded birds (1.8) was similar to that of controls (1.8) but increased over what it had been when breeding with young known-age Adélies (1.4 to 1.7).

3. Egg loss by former mates was similar (41 percent) to that of young birds (45 percent) and much greater than that of controls (31 percent).

4. The proportion of infertile eggs in the clutches of former mates (30 percent) was similar to that of young birds (21 percent) but was much greater than that of controls (8 percent).

5. Overall productivity of former mates was 0.5 fledglings per pair compared to 0.8 for controls and 0.2 to 0.4 for young Adélies.

The poor reproductive success of young, inexperienced birds stands out particularly when they pair together. Unfortunately, when we had three- and four-year-olds to study we had no birds older than eight years and vice versa. It seems unlikely that many pairings of birds greatly different in age would have resulted, given the above analysis, but the few that might have occurred could have provided the opportunity to determine the degree to which young birds dilute or old birds reinforce each other.

The ineptitude of young birds is indeed reinforced when they pair together. In combinations involving three- and four-year-olds, the tendency to produce only one egg was high (table 8.5). Out of seven such pairings, only two (29 percent) resulted in two eggs being laid, and in both cases the three- or four-year-old paired with a bird five years of age or older. In fifty-five pairings involving older birds, fifty-two produced two-egg clutches (95 percent). In the raising of chicks to crèche age, any age combination including a bird four years old or younger performed below the population average (chap. 7), but age combinations where both birds were five or older performed at or above the population average (cf. tables 8.6 and 7.5). These patterns may be consistent with that in the gannet, where young birds that would not otherwise breed do so on the relatively rare occasion that they pair with a much older partner (Nelson 1978*b*). Those younger gannets could also be high quality individuals, as in kittiwakes (Wooller and Coulson 1977).

THE DURATION OF PAIR BONDS AND ITS INFLUENCE ON REPRODUCTIVE SUCCESS

The number of seasons that a pair remains together is known to influence reproductive success in several species: birds retaining the same mate average higher success than those that change (Richdale 1957, Coulson 1966, Wood 1971, and Mills 1973). For the Adélie Penguin, Penney (1968) found that changing mates at Wilkesland had no effect on overall breeding success (percentage of pairs that fledged chicks) in one season (1959–1960) but had a definite negative effect in another (1960–1961). In the second

TABLE 8.5 Mean clutch size (±SD) for pairs in which both partners were of known age (in years); number is in parentheses.

AGE OF BIRD	AGE OF PARTNER							
	4	5	6	7	8	9	10	11+
3	1.0±0.0 (2)	1.0 (1)	2.0 (1)					
4	1.0 (1)	1.5±0.7 (2)						
5		2.0±0.0 (4)	2.0±0.0 (3)	2.0±0.0 (3)				
6			2.0±0.0 (9)	2.0±0.0 (6)	1.7±0.6 (3)	2.0 (1)	2.0 (1)	2.0 (1)
7				2.0±0.0 (8)	1.8±0.5 (4)	2.0±0.0 (4)	1.0 (1)	
8						2.0 (1)	2.0 (1)	
9							2.0±0.0 (2)	
10								2.0±0.0 (3)

TABLE 8.6 Mean number of chicks (±SD) raised to the crèche for pairs in which both partners were of known age (in years); sample is in parentheses.

AGE OF BIRD	AGE OF PARTNER							
	4	5	6	7	8	9	10	11+
3		0.0 (1)	0.0 (1)					
4	0.5±0.7 (2)	0.5±0.7 (2)						
5		1.5±1.0 (4)	1.3±0.6 (3)	1.0±1.0 (3)				
6			0.7±0.8 (6)	0.8±1.0 (3)	1.5±0.7 (2)	1.5±1.0 (4)		2.0 (1)
7				1.1±0.9 (7)		2.0 (1)	2.0±0.0 (2)	
8								2.0 (1)

season much of the effect resulted from the failure of split or disunited birds to pair in time to breed. Over four seasons at Cape Bird, Spurr (1975*b*, 1977) found no effect from changing mates on overall productivity among birds that bred after the mate change but also noted failure to breed in a high proportion of birds who did not retain their previous mate. All who have studied the phenomenon of faithfulness to mate in Adélies agree that asynchrony of return and death of a partner are the major factors leading to split and disunited pair bonds, respectively (Sladen 1958, Sapin-Jaloustre 1960, Penney 1968, Sladen and LeResche 1970, Spurr 1975*b*).

LeResche and Sladen (1970) at Cape Crozier noted breeding failure in birds split or disunited from their mate of the previous year. We now have much more data to add to this whole subject. In 247 Adélies who bred in more than one season, we first compared the clutch size of birds relative to the number of seasons they bred and the number of mates during those seasons (table 8.7). Clutch size increased markedly with the number of breeding seasons and was especially low in the year of first breeding compared to the others (see also tables 7.4 and 7.5). Retaining the same mate seemed to have a slight effect, but the increased clutch size was not statistically significant (P>.05). Next, we compared overall breeding success in terms of the percent of pairs fledging at least one chick and the average number of chicks fledged per breeding pair (table 8.8). In only one comparison was there a statistical difference: birds breeding for their third (or more) season with the same mate bred successfully more often (83.3 percent) than birds breeding in their second season but with a new mate (58.3 percent). It thus appears that Adélie Penguins find little advantage in retaining the same mate from one season to the next. Because asynchrony of return and death are the major causes for losing a mate (see above), being able to switch to a mate with similar synchrony would be advantageous. In so doing, Adélies continue to mate with birds of the same age throughout their reproductive period (see above, pp. 157 to 158). Keeping the same mate is apparently advantageous only in avoiding the need to compete again for a new one (cf. Penney 1968; Spurr 1975*b*, 1977; Ainley 1978). Mortality among breeding birds is so high, however, that the likeli-

TABLE 8.7 Mean clutch size of Adélie Penguins relative to the number of breeding seasons and the number of mates; sample is in parentheses; Cape Crozier, 1964 to 1975.

Number of seasons with mate	NUMBER OF SEASONS BRED		
	1	2	3+
First	1.5 ± 0.4* (101)	1.7 ± 0.4 (43)	1.8 ± 0.4 (36)
Second		1.8 ± 0.4 (39)	1.8 ± 0.4 (18)
Third+			1.9 ± 0.3 (10)

*Statistically smaller than all other categories (P<.05, t-test); no other comparisons were significant.

TABLE 8.8 The mean number of chicks fledged and the percentage of birds breeding successfully (fledging at least one chick) relative to the number of breeding seasons and the number of mates involved; sample is in parentheses; Cape Crozier, 1963 to 1974.

Number of seasons with mate	NUMBER OF SEASONS BRED			
	1	2	3+	Total
First	1.0 ± 0.7 75.2% (101)	0.9 ± 0.9* 58.3% (36)	0.9 ± 0.9 58.3% (24)	1.0 ± 0.7 68.9% (161)
Second+		1.0 ± 0.8 68.4% (38)	1.2 ± 0.7* 83.3% (18)	1.1 ± 0.7 73.2% (56)

*Percent breeding successfully was statistically significant (P<.05).

hood of losing a mate is also high (Ainley and DeMaster 1980; chap. 9).

The phenomenon of mate retention and its consequences has thus a different pattern in Adélie Penguins of the southern Ross Sea (Cape Bird, Cape Crozier) than in other species of long-lived seabirds or even in the Adélie Penguin farther north (at Wilkesland: Penney 1968). Not only is retaining the same mate advantageous but, in those other species, keeping the same mate from one year to another is much more likely than it is in Crozier Adélies. Richdale (1957), Coulson and White (1960), Wood (1971), and Mills (1973) all found that about 80 percent of older individuals in the species they studied retained their mates from one season to the next. This was also the figure that Penney (1968) reported for Adélies on the Wilkesland coast. Such is not the case at Cape Crozier (table 8.9). Only 18 percent of three-year-old breeders that returned the next season then bred with the same mate; in all older Adélies, the number retaining mates increased to 51 percent. What a marked difference from figures reported for species including Adélies at Wilkesland (Penney 1968) and skuas at Cape Crozier (Wood 1971)! We know, in addition, that no banded Crozier Adélie bred with the same mate for more than four years (i.e., no birds paired in 1969–1970 were still paired in 1974–1975). In fact, in a sample of 100 pairs of banded birds, only 6 bred three seasons with one mate; of twenty-two birds for whom we have records for four or more seasons of breeding, one-third bred with four different mates and half bred with three different mates (table 8.10). With

TABLE 8.9   The percentage of birds breeding with a different partner in the next season; cases where both partners returned.

Age during first season (yrs)	Same partner n	Different partner n	Total	Percent changing
3	2	9	11	81.8
4	29	21	50	42.0*
5	34	37	71	52.1*
6	18	18	36	50.0*
7	20	22	42	52.4
8–12	23	23	46	50.0*

* For a comparison between this and three-year-olds, P<.05 (*t*-test).

TABLE 8.10 The percentage of individuals (sample in parentheses) breeding with various numbers of partners among Adélies known to have bred in more than one season; Cape Crozier, 1963 to 1969.

Minimum no. of partners	NUMBER OF SEASONS BRED			
	2 (51)	3 (27)	4 (18)	5+ (4)
1	49.0	22.2		
2	51.0	44.4	22.2	
3		33.3	61.1	
4			16.7	100.0

such low fidelity, it is not surprising that changing mates has little effect on the reproductive success of Adélie Penguins at Cape Crozier. These conclusions are contrary to those we made earlier (LeResche and Sladen 1970); we see now that comparing figures at Crozier with those at Wilkesland was invalid. The shortness of the breeding season and the consequent importance of arrival and breeding cycle synchrony are no doubt the reason Adélies of the southern Ross Sea are unique in regard to the phenomenon of mate fidelity among the long-lived seabirds so far studied and reported.

WEAK PAIR- AND SITE-BONDS OF YOUNG BREEDERS

Penney (1968), on the one hand, stressed as characteristic of Adélies the synchrony of behavior between members of a pair and the strong faithfulness of mature birds to previous mates and breeding sites. LeResche and Sladen (1970), on the other hand, described "the tenuous nature of . . . pair- and site-bonds" in *young* Adélies. Previous chapters of the present report have discussed the correlation of breeding site with natal site and area of previous experience in the rookery, and they have indicated that initial choice of mate is somewhat a matter of chance, placement, and timing. In this section we discuss the alteration of breeding sites by young birds and their tendency to change mates more often than established breeders. The following section describes how nest and site shifts may occur during breeding seasons as well as between seasons.

Behavioral differences between young and established breeders are striking after the first breeding. Of 192 pairs, each involving one nonestablished known-age bird (table 8.11), only 40 percent returned the following season compared to 60 percent of 277 "established" pairs at Wilkesland (Penney 1968) and 60 percent of 10 established pairs at Hope Bay (Sladen 1958). In an additional 43 cases, 22 percent of pairs split because of the nonreturn of the known-age bird's mate. The remaining 20 percent of pairs were split when neither known-age bird nor mate returned.

Of 554 breeding birds in Penney's sample, 77 percent returned the following season. In our samples, of 192 young known-age breeders, 63 percent returned the following season; and of 192 *mates* of young breeders, only 58 percent returned.

When both known-age bird and mate returned (n =

TABLE 8.11   Fate of 192 breeding pairs of Adélie Penguins with one member of known age (values in parentheses are percentages).

	Young breeders (age in years)					Established
	7	6	5	4	Total	adults*
Both returned	12(52)	19(32)	34(42)	12(43)	77(40)	165(60)‡
Both returned and bred	10(43)	14(23)	20(25)	7(25)	51(27)	
Only known-age bird returned	2(09)	18(30)	18(22)	5(18)	43(22)	
Only mate returned	7(30)	13(22)	12(15)	3(07)	34(18)	98(35)
Neither returned	2(09)	10(17)	17(21)	9(32)	38(20)	14(05)‡
Total pairs in sample†	23	60	81	28	192	277

*Calculated from Penney (1968).
†Less second line.
‡Adult-young difference significant (P<.05, *t*-test).

77), the incidence of breeding was 72 percent for known-age birds and 58 percent for mates of known-age birds. Both figures are appreciably lower than the nearly 100 percent breeding incidence found by Penney in 330 "established" breeders ($t \geq .95$, $P < .05$).

Eliminating nonbreeders, analysis of cases where known-age birds and mates returned and the known-age bird bred (table 8.12) indicates marked differences in mate and site tenacity between young unestablished breeders and presumably established breeders. In this situation, only 56 percent of young breeders compared to 84 percent of established adults retained their previous mate ($P < .05$). Fifty percent of 26 young breeders who did not pair with their former mate retained their former site within one meter (vs. 78 percent in adults); the remainder moved more than a meter.

This contrast between unestablished and established breeders is evident from the history of one colony of about 150 breeding pairs at Cape Crozier (fig. 28). In five breeding seasons, three young females bred with eight (possibly nine) different mates. One of these paired with two different young birds in consecutive seasons. Only once did a pair remain united for two seasons, even though in all but two instances the mate from the previous year was present and available for breeding. In Sladen's (1958) sample of ten presumably established pairs banded in 1946, at least six were together the following year and only two mated with other birds when the previous mate was available. Five stayed together for three seasons. A plot analogous to figure 28 (fig. 29) contrasts markedly with the behavior of young birds.

Penney (1968) suggested asynchrony of return to the rookery as a primary factor in the disuniting of pairs. Our data generally support this in eleven cases of disunited known-age birds and four cases of reunited pairs for which arrival dates were precisely known in 1967–1968. Data from 1968–1969 (Ainley, unpub. data) show the same pattern. In "about half" of Penney's disunited pairs, return was "widely asynchronous," with seven males and eight females returning seven or more days after the partner's arrival. Younger birds disunited from mates had even greater asynchrony in arrival in our study: partners in eight of ten pairs that dis-

TABLE 8.12.   Mate and site faithfulness in Adélie Penguins when both members of a pair returned and the known-age partner bred (n = 55); Cape Crozier, 1965 to 1968.

| | AGE (IN YEARS) AND SEX OF KNOWN-AGE BIRD | | | | | | | | | | | | Totals | Adults* |
| | 7 | | | 6 | | | 5 | | | 4 | | | (percent) | (percent) |
	♀	♂	Sex?	♀	♂	Sex?	♀	♂	Sex?	♀	♂	Sex?		
Known-age bird														
Retained mate	3	1		4	2		9	2	1	2			24 (56)	(84)†
Disunited	2	2		10	2		9	0	0	5			31 (44)	(16)
Retained site within 1 meter	3	3		6	1		9	2	1	1			26 (50)	(78)†
Moved more than 1 meter	2	0		7	3		8	0	1	6			27 (50)	(22)

*From Penney (1968).

†Adult-young difference significant, ($t = 2.53$, $P < .05$); male-female differences in mate and site retention not significant.

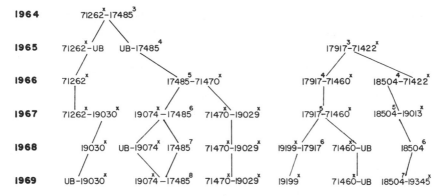

FIGURE 28   Typical breeding histories of Adélies at Cape Crozier.

united arrived seven or more days apart, and in five of the pairs arrival was separated by ten or more days.

Asynchrony of arrival did not always lead to switching of mates. Two of the four cases in which known-age birds retained mates involved males arriving fifteen to eighteen

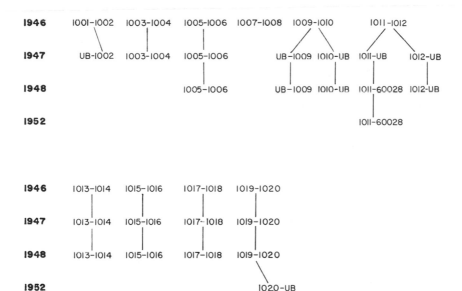

FIGURE 29   Typical breeding histories of adult Adélies at Signy Island (data from Sladen 1958).

TABLE 8.13   Site retention by young Adélie Penguins in 42 cases when the mate did not return; Cape Crozier, 1965 to 1968.

| | KNOWN-AGE PARTNER | | | |
	Female	Male	Total	Percent
Bred	15*	2*	17	40
Bred within 1 meter of previous site	2	1	3	21
Bred farther than 1 meter from previous site	11	0	11	79
Did not breed	18	7	25	58

*One male and two females bred—site change unknown.

days before their mates. In all cases when pairs reunited, the male arrived first; in all cases when pairs split, the female arrived first. This agrees with data in chapters 4 and 6 indicating that females seldom remain alone on a nest but almost always pair within a day of arrival at the rookery; in contrast, males often occupy territory alone for some time before pairing. Whether the two early-arriving males mentioned above spent fifteen and eighteen days alone on their nests out of "faithfulness" to a previous mate or out of inability to secure another mate is open to speculation.

Instances (n = 77) in which one of a pair did not return the following year also indicate a difference between mates of young birds and typical established breeders. Only 11 percent of Penney's (1968) presumably established "bereft" breeders failed to breed; but 60 percent of young birds did not breed, and 50 percent of mates of nonreturning youngsters failed to mate (tables 8.13 and 8.14). Thus young birds and their mates were markedly less successful in procuring new mates than were established breeders, which confirms circumstantial evidence given by Sladen (1958: tables VIII and IX) and more substantial evidence given by Ainley (1978).

TABLE 8.14 **Site retention* by the mate in 32 cases when the known-age Adélie Penguin did not return; Cape Crozier, 1965 to 1968.**

| | MATE* | | | |
	Female	Male	Total	Percent
Bred	2	14	16	50
Bred within 1 meter of previous site	0	12	12	38
Bred farther than 1 meter from previous site	2	2	4	13
Did not breed	5	11	16	50

*Differences in site retention between mates and young birds not significant (P> .10, *t*-test).

THE EFFECTS OF RESEARCH METHODS

Scientists who conduct research on avian breeding biology usually assume that they have no effect on the factors they measure. Robert and Ralph (1975), however, demonstrated that the frequency of visits to Western Gull *Larus occidentalis* nests to check for eggs and chicks had a significant effect on final results. Schreiber (1979) found the same to be true for Brown Pelicans *Pelecanus occidentalis* and then proceeded to review in detail the subject of researcher effects in avian natural history studies

It is well known that gulls and pelicans readily fly from their nests when humans approach (thus leaving eggs and chicks exposed to predators), but it is generally assumed that penguins are oblivious to the presence of humans because they do not flee, hence making them "ideal subjects" for natural history studies. Still, we wanted to know whether our activities altered the ability of Adélie Penguins to rear young because, as a result of their previous contact with humans, three types of Adélies occurred at Crozier that were recognizable by their responses to us: (1) birds that rarely experienced humans were very aggressive toward our approach, much as they would be to that of another penguin or skua; (2) birds that had been banded, including young ones returning for their first time, were leery of us; and (3) birds that had been banded and had had several subsequent experiences with us (when we visited their nests) were "unaffected" by our presence but were not aggressive toward us either. Robert and Ralph (1975) and Schreiber (1979) also identified habituation to the researcher in the species they studied.

We selected 2 sets of control nests during the 1968–1969 and 1969–1970 seasons (see chap. 2). In one sample of 50 nests within the most heavily studied colonies, we treated the occupants the same way as we did known-age, banded birds. We regarded these as "disturbed" controls. In a sample of 100 nests located in a little-studied part of the rookery, we assessed productivity on the basis of weekly observations rather than the almost daily visits used to check the others. We regarded these as "undisturbed" controls. In neither sample were birds banded. We found no significant differences in productivity between the two groups (P>.05, *t*-test), a result that was somewhat surprising to us (table 8.15) given the obvious behavioral differences in the three groups of Adélies mentioned above.

The fact that some colonies were less attractive to young birds prospecting for nest sites and that those least attractive were closest to our hut (see chap. 4) led us to investigate the year-to-year reproductive output of several colonies as an indirect measure of adult population size in them. The number of chicks present in these colonies on 7 to 10 January each year indicated that colonies in our study areas B and C were declining in size (fig. 30). Colonies within 200 meters of our hut declined 90 percent in the number of chicks produced; within 200 to 800 meters, 68 percent; and within 800 to 1,000 meters, 33 percent. Decline resulted from negative rates of recruitment, some or all of which in the most distant colonies (all in area B) in turn resulted from encroaching snow fields. In the nearest colonies this was because of the removal of birds for experiments (e.g., Emlen and Penney 1964, 1966), the fact that helicopters landed nearby and took off over them once every two or three weeks (nesting adults fled, leaving eggs and young exposed to skuas), and, possibly, their proximity to

TABLE 8.15 Comparative productivity of 50 nests visited once per day ("disturbed") and 100 nests visited once per week ("undisturbed"), during the two seasons; nest sites were not the same.

	"DISTURBED" NESTS			"UNDISTURBED" NESTS		
	1968–69	1969–70	Total	1968–69	1969–70	Total
Percent nests deserted	26	10	18	32	9	20
Mean clutch size	2.0	1.9	1.9	1.6	2.0	1.8
Percent eggs lost	33	25	26	25	28	27
Chicks alive per pair, 1 Jan.	1.3	1.0	1.2	1.2	1.1	1.2

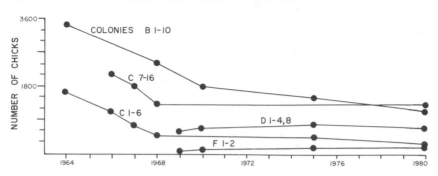

FIGURE 30   Counts of live chicks in specific colonies at Cape Crozier on about 10 January during successive years.

rather subdued human activities near the hut. Other factors had to be involved, however, because declines in C and B colonies continued from 1975 to 1980, a period when researchers were not present at Crozier (see below and chap. 9). In contrast, colonies surveyed in areas D and F, which were visited by humans only a few times each year, showed slightly increased chick output (900 to 1,010 chicks), between 1969 and 1975. F colonies, however, remained unchanged, and D colonies declined slightly in size from 1975 to 1980. Unfortunately, data for earlier years are lacking, and the overall increases for D and F occur when the decline in area B leveled off. Moreover, although people other than ourselves still conducted penguin research at Crozier, sometime between 1969–1970 and 1974–1975 new colonies appeared in at least areas C, B, and N and even in isolated F.

It seems likely that human activities, though not necessarily our data collection techniques, affected the recruitment of young birds, especially in the upper part of area C (close to the hut and helicopters) and increased their tendency to wander (see chap. 4). Fortunately, Cape Crozier was large enough to absorb a flow of birds from some areas to others; the tiny rookery at Cape Royds, however, declined in size from 1956 to 1965, which, according to Thomson (1977), was totally the result of too many unsupervised people visiting it.

Other factors could also have contributed to some of the above population declines. One must note that an entire but small Adélie rookery at Cape Barne, near Cape Royds, disappeared some time before the Scott/Shackelton expeditions without any influence from humans. Furthermore, the decline at Royds began in 1956, if not before, and reversed in the late 1960s, only a few years before declines leveled off at Crozier. Such a rapid onset of decline for Cape Royds— one year after the first visitors—is quite unbelievable as a response to disturbance. Is it possible that some factor other than human activity was responsible for or contributed to declining penguin populations in the southern Ross Sea during the 1960s and before? This will be discussed more fully below and in the following chapter.

THE EFFECT OF WEATHER

The effects of weather and sea ice conditions on Adélie Penguin breeding biology were first described in detail by Ainley and LeResche (1973), Spurr (1975b), and Yeates (1968, 1975). Calm conditions during spring and early summer were found to be detrimental because wind is required to blow sea ice away from rookeries, thus providing open seas and the opportunity for quick travel by swimming. As shown in chapter 3, the travel of inexperienced birds is affected more strongly than that of experienced ones. Fast feeding trips allow fat reserves to be used in breeding activities rather than in slow travel over ice. In addition, heavy pack ice and the resulting slowed travel result in smaller meals being fed to chicks (Emison 1968). Stonehouse (1967) surmised that many Adélie rookeries exist at all only because of the existence of anomalous, persistent areas of open water near ice-free land. Some of those areas occur because of strong currents, as at Cape Royds, and others because of strong winds, as at Cape Crozier.

Even winds of well over 100 mph have beneficial effects for Adélies; but when they reach 140 mph penguins have difficulty maintaining their footing, and other problems ensue. When such winds occurred at Crozier in early November 1967, during the period of peak laying, eggs were blown from many nests during nest reliefs, and a number of birds were killed when they lost their footing and were blown downhill (Sladen, LeResche, and Wood 1968). The effect on known-age birds, however, was relatively minor because the oldest birds that year were only six years of age; being young, many birds laid eggs later in the season. Thus we have little idea about the overall effect of this storm on Adélie productivity.

A comparison of breeding productivity within age classes showed that during 1967 and, especially, 1968, productivity was low (table 8.16). During all other years of study (1969, 1974, and 1975), it was much higher. Contrasting 1968 and 1969, the years when differences in breeding success were most extreme, Ainley and LeResche (1973) showed that the heavy, persistent pack ice during the earlier year and the very small amount of ice in the later one were ultimately responsible for the breeding differences. Spurr (1975b), working at Cape Bird, which is in an area of more persistent ice 90 km from Crozier, also found Adélie reproductive success to be low in 1968 compared to his three other seasons of study: 1967, 1969, and 1970. Dates of arrival indicate that pack ice was relatively heavy near Crozier in 1967 and probably in 1966, too (table 3.2). According to Emison (1968) this was the case at Crozier in 1964 as well; he found ice conditions to be more favorable in 1965, but how they compared with the "light ice" years of 1969, 1974, and 1975 is unknown.

Thus direct and indirect data at Crozier indicate that ice was heavy and breeding productivity was low in at least four of the five years immediately preceding 1969 but that the opposite was true in all three years studied after 1968. This change in trends is significant in two ways. First, since our data are based largely on two "good" years and two "poor" ones, we may not know what the average breeding productivity really should be, an important point when trying to make life table calculations (see chap. 9). Second, our data show declines in the sizes of Adélie colonies from the 1964–1965 to the 1969–1970 seasons and then a reversal or, at the least, a lessening in the rate of decline in later years (fig. 30). We also detected the formation of new colonies after 1969, a phenomenon that did not occur in the years of study preceding 1969. Could the Crozier population have been declining at least in part because of lowered productivity during the 1960s (and even earlier)? That is another ques-

TABLE 8.16 Breeding productivity by age for several years at Cape Crozier; data were from pairs nesting in the western, most intensively studied half of the rookery.

Year	Total no.	No. breed	% breed	BREEDING PRODUCTIVITY MEASUREMENTS			
				% lay 2 eggs	% do not desert*	% fledging a chick	Chicks per pair
AGE 3							
1967	360	10	2.8	50.0	70.0	50.0	0.02
1968†	343	7	2.3	25.0	50.0	37.5	0.01
1969	258	20	7.8	45.0	85.0	40.0	0.04
AGE 4							
1967	202	41	20.8	64.3	88.1	45.2	0.11
1968†	291	44	15.1	45.5	59.1	36.4	0.07
1969	250	68	23.2	69.1	89.7	55.9	0.16
AGE 5							
1967‡	108	51	47.2	78.4	88.2	45.1	0.37
1968	161	61	37.9	52.5	62.3	37.7	0.16
1969	161	87	54.0	79.3	94.3	71.3	0.47
1974	137	80	58.4	77.5	96.2	38.0	0.49
AGE 6							
1967‡	36	25	69.4	76.0	96.0	72.0	0.58
1968†	88	38	43.2	60.5	55.3	23.7	0.12
1969	116	93	80.2	91.4	95.7	73.1	0.90
1974	232	168	72.4	79.8	92.3	71.4	0.70
1975	304	239	78.6	70.3	92.1		

TABLE 8.16 (*continued*)

			AGE 7				
1968†	28	17	60.7	64.7	82.4	52.9	0.50
1969	60	50	83.3	92.0	94.0	70.0	0.75
1974	222	195	87.8	86.2	94.4	69.7	0.86
1975	296	253	85.6	83.3	92.9		
			AGE 8				
1969	23	21	91.3	95.2	90.5	76.2	0.91
1974	78	69	89.7	85.5	95.7	71.0	0.86
1975	253	227	89.7	78.4	97.8		

*During incubation.

†Comparing productivity measurements between 1968 and any other year within a particular age group, $X^2 > 27.40$ (P<.05).

‡Comparing productivity measurements between 1967 and 1969, among five-year-olds, $X^2 = 13.00$, and among six-year-olds, $X^2 = 15.46$ (P<.05); no other comparisons within age classes are significant.

tion important to understanding the demography of Adélie Penguins at Cape Crozier.

The especially unfavorable ice conditions in 1968 may have affected the breeding success of younger birds more strongly (table 8.16). The number of chicks fledged (actually, raised to crèche age) for three- through six-year-olds was usually more than twofold lower in 1968 than in other years, but for seven-year-olds it was lower by less than onefold. Similarly, the rate of nest desertions during incubation, mostly the result of insufficient fat reserves in the incubating bird or of tardy return of its mate (or both), was very high in four- through six-year-olds during 1968 relative to other years but was less extreme for seven-year-olds. Results for three-year-olds, as expected, were less clear because many of these females were probably paired with much older mates. These differences, though the data do not span enough years or age classes to be ideal, may result from the much higher proportions of first-time breeders in the younger age classes.

CHAPTER SUMMARY

In addition to age and experience, several factors can increase or decrease the productivity of an Adélie Penguin. If it nests at the outer edge of a colony, its nesting success will probably be reduced but not to a degree that it will look for a more central nest site the next year. Since colony conformation changes rapidly, what may have been a central site one year may not be the next. And besides, as a bird ages it gains the experience to overcome problems associated with peripheral nest sites. Similarly, heavy pack ice reduces productivity, but if an individual is older it can cope with such conditions more successfully. The presence of prying scientists at Crozier did not seem to alter the breeding success of Adélie Penguins but may have reduced the recruitment of young birds into certain colonies.

In most seabirds, switching mates has a depressing effect on productivity, but this is true only slightly in Adélie Penguins at high latitudes. For them, time is so short during a breeding season that synchronous behavior is more important than familiarity with the mate. Close coordination is necessary because breeding partners spend a total of only several hours together after egg laying; it is established by two birds of opposite sex arriving at the same colony at the same time during the egg-laying period. Asynchronous return in the spring and the death of one bird are the two most important causes for mates being changed, something that occurs frequently in this species. Young Adélies are more likely to switch mates than are older ones.

9
DEMOGRAPHY OF THE CROZIER POPULATION

 So far we have been concerned largely with the terrestrial breeding biology of the Adélie Penguin. The number of fledglings produced by birds of given ages is the ultimate result of breeding; it is affected strongly by rookery activities and success at obtaining food. We will analyze fecundity in the present chapter, and we will also discuss how productivity interplays with subadult and adult mortality to bring about changes or stability in population size. Unlike fecundity, mortality is mainly related only to the activities of Adélies at sea—if they can cope, they survive; if not, they die. In contrast to our detailed analyses of factors affecting rookery activities (the previous five chapters), we are less able to dissect those affecting survival because the pelagic lives of these birds have been far less accessible to us. Since Adélies spend but 10 percent of their life on land (Ainley 1980), it would be naive to say that marine ecology is only a minor part of their lives or that understanding their breeding biology is the key to knowing these creatures. We have some information on overall ecological patterns of this species at sea, but only during summer. What little direct and indirect knowledge we have indicates that age and experience relate importantly to the behavior of Adélies in their

marine habitat (see especially, summary of chap. 3 and Ainley and O'Connor in press).

The mortality and survivorship of Adélie Penguins in the Cape Crozier population were recently analyzed by Ainley and DeMaster (1980). For individuals six years of age and older, annual survivorship was 58 to 89 percent, a range of figures including the adult mortality estimate suggested by Stonehouse (1967) for Adélies at Cape Royds and the breeding adult estimate by Spurr (1975*b*) at Cape Bird. The figure, however, at least for the Crozier population, is probably biased downward (see below). Annual survivorship in the longer-lived Royal and Yellow-eyed penguins is about 87 percent (Carrick 1972, Ainley and DeMaster 1980).

Ainley and DeMaster (1980) found that survivorship in the Crozier population was lower among younger breeders and also among breeders (61 percent) compared to nonbreeders (78 percent) regardless of age. It was especially low in first-time breeding three-year-old females (25 percent) and four-year-old males (36 percent). Such patterns are not unique to Adélies. King Penguins *Aptenodytes patagonica* that raise chicks to fledging have higher mortality than those that do not (Stonehouse 1960). Northern Fulmars *Fulmarus glacialis* that commence breeding at a young age have higher mortality in their first breeding year than those that begin breeding at older ages (Dunnet and Ollason 1978, Ollason and Dunnet 1978). The same is true for kittiwakes (Coulson and Wooller 1976, Wooller and Coulson 1977). Nelson (1978*b*), however, speculated that young, first-time breeding gannets were under no greater stress than older breeders, but he had no data on survivorship to substantiate this. Only a few Adélies reached sixteen to nineteen years of age, and those that did so were individuals that first bred at a relatively late age (six or older; table 9.1), and they tended to be nonbreeders or failed breeders during many of their subsequent seasons (see below and Ainley 1978). Such patterns lead us to determine why young Adélies even attempt to breed given that their chances of doing so successfully *and* surviving are so low. Obviously they find it difficult to cope simultaneously with demands placed on them by both the sea and the duties of breeding.

TABLE 9.1   The minimum age at death relative to the age at first breeding for male Adélie Penguins; the percentage of birds attaining certain ages is shown.

Age first	MINIMUM AGE AT DEATH			Total
bred *(yrs)*	*5-7*	*8-10*	*11-13+*	birds
4	6	77	17	13
5	9	34	57	35
6	5	3	92	37
7-8			100	16

WHY THREE-YEAR-OLDS RISK BREEDING

It appears from table 9.2 that birds that first breed at a young age tend to breed successfully in more subsequent seasons (if they survive of course) than birds that breed first at older ages. Thus a larger proportion of birds that first bred as three- or four-year-olds during the 1965 to 1969 period bred successfully in a *greater* proportion of later years than those that first bred at older ages. Conversely, a larger proportion of birds that first bred at an older age (e.g., six years), bred successfully in a *smaller* proportion of subsequent seasons. Birds breeding successfully in their sixth or more season were observed doing so during 1974–1975 and 1975–1976 and would have to have first bred early in the 1965 to 1969

TABLE 9.2   The number and percentage, in parentheses, of birds breeding successfully in a given number of seasons relative to the age at which they first bred.

Age *(yrs)* of	NUMBER OF SEASONS SUCCESSFUL			Total
first breeding	*2*	*3*	*6+*	birds
3	6 (38)	3 (19)	7 (44)	16
4	20 (40)	9 (18)	21 (42)	50
5	19 (40)	10 (21)	18 (38)	47
6	8 (47)	4 (24)	5 (29)	17

period. This would actually decrease their chances of surviving in 1974–1975 merely by the accumulation of years. The oldest known-age birds in 1965 were four, and in 1969 the oldest were eight. This pattern indicates the selective advantage of breeding among the youngest, mature Adélies in spite of high mortality, namely because those that survive are highly productive in later years. In other words, birds that breed at an early age tend to be qualitatively better breeders because of some unknown behavioral or physiological characteristics.

These trends are confirmed by the fact that a higher proportion of females first breeding at three years of age *attempt breeding* in more subsequent years than birds first breeding at older ages. Note that we are here referring to breeding attempts rather than successful breeding, as in the preceding paragraph (tables 9.3 and 9.4). The absolute number of breeding years is compared for females in table 9.3, but to increase sample size the maximum possible number of breeding years is compared in table 9.4. In both samples, all birds had to be three years of age by the 1968–1969 season. An insufficient sample of males was available for inclusion in table 9.3, but table 9.4 shows results for males similar to those for females. These tables compare birds first breeding at the youngest ages and those first breeding at older ages in the proportion breeding the largest number of subsequent years. They show a significant difference only for males, possibly because sample sizes are more adequate for them (in that males fail to breed much more often than females). Comparing what they called "continuous" with "intermittent" breeders, Wooller and Coulson (1977) found a higher proportion of continuous breeders among kittiwakes that first bred at older ages than among those that did so at younger ages. They did not, however, compare on the basis of the number of nonbreeding years as we did for Adélies. Virtually all male Adélies, and perhaps a higher proportion of females than in kittiwakes, are intermittent breeders. This is because Adélies much more frequently must find new mates and because a coincident tendency to skip breeding exists in such circumstances (chap. 8; Spurr 1975*b*).

TABLE 9.4   **The percentage of Adélie Penguins breeding for the maximum possible number of years (greater than one) relative to their age at first breeding, 1965 to 1975.**

Age first bred	MAXIMUM YEARS BRED		
(yrs)	2–6	7–9*	n
	Female		
3	45	55	20
4	56	44	63
5	53	47	45
6–7	59	41	22
	Male		
4–5	58	42	48
6	67	33	36
7–8	75	25	16

* Comparing the proportion for youngest breeders with the weighted value for older ones (females, 0.44; males, 0.30) results in the following values of t: females 0.918 (P>.05), males 6.992 (P<.05).

TABLE 9.3   **The percentage of females breeding for a known number of years (greater than one) relative to their age at first breeding, 1965 to 1975.**

Age first bred (yrs)	YEARS KNOWN TO HAVE BRED		
	2	>2*	n
3	43	57	7
4	63	37	19
5+	60	40	5

* Comparing the proportion for three-year-olds with the weighted value for four years and older (0.38), $t = 0.891$ (P>.05).

Ainley and DeMaster (1980) demonstrated that the mortality rate of breeders declined with age but was still higher than that of nonbreeders and that the mortality of nonbreeders remained unchanged with increased age except for a sharp rise among the very oldest birds. Those results and the ones presented above indicate that if adult Adélies are to replace themselves they must indeed participate in a race between producing young and surviving long enough to do so. Assuming that the infertility rate among two-year-old Adélies would be as low as it is in two-year-old Yellow-eyed Penguins, where an incredible 65 percent of eggs incubated to term fail to hatch (see chap. 7), and given the very high mortality among the youngest breeding Adélies, one can see that for Adélies younger than three years to breed would clearly have little selective advantage.

FECUNDITY

The interplay between productivity and mortality will determine whether and to what degree the Crozier population is increasing, decreasing, or unchanging. To determine stability, or growth (λ), estimates for two factors are needed: fledging rates for parents of known ages and survival rates for these same age groups. In effect, however, we are dealing with two populations, a tagged and an untagged one, and it is necessary to determine how well the tagged population represents the other in calculations of the above values.

In comparisons of productivity between banded birds and controls, agreement was quite close (see chap. 8). The overall productivity of known-age Adélies is summarized in table 9.5. By combining these data with others (table 9.6) we estimate that 0.8 chicks (2,418.2 chicks/3,057 pairs) were fledged per breeding pair, a figure in agreement with Taylor's (1962) estimate of 0.9 chicks for one season, 1959–1960, at Cape Royds. Using data contained in Spurr's (1975*b*) tables 15 and 16, we calculate chick production at Cape Bird over four seasons, 1967–1968 to 1970–1971, to be rather consistent and to lie somewhere between 0.6 and 1.1 chicks per pair (midpoint of range is 0.85). These similarities and the small difference between control and banded Adélies at Crozier lead us to believe that our productivity data on banded birds adequately describe unbanded ones.

The data in table 9.6 were then used to determine the number of female chicks produced by all females (including

TABLE 9.5 **Fledging success relative to parent's age among adults attempting to breed (= eggs laid by a pair); Cape Crozier, 1965 to 1974.**

Age (yrs)	MALE PARENT		FEMALE PARENT		Weighted average
	No. fledged $\bar{x} \pm SD$	n	No. fledged $\bar{x} \pm SD$	n	
3	0.0	0	0.3 ± 0.5	50	0.3 ± 0.5
4	0.2 ± 0.5	34	0.4 ± 0.6	133	0.4 ± 0.6
5	0.4 ± 0.6	174	0.6 ± 0.7	228	0.5 ± 0.7
6	0.8 ± 0.7	216	0.9 ± 0.7	221	0.9 ± 0.7
7+	1.0 ± 0.8	303	1.0 ± 0.7	262	1.0 ± 0.8
Total	0.7 ± 0.7	727	0.7 ± 0.7	894	0.7 ± 0.7

nonbreeders) in an age group. This is a convention used in demographic analysis. When this information (table 9.7) was in turn combined with the survivorship data in Ainley and DeMaster (1980: table 4) the resultant net reproductive rate (R_0; see below) was 0.116. This figure implies that the existence of Adélie Penguins at Crozier was problematic or that something was wrong with the data. The population was probably declining, as discussed in chapter 8, but not as abruptly as indicated by the R_0 calculated, and the problem probably resided in the survivorship data.

SURVIVORSHIP AND AGE STRUCTURE

We reviewed the data in Ainley and DeMaster (1980) to identify any biases not previously apparent in (1) the derivation of the survivorship values, (2) the probability of sighting, and (3) the assessment of band loss. We also (4) questioned whether banding itself was causing mortality. The following resulted from this inquiry:
a. Probability of sighting differed, as would be expected, between that part of the rookery visited by us daily and that part visited less frequently. In the former, for birds five years of age and older during the 1974–1975 and 1975–1976 seasons, probability of sighting averaged 0.977 compared to 0.888 in the latter (P<.05; *t*-test). Ainley and De-

TABLE 9.6. Chick production in a breeding population of Adélie Penguins; Cape Crozier, 1968 to 1975.

Age (yrs)	Cohort n*	Adult survival, %†	Corrected cohort, "n"	Proportion adults breeding‡	Breeding population, pairs	Fledglings produced, $\bar{x}$§	Total fledglings
3	7,400	0.212	1,569	0.09	141	0.3	42.3
4	6,880	0.148	1,018	0.30	305	0.4	122.0
5	10,400	0.104	1,082	0.52	563	0.5	281.5
6	14,380	0.072	1,035	0.73	756	0.9	680.4
7+	61,160	0.025	1,520	0.85	1,292	1.0	1,292
Total					3,057		2,418.2

* From Ainley and DeMaster (1980, tables 1 and 7).
† From Ainley and DeMaster (1980, fig. 4).
‡ From table 6.5.
§ From table 9.5.

TABLE 9.7 **Data on fecundity (mx) in Adélie Penguins; Cape Crozier, 1967 to 1974.**

Age (yrs)	Fledglings per breeder	Percent breeding	Female fledglings per bird
3	0.3	17	0.026
4	0.4	49	0.098
5	0.5	68	0.204
6	0.9	82	0.369
7+	1.0	90	0.450

Master (1980) were thus justified in restricting their data to those collected from intensively studied areas, and we continued with that procedure.

The probability of sighting also varied according to the age of the birds. These probabilities were calculated using the formula,

$$1 = \frac{n_{i+1} \, s^{i+1} \, p_{i+1}}{n_i \, s^i \, p_i},$$

where n = number of birds seen of an age group in year i, s = age specific survivorship, and p = probability of sighting. The formula reduced to

$$p_i = \frac{s \, p_{i+1} \, n_i}{n_{i+1}}$$

For the purposes of estimation we assumed that $P_2 \neq P_3$, $P_3 \neq P_4$, $P_4 = P_A$, and that s is constant for all ages greater than one. The following estimates were made: P_A equaled 0.98 (table 9.8); P_2 and P_3 equaled 0.215 and 0.902, respectively (table 9.9); and s equaled 0.894 (see section d, below).

b. Banding or, more properly, the bands themselves apparently caused some mortality. For known-age birds *re-banded* as four- through seven-year-olds during the 1964–1965 to 1967–1968 seasons, their survival to the first year after rebanding differed markedly compared to their survival from first to second, second to third, and third to fourth years after rebanding (table 9.10). The survival of birds with new bands was 72 percent of the survival rate of those birds

TABLE 9.8   Estimation of the probability of sighting [p(sight$_i$)] for adult Adélie Penguins; Cape Crozier, 1974 to 1976.

Age (i) (yrs)	n$_i$	n$_{i+1}$	p(sight)
5	348	360	0.967
6	435	442	0.984
7	316	325	0.972
8	78	78	1.000
9	50	51	0.980
10	44	46	0.957
11	30	30	1.000
12	24	24	1.000
All*	1,325	1,356	0.982

* Weighted mean = 0.977.

TABLE 9.9   Estimation of the probability of sighting [p(sight$_i$)] for young Adélie Penguins; s and p$_A$ equal 0.894 and 0.98, respectively; Cape Crozier, 1967 to 1969.

Age (i) (yrs)	n$_i$	n$_{i+1}$	p(sight)
2	206	773	0.215
3	951	924	0.902

with bands older than one year. Based on observations of captive Adélie Penguins at Sea World (San Diego; S. Dreischman pers. comm.), mortality may occur from complications arising when the wing swells during molt and the band constricts blood flow. We assumed that the increased mortality (i.e., 28 percent more birds die than should) occurs only once: during the first molt, which happens after an Adélie's first year of life, when it is thirteen to fourteen months old. Whether an additional but lower band-induced mortality affects survivorship in older birds, we do not know.

TABLE 9.10   A summary of data on annual survivorship as a function of the number of years following rebanding.

| | YEARS AFTER REBANDING | | | |
	1	2	3	4
No. rebanded birds	364	309	222	139
No. survive	196	231	166	100
s_x weighted	0.538	0.748	0.748	0.719
Range in values	0.45–0.61	0.66–0.77	0.72–0.80	0.69–0.80
No. cohorts analyzed	7	6	4	3

For banded and nonbanded birds, s_o was estimated as follows:

$$1_{x(2)} = \frac{n_2}{[1\text{-}p(\text{band loss})_2]\, p(\text{sight}_2)\, n_o},$$

where $p(\text{band loss})_2$ equals the probability of losing a band in two years; $p(\text{sight}_2)$ equals the probability of seeing a two-year-old at the rookery, given that it is alive; n_2 is the number of two-year-old penguins seen; and n_o is the number of chicks originally banded. In 1965–1966, 3,800 chicks were tagged, and two years later 153 two-year-olds were observed at the Cape Crozier rookery. Band loss in two years was estimated to be 0.01 (Ainley and DeMaster 1980), and $p(\text{sight}_2)$ was estimated to equal 0.215. Therefore, $1_{x(2)}$ equals 0.189. Let

$$1_{x(2)} = (fs_o)\, s_i,$$

where f equals the ratio of the annual survivorship of a banded individual to that of a nonbanded individual, and s_i equals the annual survivorship of an individual of age i to i+1. If we assume $s_o = s_i$ and let f equal 0.72 and $1_{x(2)}$ equal 0.189, s_o equals 0.513. This is the probability of a nonbanded fledged chick surviving one year. The survival rate for a banded chick equals 0.369 (0.513 × 0.72; s_i for a banded chick is assumed to equal s_i for a nonbanded chick, or 0.513).

c. The data on band loss presented in Ainley and De-Master (1980) could not be improved. We still question, though, whether they were adequate because values seem a little low compared to other studies in which aluminum bands were used (e.g., Kadlec and Drury 1968). In addition we wonder what the degree of independence was between sightings of bands vs. web punches, in that truly naive persons (i.e., ones having no idea where banded birds resided) were not available to search for web punches (upon sighting a bird with a punched web only then was the observer supposed to look for its band; see chap. 2). Further, we do not know whether some punched webs healed over (*probably* not) or whether punched webs induced any mortality (again, *probably* not).

d. The minimum survival estimates in Ainley and De-Master (1980: table 4) were invalid because only two consecutive years of observation were available and that was insufficient. We added 1967–1968 observations to the 1968–1969 and 1969–1970 data used in Ainley and DeMaster to determine new survivorship estimates for four- through seven-year-olds (table 9.11). These were not minimum survival estimates (Stirling 1971). The degree of annual variation in these figures is similar to those for breeding Adélies at Cape Bird (Spurr 1975b). We did not use 1974–1975 and

TABLE 9.11 Estimation of adult survivorship; Cape Crozier, 1967 to 1969.

Age (yrs)	Year	Y_i	Y_{i+1}	Banding mortality	Band loss	Emigration	Total	s_x
4	1967–68	232	222	0	1	2	225	0.970
5	1967–68	129	109	12	2	2	125	0.969
	1968–69	218	152	13	8	2	175	0.803
6	1967–68	35	30	2	1	1	34	0.971
	1968–69	109	76	3	5	2	86	0.789
7	1968–69	30	24	2	1	1	28	0.933
All	1967–68	396					384	0.970
All	1968–69	357					289	0.809
All	1961–69	753					673	0.894

1975–1976 data because they were but two consecutive years and because an unusually high disappearance rate (mortality) occurred among breeding birds during 1974–1975 (i.e., they failed to return from feeding at sea). For example, looking just at the incubation period, 10.2 percent (n = 254) of breeding birds disappeared in 1974–1975 compared to only 5.8 percent (n = 138) in 1968–1969 (P<.05, *t*-test).

Using a 20 X 20 Leslie model, with age extended to 19 years, estimates for s_0, s_1 and s_A were combined with fecundity (table 9.7) to calculate population growth (λ). In 1982, we finally found a 20-year-old Adélie after failing in our search during the two previous years when a 19- or 20-year-old could have been alive. In the banded population (s_0 = 0.369, s_1 = 0.513, s_A = 0.894) λ = 0.93, and in the unbanded population (s_0 = s_1 = 0.513, s_A = 0.894) λ = 0.96. The banded population was thus declining at a 3 percent greater annual rate than the other. Using these values of λ, the age structure of the unbanded and banded populations could be calculated (tables 9.12 and 9.13, respectively). Age structure in both was similar, with roughly 20 to 25 percent of each being fledged chicks and 60 percent being birds at least three years of age. This indicates relatively high productivity, which is consistent with data on breeding biology reviewed in earlier chapters, and high mortality in older age groups, which is consistent with the idea that Adélie Penguins are unique among seabirds in that they are not at the top of the food chain, as amply demonstrated by Penney and Lowry (1967), Müller-Schwarze and Müller-Schwarze (1975), and Ainley and DeMaster (1980).

CONCLUSIONS: A DECLINING POPULATION AT CAPE CROZIER

The sum of $l_x m_x$ (or R_0, the net reproductive rate) in the unbanded Crozier population was 0.616, and in the banded population it was 0.443. The value originally calculated with the survivorship data in Ainley and DeMaster was 0.116. The 3 percent difference in the two R_0 values calculated above further indicates that both the banded and unbanded populations at Crozier were declining during the 1960s, one

TABLE 9.12   **Age structure in the unbanded population of Adélie Penguins at Cape Crozier, 1961 to 1969 ($\lambda = 0.959$).**

X	P_x	l_x	$l_x(\lambda^{-x})$	$c_o l_x(\lambda^{-x})$
0	0.513	1.000	1.000	0.219
1	0.513	0.513	0.535	0.117
2	0.894	0.263	0.286	0.063
3	0.894	0.235	0.266	0.058
4	0.894	0.210	0.248	0.054
5	0.894	0.188	0.232	0.051
6	0.894	0.168	0.216	0.047
7	0.894	0.150	0.201	0.044
8	0.894	0.134	0.187	0.041
9	0.894	0.120	0.175	0.038
10	0.894	0.107	0.163	0.036
11	0.894	0.096	0.152	0.033
12	0.894	0.086	0.142	0.031
13	0.894	0.077	0.133	0.029
14	0.894	0.069	0.124	0.027
15	0.894	0.061	0.114	0.025
16	0.894	0.055	0.107	0.023
17	0.894	0.049	0.100	0.022
18	0.894	0.044	0.093	0.020
19	0.894	0.039	0.086	0.019
Totals			4.560	0.997

slightly faster than the other. Taking into consideration all data reviewed in this and in previous chapters, we conclude that the decline was probably real and was not an artifact of inadequacies in the data. With a λ of 0.96, the population should have declined by about 34 percent over ten years, a figure that is worth considering given the trends illustrated in figure 30.

CHAPTER SUMMARY

To summarize the major points of this chapter, we found the following: (1) flipper bands induced mortality after the first

TABLE 9.13 **Age structure of the banded population of Adélie Penguins at Cape Crozier, 1967 to 1969 ($\lambda = 0.9333$).**

X	P_x	l_x	$l_x(\lambda^{-x})$	$c_0 l_x(\lambda^{-x})$
0	0.369	1.000	1.000	0.240
1	0.513	0.369	0.395	0.095
2	0.894	0.189	0.217	0.052
3	0.894	0.169	0.208	0.050
4	0.894	0.151	0.199	0.048
5	0.894	0.135	0.191	0.046
6	0.894	0.121	0.183	0.044
7	0.894	0.108	0.175	0.042
8	0.894	0.097	0.169	0.040
9	0.894	0.086	0.160	0.038
10	0.894	0.077	0.154	0.037
11	0.894	0.069	0.147	0.035
12	0.894	0.062	0.142	0.034
13	0.894	0.055	0.135	0.032
14	0.894	0.049	0.129	0.031
15	0.894	0.044	0.124	0.030
16	0.894	0.039	0.118	0.028
17	0.894	0.035	0.113	0.027
18	0.894	0.032	0.111	0.027
19	0.894	0.028	0.104	0.025
Totals			4.174	1.001

year postbanding; (2) probability of sighting was age specific; (3) survivorship data in Ainley and DeMaster (1980: table 4) are at the lower range of annual variation; (4) age structure indicated high productivity, with 20 to 25 percent of individuals in the population being fledged young and almost 60 percent being birds in the breeding population; and (5) the banded population of Adélie Penguins at Cape Crozier was declining 3 percent more rapidly than the unbanded one during the 1960s (λ banded $= 0.93$, λ unbanded $= 0.96$). The overall significance of these findings in relation to those of preceding chapters is a complex matter and will be discussed in the following chapter.

10
AGE
AT FIRST BREEDING
AND THE BALANCE
AMONG DEMOGRAPHIC
VARIABLES

 In the preceding chapters we have amply demonstrated that behavioral and reproductive characteristics vary with age in the Adélie Penguin. This we expected because it is true in those seabird species where it has so far been checked, though not many studies providing appropriate detail have been conducted (see review in chap. 1). In our study we looked for age-related variation in many more factors than previous studies on other species, and in only a few factors did we not find a relationship to age—for example, incubation period and the interval between laying and losing eggs. We did not, however, exhaust all possibilities for study. We did not, for instance, determine the size of eggs laid by known-age females. Egg size is known to vary with age in the Yellow-eyed Penguin, Black-legged Kittiwake, and Red-billed Gull (Richdale 1957, Coulson 1963, Mills 1979), and we would be surprised if this were not true for the Adélie Penguin.

The following factors varied with age in the Adélie: (1) arrival date in the spring; (2) ability to overcome unfavorable sea conditions during spring migration; (3) body weight and amount of subdermal fat upon arrival (Ainley 1975a); (4) amount of time spent in the rookery during the breeding season; (5) number of visits to the rookery; (6) activities at the rookery (i.e., wandering, occupying territory, pairing, and breeding); (7) frequency of displaying (for certain displays, Ainley 1975*b*, 1978; (8) facility in social interactions (Ainley 1978); (9) breeding incidence; (10) amount of time between spring arrival and egg laying; (11) date of egg laying; (12) nest quality; (13) nest location within the colony; (14) clutch size; (15) incubation routine; (16) duration of feeding trips to sea; (17) egg loss; (18) proportion of infertile eggs; (19) number of eggs hatched (as a function of 17 and 18); (20) nestling survival; (21) age of the chick when left alone by parents; (22) fledging success; (23) weight of fledglings (Ainley and Schlatter 1972); (24) and (25) site and mate fidelity (LeResche and Sladen 1970); (26) feeding proficiency (indirect measurement); and (27) survivorship.

We also found in many of the above factors that sex and rookery or breeding experience modified the relationship to age. As examples, males arrived earlier in spring and spent more years as prebreeders and nonbreeders after breeding once; females bred at an earlier age and suffered higher mortality. One and sometimes two (but usually not more) years of previous breeding experience increased breeding success through effects on many of the factors. We surmised that experience at the rookery or in breeding was the primary factor affecting age-related changes; some changes we ascribed to added experience at sea.

We had expected that the accumulation of experience would continue to change the behavior and reproduction of Adélies over many more years than we found because this was true in Yellow-eyed Penguins (Richdale 1957) and in kittiwakes (Coulson 1972, Wooller and Coulson 1977). The rather frequent establishment of new pair bonds in Adélies of all ages, possibly resulting in the lowered reproductive success characteristic of newly established pairs in other seabird species, may have masked the effects that superior experience could have in oldest birds. While we lacked a sample to test the effect of really long pair bonds in the Adélies (because no such bonds existed at Crozier), extended pair bonds certainly increase breeding success in species where they are found (e.g., Richdale 1957; Wood 1971; Coulson 1966, 1972). Also contributing to the lack of an extended experiential effect in Adélies must be the extreme hazards of breeding, which are unrivaled in degree by any other seabird that has been adequately studied over the long term. Adélies just do not have time to accumulate experience slowly.

In chapter 3 we discussed the adaptive advantages for Adélies in delaying visits to the rookery until older than one year (two to five years for most individuals) and, when making first visits, in waiting until later in the summer. Our conclusion was that a few years pass before Adélies can feed proficiently enough to visit the rookery and survive the necessary fast. We now continue that discussion by confronting the more basic questions of why maturity is deferred in the Adélie Penguin and how deferral contributes to population regulation. The answers are not simple because factors in the physiology, ecology, behavior, and demography of the species are involved, and we have little opportunity to use comparative data from other studies. Carrick's (1972) comment that the subject of demographic relationships "remains as obstinately light on facts as it is heavy with theory and speculation" is only slightly less true now than when made fifteen years ago. As we demonstrated in the preceding chapters, several long-term studies have established a solid foundation of knowledge on how breeding biology and behavior are affected by age and experience in seabirds. Unfortunate for our purposes now is the dearth of long-term or even detailed short-term demographic data.

Since we are not theoreticians, but rather field biologists, and since we plan to stick pretty much with fact, readers will find the following discussion relatively short; and if they are hoping to find a blinding flash of insight into the ultimate answers, they may be disappointed. We think, however, that our data has allowed some progress to be made toward understanding the demographic balances in our Adélie population and perhaps to some degree in those of other seabirds as well.

Summarizing results from several studies, Ricklefs (1973) found seabirds to have the highest adult survival rates and to delay breeding the longest among the several avian groups he compared. He noted that deferred maturity is characteristic of all bird species having an adult annual survivorship of 60 percent or more and that as annual survivorship increased, so did age at the onset of reproduction. Other authors in more general ways have noted this relationship between age at first breeding and other demographic variables, particularly the annual mortality of adults (e.g., Lack 1968). Lack also found a relationship between onset of breeding and clutch size, but such a factor is not of great importance here; pelagic birds all have small clutches, yet variability in age of first breeding still exists.

Williams (1966) hypothesized that if mortality associated with reproduction is high, it may be advantageous to reduce fecundity (e.g., reduce clutch size and/or delay reproduction in order to ensure longer life). By reducing the breeding effort, the animal is better prepared to cope with factors causing mortality, and it is better to increase the number of times breeding is attempted than to rely on a few all-out efforts. Most seabirds, however, are typically not subjected to predation as adults, and rarely has it been demonstrated that breeding is particularly risky for them if at all (though, to be sure, this information is lacking for almost all seabird species). Reproduction is not especially hazardous for kittiwakes, but Wooller and Coulson (1977) felt that age of first reproduction and the level and consistency of breeding effort in later years indeed enabled annual production and survival rates to be balanced. Carrick (1972) had essentially similar ideas, suggesting that individuals or species (the accumulation of like individuals) struggled toward realizing the optimal time-energy budget that enhances survival and breeding success. Goodman (1974), using the Red-footed Booby *Sula sula* as a model, delved into this problem in the most detail of all these authors. He showed in theoretical terms how this species' low intensity reproductive effort, which includes deferment of maturity as one component, can be a manifestation of the reproductive cost relative to the effort expended rather than, as other theoreticians have suggested, a manifestation of restraint in reproductive effort as a means to achieve demographic balance. Unfortunately, however, he had only qualitative data on how age at first reproduction could be translated into reproductive costs.

This, then, is the theoretical framework upon which our discussion rests. There appears to be general agreement on it, but we still lack sufficient direct data to indicate how the balance among demographic variables is actually struck. We are particularly deficient in demographic data from tropical seabird species, which, with their characteristically lower fecundity, would offer an interesting contrast to polar/subpolar seabirds.

To answer the question of why age at first breeding is deferred beyond the first year of life in the Adélie Penguin, we must first determine the extent to which we are concerned with deferred maturity and not just deferred breeding. In some species a limitation on a resource needed in breeding, such as territory or mate, prevents a portion of the adult population from reproducing (see review in von Haartman 1971). Usually the great majority of adults prevented from breeding by lack of territory are young, and thus, in effect, they are deferred from breeding beyond the age at which physiological maturity is reached.

The possibility that this happens among seabirds has to date been demonstrated in only one population, that of the Cassin's Auklet on the Farallon Islands, California, where the number of nest cavities is limited (Manuwal 1974). Such a situation is much less likely to occur in open-nesting seabirds. The availability of suitable, unoccupied nesting area associated with the colonies of open nesters in all populations so far studied argues against its occurrence. As for a limitation on other resources, Carrick (1972) felt that in the Royal Penguin older, established individuals could behaviorally exclude unestablished birds from food resources. We have, however, already discussed why this is probably not happening in the Adélie Penguin and perhaps not in other seabirds as well (pp. 149–150).

In the Adélie Penguin at Cape Crozier, sexual maturity is reached at three or (more usually) four years of age (Ainley 1975a). By that age, however, only 4 percent of males and 40 percent of females have bred (table 6.3). What is preventing the remaining four-year-olds from breeding? Indeed, why do some not breed for the first time until eight years old? For one thing, by three years of age 28 percent of males and 20 percent of females have not yet even visited the rookery since leaving it as fledglings (table 3.1). By the mere fact of not being at the rookery, these birds fail to breed; it is possible that three- and four-year-olds that remain at sea are still physiologically immature. Furthermore, most three-year-olds, the majority of four-year-olds, and some five-year-olds that make visits to the rookery do so long after the egg-laying season. They, too, fail to breed because they still cannot feed adequately enough to accumulate the fat reserves needed to make any visits, let alone an extended visit during spring when extensive pack ice necessitates a long fast. Even greater feeding proficiency is needed if an Adélie is simultaneously to sustain itself, visit the rookery, and feed chicks. In addition, because at least one or even more years of experience are required at the rookery before breeding, many birds four, five, or even six years old visiting for their first time are not socially proficient enough to form a pair bond. This requirement thus delays breeding a little longer.

Every male Adélie that arrives during the spring occupation period is assured a territory at Cape Crozier, especially since the population has been gradually declining (ch. 9). By six years of age, however, 45 percent of males and 9 percent of females have still not bred (table 6.3), and it is not until about eight years that the incidence of breeding in males reaches the peak level of females (which for the latter was established at six years of age with 80 to 90 percent breeding; table 6.5). Though no shortage of territories exists, these statistics indicate a shortage of females to pair with territorial males.

Many of the older nonbreeding birds and virtually all of the few, older nonbreeding females do have mates but for some reason fail to produce eggs in a given season. Thus the shortage of females is much less than it first appears. In birds eight years of age and older, 17 percent of males do not breed compared to 11 percent of females ($t = 2.36$, P<.05; table 6.5). We take the difference in these percentages to be the actual proportion of males in the adult population that do not breed because of the shortfall in female numbers. Thus by this reasoning, a 6 percent surplus exists in the number of males of breeding age. These males lose the competition for mates because of inadequate social behavior; and even having the opportunity, they would still probably fail to breed or even establish a pair bond (Ainley 1978).

They were among the oldest of all first-time breeders and were nonbreeders during many of their later seasons at the rookery. By and large, they were reproductively "dead," although they were among the longest-lived Adélies (Ainley and DeMaster 1980).

The limitation on the availability of females of breeding age, resulting from their lower annual rate of survival, is consistent with trends in the Yellow-eyed Penguin and kittiwake (Ainley and DeMaster 1980, Wooller and Coulson 1977)—that is, the sex having lowest survivorship begins breeding at an earlier age. The female begins breeding earlier in the two penguins, but the male does so in the kittiwake. In all three species, relative differences in adult survivorship between the two sexes relate inversely to the frequency and consistency of breeding effort, which is consistent with Wooller and Coulson's model as discussed above (p. 201). It is highly possible, then, that the earlier onset of breeding in the less abundant sex (sex ratios start out equal) is a response to reduced competition for a superabundant resource—that is, availability of the other sex. Conversely, increased competition for a limited resource (members of one sex) could select for deferred maturity in the other sex as a means to reduce the intensity of competition. Such a hypothesis was implied by Lack (1966:261) and von Haartman (1971).

Nelson (1978b) felt that the time needed to gain the social prowess required in territory establishment encouraged longer deferment of the maturity of male gannets compared to females. On the one hand, this would be inconsistent with the situation in the kittiwake, where it is the male that begins breeding earlier and that also establishes the territory. On the other hand, such a need for time on the part of male gannets, and penguins, might extend a deferment period even longer, thus increasing the difference in maturation rate brought on by competition for a limited pool of mates. Interestingly, the difference in the average age of first breeding between the two sexes in kittiwakes is only about 0.4 years, but it is greater than one year in gannets and the two penguins. The corollary to the hypothesis indicated by this small difference is that the female kittiwake might theoretically defer breeding even longer if it had the primary responsibilities for territory establishment.

As it is, the male's responsibility for this perhaps offsets somewhat his relatively easier task of finding a mate (compared to penguin males), thus lessening the difference between the sexes in age at first breeding. Certainly, studies on many more seabird species are needed to test these hypotheses and the generality of their application among seabird species.

To this point in the discussion we have established some important facts: (1) breeding is an accomplishment difficult for Adélies to achieve; (2) breeding even once increases the likelihood of breeding successfully in the next attempt; and (3) reproductive maturity and not just breeding is deferred. To explain these facts we hypothesize that to make a breeding effort worthwhile, Adélies must spend their first few years at sea learning to feed and then spend at least one year in the rookery learning social skills. Because it is more difficult for males to enter the breeding population, more years as prebreeders are required of them. Lacking proficiency at either feeding or social skills, Adélies cannot breed successfully, and thus deferred maturity has arisen because individuals that have bred prematurely have either wasted their time or themselves. In other words, the cost of their efforts surpassed the gains by a wide margin.

Though few seabird researchers or theoreticians have had the amount of supporting fact that we enjoy, the above hypotheses are not necessarily original with us (e.g., refer back to earlier discussion in this section). More importantly though, these hypotheses are much easier to accept with regard to the Adélie Penguin because breeding for them is indeed hazardous, and there is thus a premium on proficient breeding/feeding performance (cf. Goodman 1974). Ainley and DeMaster (1980) showed that annual mortality in breeders, especially the youngest ones, is much higher than in nonbreeders and that increased predation pressure accounts for this. As indicated in chapter 9, predation is also the major factor that selects against Adélies breeding at ages younger than they do. By three in females and four in males, feeding is efficient enough that adequate physiological condition can be attained but only to such a degree that a few can breed successfully and also avoid predation. Most Adélies wait until they are even older.

In the Yellow-eyed Penguin, which also lays and

hatches two eggs, many females begin breeding at two years, but 68 percent of the eggs laid by two-year-olds are infertile (Richdale 1957). If predation during the breeding season were a significant factor for that species and if, like the Adélie, young breeders were particularly vulnerable, such "wasted" breeding effort would certainly be selected against. Various penguin species are known to be the prey of pinnipeds (reviewed by Spellerberg 1975), but the extent of prey/predator interaction has been quantified or qualified only for the Adélie. Based on present data, it appears that Antarctic species of penguins, and particularly the Adélie, are unique among seabirds in clearly not being at the top of their respective food webs.

Having now discussed the factors that directly encouraged deferred maturity in the Adélie Penguin, we can turn our attention toward the relationship of deferred maturity to other demographic variables and ultimately to population regulation. This, however, is a much more difficult task.

Ashmole (1963), mainly discussing tropical seabird species, all of which are at the top of the food web, hypothesized that by breeding in dense concentrations on islands (to avoid terrestrial predators), they experienced a limited food supply resulting from finite availability within flight range of the colony and from intense intraspecific and interspecific competition for the resource. He further hypothesized that for successful breeding, feeding efficiency has to increase over that required during nonbreeding parts of the annual cycle and that because young birds are less efficient feeders than older ones they are prevented from breeding successfully. It is this play of factors that leads to deferred maturity. Following Lack (1954, 1966), Ashmole felt that fecundity is at its maximum in seabirds (though with clutches of only one or two eggs, it is certainly low) and that food availability near breeding islands, which affected the deferment of maturity, was the major density-dependent factor regulating seabird populations. The low fecundity and deferred maturity necessitated more attempts at breeding and a longer life span. Longer life would certainly be possible for these species since breeding was not hazardous and since predation on adults was insignificant.

Ricklefs (1973), however, questioned whether fecundity in seabirds was indeed reduced below what it could be and whether onset of breeding could not be delayed more, thus increasing life span further. More generally, he questioned whether demographic rates adjusted to one another or whether environmental factors affected them independently. Little evidence existed then to allow choice of either alternative over the other, but Goodman (1974) showed that, in theory, various demographic variables were affected independently through natural selection.

Nelson (1978b), discussing sulids, most of which are tropical or subtropical, agreed with Ashmole that food limited populations. This occurred, however, not through interspecific competition as Ashmole thought but rather through periodic downward fluctuation in food supply, causing catastrophic mortality. These episodes prevented populations from ever reaching a level where competition would occur. Such a situation of mass mortality related to reduced food supply does not usually occur in penguins (except Peruvian species perhaps; see Boersma 1978); but more importantly, Nelson's idea does not explain why lessened prey stocks, owing to human fisheries, depressed sulid populations in both South Africa and Peru independently of natural cycles in prey availability (Crawford and Shelton 1978, Idyll 1973). It seems likely that the lowering of upper asymptotes in the range of sulid population fluctuations was brought about by density-dependent competition for food resources, which should be accounted for in any theories regarding population regulation in upper trophic level predators.

Returning to Ricklefs's idea, we think there may be some circumstantial evidence among penguins that indicates that fecundity can perhaps be reduced in some species, particularly the Adélie, and in accord with Goodman (1974), that demographic variables are independent of one another. In the Royal Penguin (Carrick 1972), with a two-egg clutch, fecundity is much lower than in the Adélie (i.e., 0.5 vs. 0.8 chicks per pair, respectively); and the onset of first breeding is apparently delayed longer. In the Yellow-eyed Penguin, which also lays two eggs, fecundity is again lower than in the Adélie (i.e., 0.6 fledglings per pair— Richdale 1957), but onset of breeding is earlier and survivorship is slightly higher. Thus these two species get by with lower fecundity than does the Adélie; and among the three species, age at first breeding is not consistent with relative differences in fecundity and/or survivorship. Therefore, demographic variables may be responding independently to environmental factors.

Comparisons are rarely ideal, however. It would certainly be better to have data in greater detail on the average age at first breeding and on survivorship in the Royal, and one should remember that youngest breeding Yellow-eyed Penguins lay mostly infertile eggs. Thus from practical considerations, "age at first breeding" in the Yellow-eyed is more similar to that in the Adélie than it would at first appear. It should also be noted that Richdale's population was rebounding from earlier persecution by man and increased 230 percent during the term of study. Richdale thought that enhanced survivorship during winter, as well as increased fecundity, stemming from a density-related increase in food availability, accounted for the population increase. On the one hand, the earlier age at first breeding might also be a response to this; but on the other hand, it could also relate to the fact that pinnipeds, two species of which prey on Yellow-eyed Penguins, may once have exerted greater predation pressure on the species than they do in modern times. Pinniped populations around New Zealand have been decreased tremendously by man (King 1964), perhaps more so even than those of the penguin. Thus age of first breeding may be responding to different pressures than annual survivorship, or the two variables may be responding independently to the same environmental factor. As pinnipeds continue to increase around New Zealand in response to protection, it may be instructive to investigate again the age of first breeding in the Yellow-eyed Penguin.

Other patterns in the Adélie life history also support independence of demographic variables. Since Adélies require a few years to increase feeding efficiency to a point where they can visit the rookery and additional years to increase it to where they can cope with predators and breed successfully, food-finding ability (also a function of food availability) is probably important in limiting their breeding potential through the deferment of maturity. Since predation reduces their life span, however, Adélies "must" compensate by increasing clutch size. Thus, unlike other seabirds that also feed far at sea and require several days (two to three at minimum) to gather food and return to feed chicks, Adélies lay two eggs instead of one. As argued thoroughly by Lack (1954, 1966) a bird will produce the maximum number of young possible under given conditions. Adélies can support a clutch, and particularly a brood size, that is larger than that of other oceanic birds because of the tremendous increase in food availability during summer in Antarctic pelagic habitats, a well-known phenomenon. Ainley and O'Connor (in press), in fact, present some evidence indicating that food availability is not a limiting factor for seabirds in the Ross Sea region during summer. Greater food availability could account for their higher fecundity relative to Royal and Yellow-eyed penguins, but data on relative food availability for the three species are lacking.

Further evidence for the ability of Adélies at high latitudes to deal with increased brood size is their even production of chicks from year to year and from locality to locality with no indication of mass starvation in some years in any of the several studies on breeding biology so far published. Such a catastrophe is common in tropical and temperate seabird species (Murphy 1925; Ashmole 1963; Ainley, Boekelheide, and others, unpub. data from a ten-year study of eight species in California). Still more evidence of high production is the age structure of the Crozier population, with concentration in the fledging and early age classes (ch. 9).

The large number of prebreeding Adélies relative to older individuals in the Crozier population also indicates that mortality must be heavy in younger age classes. This mortality probably occurs because of starvation during winter when stocks of euphausiids and fish prey (see review of diet in Volkman et al. 1980) are minimal and when ice covering the sea surface reduces their availability even more (Ainley and O'Connor in press). In further support of this, Spurr (1975b) noted lower survivorship among adults during one of three overwinter periods when pack ice in at least the last part of winter and early spring was particularly heavy (he had no data for ice conditions during midwinter). Predation on Adélies, particularly young ones, could also increase under such conditions because even leopard seals take advantage of the superabundance of euphausiids during summer (Hofman et al. 1977). With fewer krill available during winter (Marr 1962), the seals might then seek alternate prey including penguins.

Mortality of young Adélies during winter in relation to food availability could thus be an important density-dependent factor regulating population size. Lack (1966) hypothesized the same for several other species of polar and subpolar oceanic birds. In addition, Eberhardt and Siniff (1977) suggested that subadult survivorship was of critical importance to the rate of population growth in pinnipeds; they also found similar rates of adult survivorship among several species with widely differing ages at first breeding. If the winter survivorship of subadults is the factor most critical to Adélie population stability, this would add another dimension to the idea that increases in certain populations of pygoscelid penguins in the Antarctic are hypothetically a response to increased food availability, or a food "surplus," resulting from declining populations of large baleen whales (i.e., competitors for food: Sladen 1964, Emison 1968, Conroy 1975, Laws 1977, Volkman and Trivelpiece 1980).

The actual mechanism by which food supply limits population growth in Antarctic plankton-feeding predators has been considered only by us and by Ainley and O'Connor (in press) as it applies to birds. The data on Adélie Penguins in the Ross Sea presented, referred to, and discussed in the present contribution are rather more complete than for elsewhere in the Antarctic. For one thing, they indicate that the phenomenon of expanding penguin populations is not occuring throughout the Antarctic, or at least not in the Ross Sea, as some of the above authors may imply. They further indicate that it may be overly simplistic to explain the penguin population increase in the Scotia Sea as being a result of an increased food supply during summer, the only period when large baleen whales are present. If the depressed population state of whales is involved in this—and, for that matter, depressed populations of fur seals *Arctocephalus tropicalis* too—and if overwinter survivorship is critical to population stability in Adélie Penguins, then perhaps we should be considering the effect that summertime predators would have on the size of prey populations overwintering. The possibility that some adult krill overwinter to live through another summer (Marr 1962) indicates that summertime predation, and not just postspawning mortality, could have an impact on the size of winter krill stocks. A change in food availability during winter is thus a likely possibility by which the increase in penguin populations is coming about. To determine if this is so, we should be looking for increased annual survivorship, particularly among subadults, in the Scotia Sea populations. If, however, summertime food availability is the critical factor determining population growth in Adélies, and if summertime food availability has changed, then we might look for differences in fecundity and average age at first breeding compared to the Crozier population, as well as for changes in these rates measured over a period of years in the Scotia Sea. Of course, increased krill stocks might also reduce predation pressure on Adélies by providing more alternate and easier-to-catch food for leopard seals; if predation pressure has strong effects on age of first breeding, this could complicate matters. Nevertheless, relative differences in various changes among demographic variables would add further data on how the variables interact to affect population growth in this species.

It is certainly clear that by looking a little further into the question of how increases in Scotia Sea penguin populations could be coming about, an activity that the present contribution has made a bit less speculative, we discover that an exciting opportunity is before us to learn about the mechanisms of population regulation in penguins and perhaps other seabirds. *All* we need now is some additional long-term research. . . .

APPENDIXES

APPENDIX 1A Average date of arrival; Cape Crozier, 1967–1968.

Age (yrs)	MALE First time Date ± SD	n	MALE Returnees Date ± SD	n	FEMALE First time Date ± SD	n	FEMALE Returnees Date ± SD	n
2	30 Dec. ± 10.2	26	0.0	0	28 Dec. ± 13.4	34	0.0	0
3	14 Dec. ± 16.1	77	2 Dec. ± 16.0	12	12 Dec. ± 16.5	73	7 Dec. ± 14.7	5
4	11 Dec. ± 20.6	44	25 Nov. ± 14.1	41	5 Dec. ± 22.5	30	27 Nov. ± 18.4	34
5	29 Nov. ± 14.2	13	21 Nov. ± 15.8	34	10 Dec. ± 11.1	4	24 Nov. ± 16.3	37
6	17 Nov. ± 0.0	1	28 Nov. ± 22.1	12	27 Nov. ± 19.5	4	25 Nov. ± 20.6	14
All	15 Dec. ± 18.4	161	25 Nov. ± 16.4	99	14 Dec. ± 19.2	145	26 Nov. ± 18.0	90

APPENDIX 1B   Average date of arrival; Cape Crozier, 1968–1969.

Age (yrs)	MALE								FEMALE							
	First time			Returnees					First time			Returnees			
	Date	± SD	n	Date	± SD	n			Date	± SD	n	Date	± SD	n	
2	31 Dec.	± 9.5	23			0			2 Jan.	± 8.4	21			0	
3	21 Dec.	± 14.0	60	4 Dec.	± 15.7	26			15 Dec.	± 17.7	50	1 Dec.	± 13.9	32	
4	4 Dec.	± 23.1	26	22 Nov.	± 16.1	78			29 Nov.	± 17.8	15	23 Nov.	± 16.7	65	
5	11 Dec.	± 26.2	18	20 Nov.	± 18.7	80			25 Dec.	± 25.0	9	23 Nov.	± 18.5	53	
6	10 Dec.	± 23.3	5	15 Nov.	± 16.6	44					0	18 Nov.	± 16.7	29	
7			0	21 Nov.	± 20.4	11			7 Jan.	± 0.0	1	24 Nov.	± 20.2	11	
All	17 Dec.	± 20.2	132	21 Nov.	± 18.0	239			18 Dec.	± 20.2	96	24 Nov.	± 17.5	190	

APPENDIX 1C Average date of arrival; Cape Crozier, 1969–1970.

Age (yrs)	MALE First time Date ± SD	n	MALE Returnees Date ± SD	n	FEMALE First time Date ± SD	n	FEMALE Returnees Date ± SD	n
2	2 Jan. ± 11.1	55		0	30 Dec. ± 10.4	60		0
3	22 Dec. ± 17.5	46	5 Dec. ± 24.4	23	15 Dec. ± 19.9	50	29 Nov. ± 22.9	18
4	9 Dec. ± 17.7	25	22 Nov. ± 21.5	75	8 Dec. ± 20.7	20	24 Nov. ± 21.8	62
5	7 Dec. ± 17.8	9	16 Nov. ± 19.3	87	25 Nov. ± 32.8	3	19 Nov. ± 20.9	56
6	4 Nov. ± 4.9	3	9 Nov. ± 16.1	79	31 Oct. ± 0.0	1	11 Nov. ± 15.6	47
7		0	13 Nov. ± 22.8	41	11 Nov. ± 3.0	2	11 Nov. ± 18.8	24
8		0	5 Nov. ± 16.1	10	31 Oct. ± 0.0	1	2 Nov. ± 4.6	10
All	22 Dec. ± 19.3	138	16 Nov. ± 21.1	315	19 Dec. ± 20.7	137	18 Nov. ± 20.8	217

APPENDIX 1D   Average date of arrival; Cape Crozier, 1974–1975.

| Age | First time | MALE | | | First time | FEMALE | |
(yrs)	n	Returnees Date ± SD	n	n	Returnees Date ± SD	n
5	0	14 Nov. ± 14.2	208	0	15 Nov. ± 8.2	171
6	0	11 Nov. ± 11.7	212	0	17 Nov. ± 12.9	187
7	0	8 Nov. ± 10.7	178	0	14 Nov. ± 10.1	159
8	0	8 Nov. ± 12.8	50	0	14 Nov. ± 8.2	34
9	0	9 Nov. ± 10.6	37	0	14 Nov. ± 6.9	22
10	0	9 Nov. ± 15.0	39	0	18 Nov. ± 14.5	19
11	0	10 Nov. ± 12.6	33	0	21 Nov. ± 20.4	14
12	0	2 Nov. ± 5.2	12	0	12 Nov. ± 5.3	11
13	0	8 Nov. ± 8.0	4	0		0
All	0	10 Nov. ± 12.6	773	0	15 Nov. ± 11.0	617

APPENDIX 1E   Average date of arrival; Cape Crozier, 1975–1976.

| Age | First time | MALE | | | First time | FEMALE | |
(yrs)	n	Returnees Date ± SD	n	n	Returnees Date ± SD	n
6		10 Nov. ± 8.9	171	0	14 Nov. ± 6.1	131
7	0	8 Nov. ± 9.3	161	0	15 Nov. ± 5.6	134
8	0	6 Nov. ± 9.0	138	0	13 Nov. ± 6.1	119
9	0	6 Nov. ± 8.2	41	0	12 Nov. ± 4.1	24
10	0	5 Nov. ± 7.1	25	0	11 Nov. ± 6.9	17
11	0	1 Nov. ± 10.1	26	0	9 Nov. ± 7.0	19
12	0	4 Nov. ± 8.6	26	0	9 Nov. ± 6.9	13
13	0	31 Oct. ± 7.2	11	0	14 Nov. ± 2.0	8
14	0	4 Nov. ± 10.4	3	0		0
All	0	7 Nov. ± 9.3	602	0	13 Nov. ± 6.1	465

APPENDIX 2 Observations of 892 individual Adélie Penguins "alone at territory" (A1T) in relation to age and experience; Cape Crozier, 1963 to 1969.

AGE (yrs)	YEAR IN ROOKERY	A) NUMBER PRESENT				B) NUMBER "A1T" (percent of a)				C) NUMBER OBSERVATIONS "A1T" (percent of b)			
		Sex?	Males	Females	Total	Sex?	Males	Females	Total	Sex?	Males	Females	Total
2	First	647	17	30	694	104	4	5	113	121	6	5	132
						.16	.24	.17	.16	1.16	1.50	1.00	1.17
3	First	984	38	83	1,105	346	25	18	389	529	70	26	625
						.35	.66	.22	.35	1.53	2.80	1.44	1.61
	Second	151	11	12	174	72	7	2	81	150	18	4	172
						.48	.64	.17	.47	2.08	2.57	2.00	2.12
4	First	287	15	19	321	139	10	6	155	250	42	8	300
						.48	.67	.32	.48	1.80	4.20	1.33	1.94
	Second	254	24	25	303	142	16	7	165	84	7	7	98
						.56	.67	.28	.54	.60	.44	1.00	.59
	Third	24	5	3	32	18	4		22	137	50		187
						.75	.80		.69	7.61	12.50		8.50
5	First	55	6	2	63	26	5		31	49	17		66
						.47	.83		.49	1.88	3.40		2.13
	Second	76	7	13	96	48	6	3	57	190	61	3	254
						.63	.86	.23	.59	3.96	10.17	1.00	4.46
	Third	42	8	13	63	33	7	2	42	170	58	7	235
						.79	.88	.15	.67	5.15	8.29	3.50	5.60
	Fourth	5	6	5	16	4	4	1	9	17	26	3	46
						.80	.67	.20	.56	4.25	6.50	3.00	5.11

APPENDIX 2 *(continued)*

6 & 7																				
First	15		1	16	6	.40					6	.38	22	3.67					22	3.67
Second	13	5	2	20	10	.77	5	1.00	1	.50	16	.80	32	3.20	22	4.40	4	4.00	58	3.63
Third	19	3	3	25	9	.47	2	.67	1	.33	12	.48	30	3.33	48	24.00	1	1.00	79	6.58
Fourth	10	9	3	22	6	.60	9	1.00	1	.33	16	.73	20	3.33	58	6.44	6	6.00	84	5.25

APPENDIX 3 Observations of 892 individual Adélie Penguins "keeping company" in relation to age and experience; Cape Crozier, 1963 to 1969.

AGE (yrs)	YEAR IN ROOKERY	A) NUMBER PRESENT				B) NUMBER KEEPING COMPANY (percent of a)				C) NUMBER OBSERVED KEEPING COMPANY (percent of b)			
		Sex?	Males	Females	Total	Sex?	Males	Females	Total	Sex?	Males	Females	Total
2	First	647	17	30	694	72		4 / .13	76 / .11	82		4 / 1.00	86 / 1.13
3	First	984	38	83	1,105	211	6 / .16	44 / .53	261 / .24	346	11 / 1.83	76 / 1.73	433 / 1.66
	Second	151	11	12	174	49	2 / .18	5 / .42	56 / .32	99	2 / 1.00	6 / 1.20	107 / 1.91
4	First	287	15	19	321	81	6 / .40	11 / .58	98 / .31	143	17 / 2.83	21 / 1.91	181 / 1.85
	Second	254	24	25	303	95	6 / .25	16 / .64	117 / .39	174	19 / 3.17	44 / 2.75	237 / 2.03
	Third	24	5	3	32	11	4 / .80	1 / .33	16 / .50	42	17 / 4.25	6 / 6.00	65 / 4.06
5	First	55	6	2	63	16	3 / .50		19 / .30	21	15 / 5.00		36 / 1.89
	Second	76	7	13	96	29	7 / 1.00	6 / .46	42 / .44	35	33 / 4.71	22 / 3.67	90 / 2.14
	Third	42	8	13	63	18	4 / .50	8 / .62	30 / .48	54	24 / 6.00	41 / 5.13	119 / 3.97

APPENDIX 3 (*continued*)

Fourth	5	6	5	16	2	2	.33	4	.80	8	.50	11	42	21.00	18	4.50	71	8.88
6 & 7 First	15	0	1	16	9					9	.56	26					26	2.89
Second	13	5	2	20	5	1	.20	2	1.00	8	.40	7	2	2.00	4	2.00	13	1.63
Third	19	3	3	25	5	2	.67	3	1.00	10	.40	23	22	11.00	3	1.00	48	4.80
Fourth	10	10	6	26	4	6	.60	6	1.00	16	.62	13	13	2.17	58	9.67	84	5.25

APPENDIX 4 Nest quality in relation to age and experience at the rookery as based on 4,045 observations of nonbreeding Adélie Penguins; Cape Crozier, 1963 to 1969.

Age (yrs)	Experience	ALONE AT TERRITORY				PAIRED AT TERRITORY			
		Scoop	Poor nests	Fair nests	Good nests	Scoop	Poor nests	Fair nests	Good nests
		n (%)	n (%)	n (%)	n (%)	n (%)	n (%)	n (%)	n (%)
2	First	84 (37)	42 (18)	4 (2)	12 (5)	14 (6)	25 (11)	21 (9)	26 (11)
3	First	270 (27)	163 (16)	54 (5)	95 (9)	68 (7)	109 (11)	89 (9)	167 (16)
	Second	65 (25)	35 (14)	33 (13)	18 (7)	14 (5)	30 (12)	37 (14)	26 (10)
4	First	103 (22)	56 (12)	61 (13)	70 (15)	15 (3)	42 (9)	36 (8)	88 (19)
	Second	106 (18)	91 (15)	77 (13)	90 (15)	26 (4)	48 (8)	72 (12)	91 (15)
	Third	21 (10)	23 (11)	35 (16)	73 (34)	3 (1)	10 (5)	22 (10)	30 (14)
5	First	26 (28)	12 (13)	9 (10)	9 (10)	7 (8)	7 (8)	11 (12)	11 (12)
	Second	78 (22)	65 (19)	58 (17)	60 (17)	11 (3)	8 (2)	32 (9)	39 (11)
	Third	38 (12)	45 (15)	54 (18)	51 (17)	2 (1)	24 (8)	25 (8)	68 (22)
	Fourth	12 (10)	10 (9)	9 (8)	18 (15)	6 (5)	2 (2)	27 (23)	36 (30)
6 & 7	First	3 (8)	2 (5)	3 (8)	5 (13)	4 (10)	3 (8)	9 (23)	10 (26)
	Second	15 (22)	7 (10)	28 (40)	6 (9)			4 (6)	9 (13)
	Third	26 (20)	13 (10)	17 (13)	23 (18)		18 (14)	7 (6)	23 (18)
	Fourth	27 (18)	9 (6)	15 (10)	15 (10)	2 (1)	17 (11)	25 (17)	40 (27)
Totals		874 (22)	573 (14)	457 (11)	545 (13)	172 (4)	343 (9)	417 (10)	664 (16)

APPENDIX 5A Laying, hatching, and fledging success of male Adélie Penguins relative to their prior breeding experience; Cape Crozier, 1963 to 1974.

NUMBER OF PRIOR SEASONS BRED		EGGS LAID			EGGS HATCHED			CHICKS FLEDGED		
		1	2	3	0	1	2	0	1	2
0	n	30	110	2	45	39	58	73	56	13
	%	21.1	77.5	1.4	31.7	27.5	40.8	51.4	39.4	9.2
1	n	6	48	0	9	14	31	18	24	12
	%	11.1	88.9	0.0	16.7	25.9	57.4	33.3	44.4	22.2
2	n	2	7	0	3	1	5	4	3	2
	%	22.2	77.8	0.0	33.3	11.1	55.6	44.4	33.3	22.2
Totals	n	38	165	2	57	54	94	95	83	27
	%	18.5	80.5	1.0	27.8	26.3	45.9	46.3	40.5	13.2

APPENDIX 5B Laying, hatching, and fledging success of female Adélie Penguins relative to their prior breeding experience; Cape Crozier, 1963 to 1974.

NUMBER OF PRIOR SEASONS BRED		EGGS LAID			EGGS HATCHED			CHICKS FLEDGED		
		1	2	3	0	1	2	0	1	2
0	n	44	161	0	58	68	79	94	86	25
	%	21.5	78.5	0.0	28.3	33.2	38.5	45.9	42.0	12.2
1	n	14	61	1	31	16	29	40	24	12
	%	18.4	80.3	1.3	40.8	21.1	38.2	52.6	31.6	15.8
2	n	4	21	0	6	6	13	11	8	6
	%	16.0	84.0	0.0	24.0	24.0	52.0	44.0	32.0	24.0
3	n	0	3	0	0	1	2	1	1	1
	%	0.0	100.0	0.0	0.0	33.3	66.7	33.3	33.3	33.3
4	n	0	1	0	1	0	0	1	0	0
	%	0.0	100.0	0.0	100.0	0.0	0.0	100.0	0.0	0.0
Totals	n	62	247	1	96	91	123	147	119	44
	%	20.0	79.7	0.3	31.0	29.4	39.7	47.4	38.4	14.2

APPENDIX 5C Laying, hatching, and fledging success of Adélie Penguins of unknown sex relative to their prior breeding experience; Cape Crozier, 1963 to 1974.

NUMBER OF PRIOR SEASONS BRED		EGGS LAID			EGGS HATCHED				CHICKS FLEDGED			
		1	2	3	0	1	2	3	0	1	2	3
0	n	3	10	0	5	4	4	0	8	2	3	0
	%	23.1	76.9	0.0	38.5	30.8	30.8	0.0	61.5	15.4	23.1	0.0
1	n	0	2	0	0	0	2	0	0	1	1	0
	%	0.0	100.0	0.0	0.0	0.0	100.0	0.0	0.0	50.0	50.0	0.0
Totals	n	3	12	0	5	4	6	0	8	3	4	0
	%	20.0	80.0	0.0	33.3	26.7	40.0	0.0	53.3	20.0	26.7	0.0

LITERATURE CITED

AINLEY, D. G. 1972. Flocking in Adélie Penguins. *Ibis* 114:388–390.

———. 1974. The comfort behavior of Adélie and other penguins. *Behaviour* 50:16–51.

———. 1975a. The development of reproductive maturity in Adélie Penguins. Pp. 139–157 in B. Stonehouse, ed., *The Biology of Penguins*. London: Macmillan.

———. 1975b. Displays of Adélie Penguins: a reinterpretation. Pp. 503–534 in B. Stonehouse, ed., *The Biology of Penguins*. London: Macmillan.

———. 1978. Activity of non-breeding Adélie Penguins. *Condor* 80:135–146.

———. 1980. Seabirds as marine organisms: a review. *Calif. Coop. Ocean. Fish Investig., Repts.* 23:48–53.

AINLEY, D. G., and D. P. DEMASTER. 1980. Survival and mortality in a population of Adélie Penguins. *Ecology* 61:522–530.

AINLEY, D. G., and R. E. LERESCHE. 1973. The effects of weather and pack-ice conditions on breeding in Adélie Penguins. *Condor* 75:235–239.

AINLEY, D. G. and E. F. O'CONNOR. In press. The marine ecology of birds in the Ross Sea, Antarctica. *Amer. Ornithol. Union Monogr.*

AINLEY, D. G., and R. P. SCHLATTER. 1972. Chick raising ability in Adélie Penguins. *Auk* 89:559–566.

AINLEY, D. G., R. C. WOOD, and W. J. L. SLADEN. 1978. Bird life at Cape Crozier, Ross Island. *Wilson Bull.* 90:492–510.

AMADON, D. 1964. The evolution of low reproductive rates in birds. *Evolution* 18:105–110.

ASHMOLE, N. P. 1963. The regulation of numbers of tropical oceanic birds. *Ibis* 103b:458–473.

ASHMOLE, N. P., and H. TOVAR. 1968. Prolonged parental care in Royal Terns and other birds. *Auk* 85:90–100.

BAGSHAWE, T. W. 1938. Notes on the habits of the Gentoo and Ringed or Antarctic penguins. *Trans. Zool. Soc. Lond.* 24(3):1–306.

BEKOFF, M., D. G. AINLEY, and A. BEKOFF. 1979. The ontogeny and organization of comfort behavior in Adélie Penguins. *Wilson Bull.* 91:255–270.

BOERSMA, P. D. 1978. Breeding patterns of Galapágos Penguins as an indicator of oceanographic conditions. *Science* 200:1481–1483.

BUCKLEY, F. G., and P. A. BUCKLEY. 1974. Comparative feeding ecology of wintering adult and juvenile Royal Terns (Aves: Laridae, Sterninae). *Ecology* 55:1053–1063.

BUTLER, R. G., and D. MÜLLER-SCHWARZE. 1977. Penguin census by aerial photographic analysis at Cape Crozier, Ross Island. *Ant. J. U. S.* 12:25–27.

CARRICK, R. 1970. Ecology and population dynamics of Antarctic sea-birds. Pp. 505–525 in M. Holdgate, ed., *Antarctic Ecology.* New York: Academic Press.

———. 1972. Population ecology of the Australian Black-backed Magpie, Royal Penguin, and Silver Gull. Pp. 41–99 in *Population Ecology of Migratory Birds.* U. S. Dept. Interior, Wildl. Res. Rept. 2.

CARRICK, R., and S. E. INGHAM. 1967. Antarctic sea-birds as subjects for ecological research. *J. A. R. E. Sci. Rep.*, Spec. Issue No. 1:151–184.

CONROY, J. W. H. 1975. Recent increases in penguin populations in the Antarctic and Subantarctic. Pp. 321–336 in B. Stonehouse, ed., *The Biology of Penguins.* London: Macmillan.

COULSON, J. C. 1963. Egg size and shape in the Kittiwake (*Rissa tridactyla*) and their use in estimating age composition of populations. *Zool. Soc. Lond., Proc.* 140:211–227.

———. 1966. The influence of the pair-bond and age on the breeding biology of the Kittiwake Gull, *Rissa tridactyla. J. Anim. Ecol.* 35:269–279.

———. 1968. Differences in the quality of birds nesting in the centre and on the edges of a colony. *Nature, Lond.* 217:478–479.

———. 1972. The significance of the pair-bond in the Kittiwake. *Proc. 15th Intl. Ornithol. Congr.*:424–433.

COULSON, J. C., and E. White. 1956. A study of colonies of the Kittiwake, *Rissa tridactyla* (L.). *Ibis* 98:63–79.

———. 1958a. The effect of age on the breeding biology of the Kittiwake, *Rissa tridactyla. Ibis* 100:40–51.

———. 1958b. Observations on the breeding of the Kittiwake. *Bird Study* 5:74–83.

———. 1959. The post-fledging mortality of the Kittiwake. *Bird Study* 6:97–102.

———. 1960. The effect of age and density of breeding birds on the time of breeding of the Kittiwake, *Rissa tridactyla. Ibis* 102:71–86.

———. 1961. An analysis of the factors influencing the clutch size of the Kittiwake. *Proc. Zool. Soc. London* 136:206–217.

COULSON, J. C., and R. D. WOOLLER. 1976. Differential survival rates among breeding kittiwake gulls. *J. Anim. Ecol.* 45:205–213.

CRAWFORD, R. J. M., and P. A. SHELTON. 1978. Pelagic fish and seabird interrelationships off the coasts of Southwest and South Africa. *Biol. Conserv.* 14:85–109.

DAVIS, L. S. 1982. Timing of nest relief and its effect on breeding success in Adélie Penguins *(Pygoscelis adeliae)*. *Condor* 84:178–183.

DERKSEN, D. V. 1977. A quantitative analysis of the incubation behavior of the Adélie Penguin. *Auk* 94:552–566.

DUNN, E. K. 1972. Effect of age on the fishing ability of Sandwich Terns, *Sterna sandvicensis*. *Ibis* 114:360–366.

DUNNET, G. M., and J. C. OLLASON. 1978. The estimation of survival rate in the fulmar, *Fulmarus glacialis*. *J. Anim. Ecol.* 47:507.

EBERHARDT, L. L., and D. B. SINIFF. 1977. Population dynamics and marine mammal management policies. *J. Fish Res. Bd. Canada* 34:183–190.

EMISON, W. B. 1968. Food preferences of the Adélie Penguin at Cape Crozier, Ross Island. Pp. 191–212 in O. L. Austin, Jr., ed., *Antarctic Research Series*, vol. 12. Washington, D. C.: American Geophysical Union.

EMLEN, J. T., and R. L. PENNEY. 1964. Distance navigation in the Adélie Penguin. *Ibis* 106:417–431.

———. 1966. The navigation of penguins. *Sci. Amer.* 215:104–113.

FICKEN, M. S., and R. W. FICKEN. 1967. Age-specific differences in the breeding behavior and ecology of the American Redstart. *Wilson Bull.* 79:188–198.

GOODMAN, D. 1974. Natural selection and a cost ceiling on reproductive effort. *American Natur.* 108:247–268.

GRAU, C. R., and G. WILSON. 1980. Yolk formation in Adélie Penguin eggs. Pp. 42–45 in G. A. Knox and G. J. Wilson, eds., *University of Canterbury Antarctic Research Unit, Expedition 18.* Mimeographed.

HARRINGTON, B. A. 1974. Colony visitation behavior and breeding ages of Sooty Terns (*Sterna fuscata*). *Bird-Banding* 45:115–144.

HARRIS, M. P. 1966a. Age of return to the colony, age of breeding and adult survival of Manx Shearwaters. *Bird Study* 13:84–95.

———. 1966b. The breeding biology of the Manx Shearwater. *Ibis* 108:17–33.

HOFMAN, R. J., R. A. REICHLE, D. B. SINIFF, and D. MÜLLER-SCHWARZE. 1977. The Leopard Seal (*Hydrurga leptonyx*) at Palmer Station, Antarctica. Pp. 769–782 in G. A. Llano, ed., *Adaptations within Antarctic Ecosystems.* Houston: Gulf Publishing Co.

HUNTINGTON, C. E. 1963. Population dynamics of Leach's Petrel, *Oceanodroma leucorhoa. Proc. Internatl. Ornithol. Congr.* 13:701–705.

IDYLL, C. P. 1973. The anchovy crisis. *Sci. Amer.* 228:22–29.

KADLEC, J. A., and W. H. DRURY. 1968. Structure of the New England Herring Gull population. *Ecology* 49:644–676.

KING, J. E. 1964. *Seals of the World*. London: British Museum (Natural History).

LACK, D. 1954. *The Natural Regulation of Animal Numbers*. Oxford: Clarendon Press.

———. 1966. *Population Studies of Birds*. Oxford: Clarendon Press.

———. 1968. *Ecological Adaptations for Breeding in Birds*. London: Methuen and Co.

LAWS, R. M. 1977. The significance of vertebrates in the Antarctic marine ecosystem. Pp. 411–438 in G. A. Llano, ed., *Adaptations within Antarctic Ecosystems*. Houston: Gulf Publishing Co.

LERESCHE, R. E. 1971. *Ecology and Behavior of Known-Age Adélie Penguins*. Ph.D. diss., Johns Hopkins University, Baltimore.

LERESCHE, R. E., and J. C. BOYD. 1969. Response to acute hypothermia in Adélie Penguin chicks. *Commun. Beh. Biol.* 4:85–89.

LERESCHE, R. E., and W. J. L. SLADEN. 1970. Establishment of pair and breeding site bonds by known-age Adélie Penguins. *Anim. Behav.* 18:517–526.

LEVICK, G. M. 1914. *Antarctic Penguins*. London: William Heinemann.

LOCKLEY, R. M. 1942. *Shearwaters*. New York: Devin-Adair Co.

MANUWAL, D. A. 1974. Effects of territoriality on breeding in a population of Cassin's Auklet. *Ecology* 55:1399–1406.

MARR, J. W. S. 1962. The natural history and geography of the Antarctic krill (*Euphausia superba* Dana). *Disc. Rep.* 32:33–464.

MAYFIELD, H. F. 1961. Nesting success calculated from exposure. *Wilson Bull.* 73:255–261.

MILLS, J. A. 1973. The influence of age and pair-bond on the breeding ecology of the Red-billed Gull, *Larus novaehollandiae scopulinus*. *J. Anim. Ecol.* 42:147–162.

———. 1979. Factors affecting the egg size of Red-billed Gulls, *Larus novaehollandiae scopulinus*. *Ibis* 121:53–67.

MÜLLER-SCHWARZE, D., AND C. MÜLLER-SCHWARZE. 1975. Relations between leopard seals and Adélie Penguins. *Rapp. P.-v. Reun. Cons. Int. Explor. Mer.* 169:394–404.

———. 1977. Interactions between South Polar Skuas and Adélie Penguins. Pp. 619–646 in G. A. Llano, ed., *Adaptations within Antarctic Ecosystems*. Houston: Gulf Publishing Co.

———. 1980. Display rate and speed of nest relief in Antarctic pygoscelid penguins. *Auk* 97:825–831.

MURPHY, R. C. 1925. *Bird Islands of Peru*. New York: Putnam.

———. 1936. *Oceanic Birds of South America*. New York: American Museum of Natural History.

NELSON, J. B. 1966a. The behavior of the young Gannet. *Brit. Birds* 59:393–419.

———. 1966b. The breeding biology of the Gannet, *Sula bassana,* on the Bass Rock, Scotland. *Ibis* 108:584–626.

———. 1978a. *The Gannet.* Vermillion, S. D.: Buteo Books.

———. 1978b. *The Sulidae: Gannets and Boobies.* Oxford: Oxford University Press.

OELKE, H. 1975. Breeding behavior and success in a colony of Adélie Penguins, *Pygoscelis adeliae,* at Cape Crozier, Antarctica. Pp. 363–395 in B. Stonehouse, ed., *The Biology of Penguins.* London: Macmillan.

OLLASON, J. C., and G. M. DUNNET. 1978. Age, experience and other factors affecting the breeding success of the Fulmar, *Fulmarus glacialis,* in Orkney. *J. Anim. Ecol.* 47:961.

ORIANS, G. H. 1969. Age and hunting success in the Brown Pelican (*Pelecanus occidentalis*). *Anim. Beh.* 17:316–319.

PARMELEE, D. F., W. R. FRASER, and D. R. NEILSON. 1977. Birds of the Palmer Station area. *Antarc. J. U.S.* 12:14–21.

PATTERSON, I. J. 1965. Timing and spacing of broods in the Black-headed Gull *Larus ridibundus. Ibis* 107:433–459.

PENNEY, R. L. 1962. Voices of the Adélie. *Nat. Hist.* 71:16–24.

———. 1967. Molt in the Adélie Penguin. *Auk* 84:61–71.

———. 1968. Territorial and social behavior in the Adélie Penguin. Pp. 83–131 in O. L. Austin, Jr., ed., *Antarctic Research Series,* vol. 12. Washington, D. C.: American Geophysical Union.

PENNEY, R. L., and G. LOWRY. 1967. Leopard seal predation on Adélie Penguins. *Ecology* 48:878–882.

PERRINS, C. M. 1966. Survival of young Manx Shearwaters, *Puffinus puffinus,* in relation to their presumed date of hatching. *Ibis* 108:132–135.

RECHER, H. F., and J. A. RECHER. 1969. Comparative foraging efficiency of adult and immature Little Blue Herons (*Florida caerulea*). *Anim. Beh.* 17:320–322.

REID, B. 1965. The Adélie Penguin (*Pygoscelis adeliae*) egg. *N. Z. J. Sci.* 8:502–514.

———. 1968. An interpretation of the age structure and breeding status of an Adélie Penguin population. *Notornis* 15:193–197.

REID, B., F. C. KINSKY, H. J. CRANFIELD, and R. C. WOOD. 1967. Notes of recoveries and breeding behavior of Adélie Penguins of known age at Cape Hallett. *Notornis* 3:140–143.

RICE, D. W., and K. W. KENYON. 1962. Breeding cycles and behavior of Laysan and Black-footed Albatrosses. *Auk* 79:517–567.

RICHDALE, L. E. 1945. Courtship and allied behavior in penguins. *Emu* 44:305–319, 45:37–54.

———. 1949a. A study of a group of penguins of known age. *Biol. Monogr.* 1:1–88.

———. 1949b. The effect of age on laying dates, size of eggs, and size of clutch in the Yellow-eyed Penguin. *Wilson Bull.* 61:91–98.

232 LITERATURE CITED

———. 1951. *Sexual Behavior in Penguins.* Lawrence: Kansas University Press.

———. 1954. Breeding efficiency in Yellow-eyed Penguins. *Ibis* 96:206–224.

———. 1955. Influence of age on the size of eggs in Yellow-eyed Penguins. *Ibis* 97:266–275.

———. 1957. *A Population Study of Penguins.* Cambridge: Oxford University Press.

RICKLEFS, R. E. 1973. Fecundity, mortality, and avian demography. Pp. 366–435 in D. S. Farner, ed., *Breeding Biology of Birds.* Washington D. C.: National Academy of Science.

ROBERT, H. C., and C. J. RALPH. 1975. Effects of human disturbance on the breeding success of gulls. *Condor* 77:495–499.

ROBERTSON, W. B. 1964. The terns of the Dry Tortugas. *Florida State Mus., Bull.* 8(1):1–94.

SAPIN-JALOUSTRE, J. 1960. *Ecologie du Manchot Adélie.* Paris: Hermann.

SAPIN-JALOUSTRE, J., and F. BOULIÈRE. 1951. Incubation et dévelopement du poussin chez le Manchot Adélie, *Pygoscelis adeliae. Alauda* 19:65–83.

SCHLATTER, R. P., and W. J. L. SLADEN. 1971. Nonbreeding south polar skuas: studies at Cape Crozier, 1969–1971. *Antarc. J. U. S.* 6:103–104.

SCHREIBER, R. W. 1979. Reproductive performance of the eastern Brown Pelican, *Pelecanus occidentalis. Contrib. Sci. Natur. Hist. Mus. Los Angeles County* 317:1–43.

SCOTT, J. P. 1958. *Animal Behavior.* Chicago: University of Chicago Press.

SERVENTY, D. L. 1956. Age at first breeding of the Short-tailed Shearwater, *Puffinus tenuirostris. Ibis* 98:532–533.

———. 1957. Duration of immaturity in the Short-tailed Shearwater, *Puffinus tenuirostris* (Temminck). *C. S. I. R. O. Wildl. Res.* 2:60–62.

———. 1961. The banding programme on *Puffinus tenuirostris* (Temminck). *C. S. I. R. O. Wildl. Res.* 6:42–55.

———. 1963. Egg-laying timetable of the Slender-billed Shearwater, *Puffinus tenuirostris. Proc. Internatl. Ornithol. Congr.* 13:338–343.

SLADEN, W. J. L. 1953. The Adélie Penguin. *Nature* 171:952–955.

———. 1958. The pygoscelid penguins, Pts. 1 and 2. *Sci Repts. Falkland Is. Depend. Surv.,* No. 17. London.

———. 1964. The distribution of Adélie and Chinstrap penguins. Pp. 359–365 in R. Carrick, M. W. Holdgate, and J. Prevost, eds., *Biologie Antarctique.* Paris: Hermann.

SLADEN, W. J. L., and R. E. LERESCHE. 1970. New and developing techniques in Antarctic ornithology. Pp. 585–604 in M. Holdgate, ed., *Antarctic Ecology,* vol. 1. New York: Academic Press.

SLADEN, W. J. L., R. E. LERESCHE, and R. C. WOOD. 1968. Antarctic avian population studies, 1967–68. *Antarc. J. U. S.* 3:247–249.

SLADEN, W. J. L., and R. L. PENNEY. 1960. Penguin flipper bands used by the USARP Bird Banding Program, 1958–1960. *Bird-Banding* 29:1–26.

SLADEN, W. J. L., R. C. WOOD, and E. P. MONAGHAN. 1968. The USARP bird banding program, 1958–1965. Pp. 213–262 in O. L. Austin, Jr., ed., *Antarctic Research Series*, vol. 12. Washington, D. C.: American Geophysical Union.

SMITH, W. J. 1965. Message, meaning, and context in ethology. *Amer. Natur.* 99:405–409.

———. 1966. Communication and relationships in the genus *Tyrannus. Nuttall Ornithol. Club, Publ.* 6:1–250.

———. 1969*a*. Messages of vertebrate communication. *Science* 165:145–150.

———. 1969*b*. Displays and messages in intraspecific communication. *Semiotica* 1:357–369.

———. 1977. *The Behavior of Communicating.* Cambridge: Harvard University Press.

SOKAL, R. R., and F. J. ROHLF. 1969. *Biometry.* San Francisco: W. H. Freeman and Co.

SPELLERBURG, I. F. 1975. The predators of penguins. Pp. 413–434 in B. Stonehouse, ed., *The Biology of Penguins.* London: Macmillan.

SPURR, E. B. 1974. Individual differences in aggressiveness of Adélie Penguins. *Anim. Beh.* 22:611–616.

———. 1975*a*. Communication in the Adélie Penguin. Pp. 449–502 in B. Stonehouse, ed., *The Biology of Penguins.* London: Macmillan

———. 1975*b*. Breeding of the Adélie Penguin, *Pygoscelis adeliae,* at Cape Bird. *Ibis* 117:324–338.

———. 1977. Adaptive significance of the reoccupation period of the Adélie Penguin. Pp. 605–618 in G. A. Llano, ed., *Adaptations within Antarctic Ecosystems.* Houston: Gulf Publishing Co.

STIRLING, I. 1971. Population dynamics of the Weddell seal (*Leptonychotes weddelli*) in McMurdo Sound, Antarctica. Pp. 141–161 in W. H. Burt, ed., *Antarctic Research Series,* vol. 18. Washington, D. C.: American Geophysical Union.

STONEHOUSE, B. 1960. The King Penguin, *Aptenodytes patagonica,* of South Georgia, Pt. 1. *Sci Rept. Falkland Is. Depend. Surv.,* No. 23. 81 pp.

———. 1963. Observations on Adélie Penguins (*Pygoscelis adeliae*) at Cape Royds, Antarctica. *XIII Intern. Ornithol. Congr., Proc.:* 766–779.

———. 1967. Occurrence and effects of open water in McMurdo Sound, Antarctica, during winter and early spring. *Polar Rec.* 13:775–778.

TAYLOR, R. H. 1962. The Adélie Penguin, *Pygoscelis adeliae,* at Cape Royds. *Ibis* 104:176–204.

TAYLOR, R. H., and H. S. ROBERTS. 1962. Growth of Adélie Penguin (*Pygoscelis adeliae* Hombron and Jacquinot) chicks. *N. Z. J. Sci.* 5:191–197.

TENAZA, R. 1971. Behavior and nesting success relative to nest locations in Adélie Penguins (*Pygoscelis adeliae*). *Condor* 73:81–92.

THOMPSON, D. H. 1974. *Mechanisms Limiting Food Delivery by Adélie Penguin Parents Exclusively to Their Genetic Offspring*. Ph.D. diss., University of Wisconsin, Madison.

THOMSON, R. B. 1977. Effects of human disturbance on an Adélie Penguin rookery and measures of control. Pp. 1177–1180 in G. A. Llano, ed., *Adaptations within Antarctic Ecosystems*. Houston: Gulf Publishing Co.

TINBERGEN, N. 1960. *The Herring Gull's World*, rev. ed. New York: Basic Books.

TRIVELPIECE, W., and N. J. VOLKMAN. 1979. Nest site competition between Adélie and Chinstrap penguins: an ecological interpretation. *Auk* 96:675–681.

VOLKMAN, N. J., P. PRESLER, and W. TRIVELPIECE. 1980. Diets of pygoscelid penguins at King George Island, Antarctica. *Condor* 82:373–378.

VOLKMAN, N. J., and W. TRIVELPIECE. 1980. Growth in pygoscelid penguin chicks. *J. Zool., Lond.* 191:521–530.

VON HAARTMAN, L. 1971. Population dynamics. Pp. 391–459 in D. S. Farner, J. R. King, and K. C. Parkes, eds., *Avian Biology*. Vol. 1. New York: Academic Press.

WATSON, G. E., J. P. ANGLE, P. C. HARPER, M. A. BRIDGE, R. P. SCHLATTER, W. L. N. TICKELL, J. C. BOYD, and M. M. BOYD. 1971. *Birds of the Antarctic and Subantarctic*. Antarctic Map Folio Series, Folio 14. New York: American Geographical Union.

WEINRICH, J. A., and J. R. BAKER. 1978. Adélie Penguin (*Pygoscelis adeliae*) embryonic development at different temperatures. *Auk* 95:569–576.

WILLIAMS, G. C. 1966. Natural selection, the costs of reproduction and a refinement of Lack's principle. *Amer. Nat.* 100:687–690.

WOOD, R. C. 1971. Population dynamics of breeding South Polar Skuas of unknown age. *Auk* 88:805–814.

WOOD, R. C., D. G. AINLEY, and W. J. L. SLADEN. 1970. Antarctic avian population studies, 1969–70. *Antarc. J. U. S.* 5:127–128.

WOOLLER, R. D., and J. C. COULSON. 1977. Factors affecting the age of first breeding of the Kittiwake, *Rissa tridactyla*. *Ibis* 119:339–349.

WORTH, C. B. 1940. Egg volumes and incubation periods. *Auk* 57:44–60.

YEATES, G. W. 1968. Studies on the Adélie Penguin at Cape Royds 1964–65 and 1965–66. *N. Z. J. Mar. Freshwater Res.* 2:472–496.

———. 1975. Microclimate, climate and breeding success in Antarctic penguins. Pp. 397–410 in B. Stonehouse, ed., *The Biology of Penguins*. London: Macmillan.

YOUNG, E. C. 1981. The ornithology of the Ross Sea. *J. Royal Soc. New Zealand* 11:287–315.

INDEX

Designer: Linda M. Robertson
Compositor: Computer Typesetting Services, Inc.
Printer: Thomson-Shore
Binder: Thomson-Shore/Dekker
Text: Garamond
Display: Garamond